D1021925

AMERICAN
PHOENIX

AMERICAN PHOENIX

HEROES OF THE PENTAGON ON 9/11

LINCOLN M. STARNES
Foreword by Benjamin W. Starnes

GIRL FRIDAY BOOKS

 GIRL FRIDAY BOOKS

Published by Girl Friday Books™, Seattle

Produced by Girl Friday Productions in association with Little Martha Press
girlfridayproductions.com
littlemarthapress.com

Cover design: David Drummond
Development & editorial: Karen McNally Upson with Dan Crissman
Production editorial: Laura Dailey
Project management: Karen McNally Upson

Image credits: cover © Shutterstock/Douglas Litchfield

ISBN (hardcover): 978-1-7348802-3-6
ISBN (paperback): 978-1-7348802-4-3
ISBN (ebook): 978-1-7348802-5-0

Library of Congress Control Number: 2021905552

First edition

For those who gave their lives so that others might live free

"The United States is like a gigantic boiler. Once the fire is lit under it, there is no limit to the power it can generate."

—Winston Churchill

NOTHING MORE THAN THIS

He heard no distant trumpet
As he faced the fires alone
He wore no gleaming medals
No light upon him shone

There were no saints before him
Nor seraphs by his side
There was only prayer
To give him strength
As those around him died

He thought to turn
And run away
To reach the light
Once more
But the darkness
Held his brothers
His sisters huddled
Near the floor

Gravely wounded
And defenseless
He charged the black abyss
For home and hearth
And brotherhood
And nothing
More than this

He carried them all
To safety
From the grip
Of the demon fire
But he alone
Would pay the price
For the cause
Of something higher

They found him
In the morning
Amid the ashes
And the stone
His body
Burned and broken
His face
And name
Unknown

The arms of God
Close round him now
He's shining
In the midst
Of home
And hearth
And brotherhood
And nothing
More than this

CONTENTS

PREFACE

This project was first proposed to me by my brother, Lieutenant Colonel Benjamin W. Starnes of the United States Army Medical Corps, and his colleagues Lieutenant Colonel James Goff, USAMC, and Lieutenant Colonel Ed Lucci, USAMC, all of whom responded within the first hour to the attack at the Pentagon on September 11, 2001. They wanted to record their recollections of this event, and they asked me to assemble their memoirs into one manuscript.

I accepted, but found that when I completed their story it did not amount to enough material for a major nonfiction book. I cast around for other published accounts of this event to round out the narrative, but found to my dismay that such sources were almost nonexistent. At that point I decided to write a complete account of the attack on the Pentagon on that one day from the perspective of those who were there, incorporating the memories of my brother and his colleagues.

The task, I soon discovered, was monumental. I pored over hundreds of accounts and statements to try to find out what really happened. I also conducted a series of in-depth interviews of the principal participants. The description of the plane crash is based on numerous eyewitness accounts and on established facts contained in *The Pentagon Building Performance Report* by the American Society of Civil Engineers (January 2003), a comprehensive technical assessment of the crash and its aftereffects made by several of the world's foremost structural engineers. I also visited the Pentagon in August 2002 and investigated the site of the attack.

The full picture, however, will always remain out of reach. Many of the scenes depicted aboard American Airlines Flight 77 and in the initial moments of the crash were dramatized using a combination of what little factual information has come down to us, the statements of family and friends, personality profiles of certain individuals, and, where possible, actual eyewitness accounts. I have tried my best to do justice to the memory of those who perished.

As a result of writing this book, I found one thing that consistently reappeared time after time, and this was the courage, self-sacrifice, and heroism of Pentagon personnel who, in a matter of seconds, were thrown into a terrifying maelstrom of death and destruction and who just as quickly rose to the challenge. This is their story.

Lincoln M. Starnes

FOREWORD

AMERICA THE PHOENIX

BY BENJAMIN W. STARNES

It has been twenty years since that fateful day in September that changed our world forever in so many ways. The attack on the Pentagon on September 11, 2001, has largely been overshadowed by the nearly simultaneous attacks on the north and south towers of the World Trade Center in lower Manhattan. While often not discussed in detail, 189 people perished at the Pentagon that day, which, exclusive of the events in New York City, would have made the attack there the largest terrorist attack on American soil since the Oklahoma City bombing in 1995. The searing memories of that as my colleagues and I responded to the Pentagon are never far from my mind. As a witness, physician, husband, father, son, and soldier, the feelings I experienced that day were those of horror, sadness, anger, dejection, resilience, and pride.

The acts of heroism and bravery that ensued minutes after the impact of Flight 77 against the west wall of the Pentagon have seldom been written about. Although obscure names like Christopher Braman, Craig Powell, David Tarantino, Tony Rose, Victor Correa, Eduardo Brunoporto, Isaac Ho'opi'i, and Phil McNair are little known to American history twenty years later, they should be household names and held in reverence. These were individuals who spent their whole lives and careers working to serve their country and had secured a place at one of the most revered and protected places on earth, the "cream of the crop" working diligently at a premier establishment. Everything they did that day embodies what we know to be the best of America. Contrary to some opinions, these soldiers *were* prepared for this event. They leaped to action using their training and experience to save lives. In retrospect, the terrorists' decision to aim the jet at the Pentagon was foolish, as it only emboldened those serving in uniform for a decade or more to come. The terrorists doubted America's resolve to stand together. They were wrong.

In February 2020, a new and invisible threat reached our shores. The COVID-19 pandemic wreaked havoc and destruction on our families, our economy, and our way of life. Having been a witness to the valiance of the heroes at the Pentagon and those serving on the front lines of the COVID-19 pandemic, I have seen Americans at their best. Courageous, fearless, self-sacrificing, unwavering, and unafraid, these heroes provide us with a strong example of what we are capable of when we are united together and care for one another. As Abraham Lincoln once said, "This, too, shall pass." America will forever rise again as an American phoenix. The acts of selflessness displayed in this book give the reader some insight as to why this is truth.

My brother, Lincoln Starnes, spent years after 9/11 compiling all of these stories, conducting interviews, and assembling the story of the Pentagon. It was a massive effort and a labor of allegiance and reverence. He is not someone who would normally talk about himself or tout his own efforts, but I strongly believe he wrote this book out of his profound love of this country. He shelved the project shortly after completing it because of lack of interest by publishers and media organizations. America seemed to simply want to move on from that day. After a few glasses of whiskey late one night in the summer of 2018, Linc and I decided to proceed with publishing this book to ensure the legacy of these heroes would not be forgotten.

MAP OF THE PENTAGON
SEPTEMBER 11, 2001

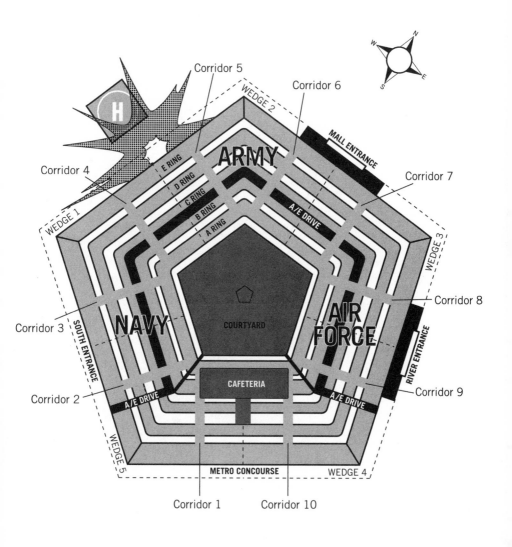

TERRORIST ATTACKS OF SEPTEMBER 11, 2001

A TIMELINE

7:59 a.m.—American Airlines Flight 11 leaves Boston for Los Angeles

8:14 a.m.—United Airlines Flight 175 leaves Boston for Los Angeles

8:20 a.m.—American Airlines Flight 77 departs Washington Dulles for Los Angeles

8:42 a.m.—United Airlines Flight 93 departs Newark for San Francisco

8:46:40 a.m.—American Airlines Flight 11 crashes into the north tower of the World Trade Center

9:03:11 a.m.—United Airlines Flight 175 crashes into the south tower of the World Trade Center

9:17 a.m.—FAA shuts down all New York City–area airports

9:21 a.m.—Port Authority closes all bridges/tunnels into and out of Manhattan

9:24 a.m.—FAA notifies NORAD of the possibility that American Airlines Flight 77 has been hijacked

9:24 a.m.—NORAD scrambles three F-16 fighter jets from Langley AFB Virginia

9:25 a.m.—FAA initiates national "ground stop," grounding all departing flights and closing airports nationwide

9:28 a.m.—United Airlines Flight 93 is hijacked over Ohio

9:30 a.m.—F-16 fighter jets take off for Washington, DC, from
Langley AFB Virginia

9:31 a.m.—President Bush, speaking in Sarasota, Florida, states that
the attacks are the work of terrorists

9:37:46 a.m.—American Airlines Flight 77 crashes into the west wall
of the Pentagon

9:48 a.m.—The US Capitol and White House West Wing are
evacuated

9:55 a.m.—Fighter jets from Langley reach Washington and begin
patrols

9:57 a.m.—Passengers of United Airlines Flight 93 stage a revolt to try
to take back the plane

9:58:59 a.m.—South tower of the World Trade Center collapses

10:03:11 a.m.—United Airlines Flight 93 crashes into a field near
Shanksville, Pennsylvania

10:15 a.m.—Section of the west wall of the Pentagon collapses

10:28:25 a.m.—North tower of the World Trade Center collapses

11:00 a.m.—New York City mayor Giuliani evacuates lower
Manhattan

1:04 p.m.—President Bush places US military on worldwide alert
from Barksdale AFB Louisiana

2:50 p.m.—Air Force One arrives at Offutt AFB Nebraska

2:51 p.m.—Navy sends missile-equipped destroyers to New York City
and Washington, DC

3:06 p.m.—President Bush is taken from Air Force One to an
underground facility at Offutt AFB Nebraska

5:20:52 p.m.—Forty-seven-story 7 World Trade Center collapses to
the ground

7:00 p.m.—President Bush returns to White House on Marine One

8:30 p.m.—President Bush addresses the nation

PROLOGUE

The open-air touring car pulled to a stop in front of a broken-down fence that looked as if it had been there for a century. To the east stood the abandoned remains of Hoover Field, a leftover from the days before the Great Depression. To the southeast lay a wide-open floodplain leading up to the Potomac River, with a shantytown known as "Hell's Bottom" ringing the shoreline. To the west, behind the limousine on a hill, were the graves of Arlington National Cemetery, shining white in the noonday sun.

Two US Secret Service agents opened the door and helped President Franklin Delano Roosevelt into his wheelchair. The fifty-nine-year-old Roosevelt, his body long since ravaged by polio, looked up at the blue sky and flashed his trademark grin.

"Good day for a ride in the country," he remarked as he rolled around in his wheelchair.

Bounding out of the car behind the president came his dog, Fala, the little Scottish terrier who was never far from his side, and behind the dog, Brigadier General Brehon Somervell, chief of construction for the War Department, and Gilmore Clarke, head of the District of Columbia Commission on Fine Arts. Both men stepped out of the car and flanked the president.

This was not a simple noontime stroll with colleagues. Roosevelt knew that America was inching closer to war. In June, Hitler's armies had invaded Russia, and the United States was now sending millions of dollars' worth of armaments and food to its new ally. A bill to extend the military draft to a minimum commitment of thirty months had just passed the House by a single vote, giving Roosevelt the slim victory he needed over the isolationists. He could now begin building a fighting army. There was only one problem: the War Department was spread over some seventeen buildings in and around the capital. The president knew that to prepare the nation for war, he would have to consolidate the high command of the United States Armed Forces into a single building to improve communications and efficiency.

Somervell, a brash and serious man who had a reputation as one of the most outspoken generals in the United States Army, had come up with a plan for a four-story, fireproof, air-conditioned building that would house roughly forty thousand workers, and for the past two weeks, he had been trying to persuade FDR to select a site known as Arlington Farms that was closer to the entrance gates to the cemetery. Clarke, who represented the DC fine-arts crowd, opposed the Arlington Farms site because he thought it tantamount to a desecration of hallowed ground. He sensed that Roosevelt was growing weary of Somervell. Just a few moments before, as they were crossing the memorial bridge, Somervell had challenged the president on his choice of a site, and Roosevelt had been forced to remind the general in no uncertain terms that he was still the commander in chief and that it was his decision alone. Observing the altercation, Clarke was certain that this time Somervell had gone too far.

As they approached the site that Clarke favored, Roosevelt took a drag from his cigarette, encased in a slender black holder with an ivory tip, and peered through his spectacles at the dish-shaped swath of land before him. In the distance, he could see the wide Potomac River, a shimmering band of sunlight catching it in its bend. He began to imagine the new building and how it would look set against the white monoliths of the nation's capital. Roosevelt knew that this area had once been rolling pastureland, part of the ancestral home of Robert E. Lee, but in the years since, it had become a virtual slum. He was quiet for a while, surveying the old run-down Hoover Field, named for his predecessor, a man who had faded into history as a president held in utter contempt by the American people—something Roosevelt did not want for himself.

"My dear Clarke, we are going to put the building over here, aren't we?" Roosevelt said, pointing to the swamp in front of him, in a loud-enough voice that Somervell could hear that his choice had been rejected.

"Yes sir!" Clarke said, smiling. "But one thing if I may, Mr. President," he said.

Roosevelt looked at him. "Yes?"

Clarke pointed at the swamp. "Combining all our military offices into one building will present the largest target in the world for enemy bombs."

Roosevelt reached down and stroked Fala, then flashed his famous smile. "Well, I like it," he replied, taking another look at the scene in front of him. "You know why? Because nothing like it has ever been done before."

A few weeks later, the disgruntled Somervell returned to the site and plunged a shovel into the earth to break ground for construction of the new building, which would be called the "Pentagon" for its distinctive five-sided shape. The date was September 11, 1941, a beautiful fall day.

I

SEPTEMBER SKIES

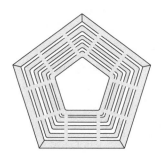

FIRE STATION, WEST WALL OF PENTAGON—
SEPTEMBER 11, 2001, 0800 HOURS

Like the others, Alan Wallace would remember how blue the sky was; a clear autumn high with no clouds, the harsh sun of August giving way to the mellow sun of September, the west wall of the Pentagon covered in cool morning shadow, the American flag asleep against its pole with no breeze to disturb it. On a hill across the highway, he could see the gravestones of Arlington National Cemetery, partially hidden by trees, the final resting place of so many who had fought and died for America. He thought how beautiful it was, the sunlight filtering through the branches, the white marble glowing against the green grass as if the souls of these departed patriots were very much alive, keeping silent watch.

There was a slight chill in the air, but the warmth of the sun seemed to counter it perfectly. It was the kind of day where you could literally breathe freedom; where the whole country from the Atlantic to the Pacific seemed to display itself in all its glory, the heavens smiling down in satisfaction.

Wallace watched the steady stream of cars on Washington Boulevard as they passed under a green highway sign, each of them going in different directions and to different places. Directly in front of him were two big oak trees, their leaves just beginning to fade with the recent onset of cool nights, and near the firehouse, a bull bay magnolia tree, its white blossoms withering on the branches. Summer was almost gone.

Like most former servicemen, Wallace thanked God for every day above ground. As a navy corpsman in Vietnam, he had escaped death many times and considered himself lucky to still be alive. He breathed in the morning air and then turned and went back to work on his fire truck, an Emergency Titan 3000 assigned to the fire station that supported the Pentagon helipad. The members of the regularly assigned fire team were taking an airfield firefighting course this week over at Fort Myer, and Wallace and his crew had come to the Pentagon to assume their watch for them.

President Bush was due to land at noon on Marine One from Jacksonville, Florida, and Wallace had to make sure everything was in order. Normally, whenever the president flew in, everyone was placed under what was called a "Code One Standby," which required increased security. Wallace's peace of mind was interrupted by thoughts of what he knew was going to happen: lots of vehicles, Secret Service all over the place, Pentagon SWAT and US Park Police covering every angle, the ever-present DC cops on motorcycles, and, of course, the two presidential limousines. This entourage would be descending on the area shortly. The firehouse was a plain square building parallel to the west wall with a truck bay on the south end, a lounge and equipment room on the north end, and an air traffic control tower above. The station had been there as long as they had been transporting military personnel with helicopters, but it had been newly renovated the previous February. Next to it was Wedge Two of the massive edifice of the Pentagon, one of the most recognizable structures in the world and symbolic of the strength and power of the United States.

Completed in 1943, the Pentagon is divided into five chevrons or "wedges." The complex itself comprises five pentagonal rings separated by "light" alleys that lie between the rings and are open to the sky. Each ring is five stories high and identified with a letter, E being the outermost ring, followed by D, C, B, and finally A, the last and innermost ring. Between the C and B Rings is a service road known as A/E Drive. Supplies and food are delivered to the complex via this road. In the center of the complex is a five-acre courtyard with a kiosk in the center, known during the Cold War years as "Ground Zero" because of all of the Soviet missiles supposedly aimed at it. Bisecting each chevron are two main corridors that link the rings to each other and connect the courtyard in the center with the outer wall. Due to the building's unique construction, a person can walk from any one point of the building to the opposite side within ten minutes.

Somewhere on the east side of the Pentagon, in a location still classified to this day, is the National Military Command Center, known as the NMCC. The NMCC is accessible only to those personnel with a high-level security clearance. It supports the National Command Authority, composed of the president, the secretary of defense, and the chairman of the Joint Chiefs of Staff. From this suite, all command decisions of the president regarding the military are disseminated to the various branches of the service throughout the world. The communications requirements for the NMCC are substantial, and it has long required its own separate power source in order to fulfill its mission. Within the NMCC is a fortified and highly secret area known locally as "the tank," which is required to be manned twenty-four hours a day.

On the west side of the Pentagon, the first and second floors of Wedge One and Wedge Two are enormous suites that have no light alleys between them, the light alleys beginning on the third floor.

Wallace knew that on the first floor, stretching from the west wall almost to A/E Drive between B Ring and C Ring, was the brand-new Navy Command Center, recently relocated from the fourth floor and from the old Navy Annex a mile to the south. This suite contained several classified areas with no windows and with heavy steel doors, many of which opened and closed electronically. Secured within were the offices of Meteorology, Communications, Operations, and Naval Intelligence. On the second floor, directly above, was the Army Personnel Center, which was in the final stages of relocating from Wedge Three.

Earlier that morning, Alan Wallace had remembered that in the past, the president's advance team had a bad habit of parking in front of the fire station and blocking the exit, so he had pulled the fire truck out of the bay and parked it within twenty feet of the west wall between Corridors Four and Five, just to the left of the new Navy Command

Center. As he looked around, he saw the Ford passenger van he had brought up from Fort Myer parked along the west side of the firehouse facing north. For a moment, he considered moving it but then decided to leave it where it was. It wasn't likely to get in the way.

DULLES AIRPORT, WASHINGTON, DC—0809 HOURS

American Airlines Flight 77, a large Boeing 757 passenger jet with service to Los Angeles, pulled back from its gate and prepared to taxi to the runway. Its wings and fuselage held nearly 11,500 gallons of jet fuel, maximum capacity for the long trip to the West Coast.

At the controls was Captain Charles F. "Chic" Burlingame, one of the most experienced pilots at American Airlines. Burlingame had been with American for twenty-two years after retiring from the navy, where he piloted F-4 Phantom fighter jets. The next day would be his fifty-second birthday, and he was looking forward to attending an Anaheim Angels baseball game by himself. He had wanted to bring his wife, Sheri, along with him, but he hadn't been able to find two good seats at the stadium.

Burlingame was all-American, having grown up in Orange County, California, playing baseball and earning the title of Eagle Scout. But his greatest dream had always been to fly. As a child, living in England, where his father was stationed, he had made a huge model airplane out of old scrap wood and then had his photo taken with his parents. On the wings of the plane were the letters "USA."

The culmination of Burlingame's dream came when he graduated from the navy's "Top Gun" fighter-pilot school at Miramar, California. After a distinguished career, he retired from the navy and entered the reserves, where he was one of the first to volunteer for service during the Persian Gulf War.

Behind Burlingame, in the first-class cabin, two Saudi brothers, Nawaf al-Hazmi and Salem al-Hazmi, settled into their seats. Nawaf, born in Mecca, Saudi Arabia, was a longtime follower of Osama bin Laden, who in 1998 had issued a general fatwa, or holy war, against the United States. Nawaf had crisscrossed the globe for several years, working on various terrorist operations for Bin Laden's outfit, known as al-Qaeda or "the Base." He harbored a deep and abiding hatred for America and was an associate of Tawfiq bin Attash, alias "Khallad," who helped blow up the USS *Cole* in the port of Aden in October 2000.

Sitting in the first-class section this morning, Nawaf looked around nervously. At the security screening, he'd set off the metal detector, but the guard had miraculously allowed him to pass. Now, without arousing suspicion, he reached around and felt his back pocket with his hand. The knife was still there, clipped to the inside. He was glad he had been the one screened and not Salem, his loudmouthed brother, who might have started something right there at the checkpoint. Salem was young and impatient and had a drinking problem, but when the time came to put their plan in motion, Nawaf knew his little brother could be counted on.

Four rows in front of the Hazmi brothers, in seat 1B near the cockpit, was a slender young Saudi named Hani Hanjour. The son of a grocer from the city of Ta'if, Hanjour was short, standing only five feet five inches tall, and a shy sort of fellow who attended mosque regularly but otherwise kept to himself. To his family, he was gentle and soft-spoken and not one to resort to violence. To the FBI, though, he fit the profile of an increasing number of young men, mostly unmarried and with few prospects, who were being persuaded to give their lives for a fanatical brand of the Islamic religion, a sect called Wahhabi.

As the plane readied for takeoff, Hanjour must have reflected back on how he had arrived at this momentous point in his life. It all started in Afghanistan, where he had gone in the late 1980s to fight the Soviets. Arriving after their withdrawal, he worked as a volunteer in a relief agency, but after a short time, he left this and drifted, ending up in the al-Faruq camp of al-Qaeda in the mountains of northern Afghanistan sometime in 2000, one of many new recruits. It wasn't long before Bin Laden himself discovered that Hanjour was a trained pilot and yearned to do something important with his life. He fit the classic profile of a suicide operative. The fact that he could fly and was easily manipulated made him a rare find, and Bin Laden immediately pulled him aside for what was being called the "planes" operation. In the ensuing weeks, Hanjour met a man named Khalid Sheik Mohammed, who trained the timid Saudi in the special code used by the organization and set him up with a bank account and an itinerary. Now, only months later, he was ready to give his life for jihad.

Seated behind Hanjour, Nawaf al-Hazmi intently watched the cockpit door. He knew that standard airline procedure was for it to be locked during flight, but he also knew that the attendants had a key to it and would sometimes peek inside and speak with the pilots. He was also aware that they sometimes carelessly left it open. He had been told in training to concentrate on getting into the cockpit first before attempting to take control of the plane. As he watched the movements of the flight attendants, he remembered Khalid Sheik Mohammed sending him and the others to a camp where a man named al-Jordani brought out a camel and a sheep and had them butcher the animals with their knives to see if each man had the stomach to draw blood, in case they had to use them on people. Nawaf knew that Mohamed Atta, the leader of this American operation, considered him his second-in-command. He was not going to fail. He and his brother would be the ones to rush the cockpit and take control while Hanjour followed behind. In the coach section in the back were Khalid al-Mihdhar and Majed Moqed, the rear guard who would control the passengers when the time came. It would not be long now.

OFFICE OF THE SECRETARY OF THE ARMY, SECOND FLOOR BETWEEN CORRIDORS FOUR AND FIVE—0815 HOURS

Lieutenant Colonel Theodore "Ted" Anderson had served in Operation Desert Storm and the invasion of Iraq in the early 1990s. He was a soldier's soldier, a man committed to duty and to upholding the code, a man of integrity. These days, he found himself serving as a congressional aide to the secretary of the army. His job was to keep abreast of all congressional activities regarding the army and to keep the secretary updated on a regular basis. This morning, he sat in his office, speaking to a liaison with the European desk about matters relating to the Balkans in Eastern Europe. When he finished this call, he went to the gym and worked out and then had breakfast with some close friends. As he sat eating, Anderson thought about his wife, a schoolteacher who taught at Mac Williams Middle School in Fayetteville, North Carolina. Her students would just be arriving for class about now.

ARMY PERSONNEL CENTER, E RING, SECOND FLOOR, WEDGE ONE, THE PENTAGON—0820 HOURS

Colonel Phil McNair sat at his desk, sipping from a mug of hours-old coffee. He had left his home in Stafford, Virginia, some forty miles to the south, before dawn and arrived at his desk just before 6:00 a.m. As usual, he turned on the coffeepot, unlocked the doors to the offices and conference rooms, and greeted the general as he arrived. The Adjutant General's Office had just been moved to this freshly renovated part of the Pentagon the previous June, so everything was new. Through two windows across the room, McNair could look out at Washington Boulevard and the gravestones of Arlington National Cemetery. The helipad was almost directly underneath the windows in Adjutant General Timothy Maude's office, and McNair and the others would sometimes peer out at VIPs and dignitaries coming and going.

The bustling capital metro area was a far cry from the bayou he'd grown up in. When McNair was a teenager in Midland, Texas, he once built a surfboard in shop class so he could go surfing on the surrounding sand dunes. A few years later, his father moved the family to Louisiana, and young Phil found himself working as a roustabout on an oil rig in the swamp, surrounded by alligators. Working for Texaco drilling in the tributaries of the Mississippi River was not what the ambitious McNair had in mind for a career, so after graduating from Louisiana State University, where he headed a Reserve Officers' Training Corps (ROTC) brigade, he joined the regular army, beginning a long career with the Adjutant General's Corps. McNair eventually found himself assigned to the Pentagon, serving as executive officer to Lieutenant General Timothy Maude, the deputy chief of staff for personnel or DCSPER. McNair's main job was to handle all correspondence for Maude, handing out directives and keeping him up to date on all news. McNair's desk was located in front of a small conference room a few feet to the right of Maude's office and to the right of

Maude's secretary, Deborah Ramsaur. Anyone wanting to see Maude had to go through McNair first.

Across the hallway from Maude's office was a large conference room where McNair would be holding his executive officers' meeting at 9:00 a.m. this morning. Before he could get ready for this, he had to prepare the smaller conference room next to it for a meeting Lieutenant General Maude had scheduled, also for 9:00 a.m. The meeting was to be a briefing on the Army Retirement Services Program, and several vendors and contractors would be attending.

Peering into the small conference room, McNair noticed that there weren't enough chairs, so he went across the hall to the large conference room and dragged two more inside. He knew that Sergeant Major Larry Strickland, scheduled to be at McNair's meeting, had decided to sit in on the meeting with Lieutenant General Maude instead, so McNair added an extra chair.

"I'm going down to the shops to run some errands," Kip Paul Taylor called out to McNair from Lieutenant General Maude's office. A lieutenant colonel in the Adjutant General's Corps, Taylor had served in a wide range of military assignments all over the world. Taylor was the only one in the office who could handle the general when he was in one of his "moods." His easygoing personality could turn a very bad day into a good one.

"Hold on," McNair said, grabbing a bag of dirty laundry and handing it to Taylor. "Mind running these by the dry cleaner's?"

"No problem," Taylor replied as he grabbed the bag and left. That would be the last time McNair would ever see him.

ARMY PERSONNEL CENTER, E RING,
SECOND FLOOR—0820 HOURS

Lieutenant Colonel Brian Birdwell had been in his office since 6:30 a.m. It sat on the north side of the main fourth corridor, on the second floor, adjacent to the Army Personnel Center. A Texan and a devout Christian who kept a Bible on his desk, Birdwell wasn't someone who just attended church on Sundays; he lived and breathed his faith. He was also a family man. His wife, Mel, was at home this morning with their thirteen-year-old son, Matt, whom the couple was homeschooling.

Like Ted Anderson, Birdwell, who held the same rank, had served in Desert Storm and in Central America during the 1990s. He was a career army officer with twenty years of service.

ARMY RESOURCE SERVICES OFFICE, E RING, FIRST FLOOR—0825 HOURS

September 11, 2001, was Sheila Moody's second day on her new job at the Pentagon. For the previous six years, she had lived with her family in Rome, New York, where she worked as an accountant for the army finance office. In July, she had been offered a job at the Pentagon, so the family moved to Washington, DC. Even though she had been one of very few African Americans in Rome, Moody missed the town and its people.

As Moody sat in her cubicle, Louise Kurtz walked by, and the two began talking. Moody soon learned that it was also Kurtz's second day on the job, and more surprisingly that she, too, had previously lived in Rome. As the two talked, Moody learned that Kurtz had once worked with many of the people Moody had just said goodbye to only a few days before. It was a strange coincidence.

METEOROLOGY OFFICE, NAVY COMMAND CENTER, D RING, FIRST FLOOR—0825 HOURS

Aerographer's Mate Second Class Matthew Flocco, USN, scanned the morning weather reports that cluttered his desk. Flocco had just transferred to the morning shift a few days earlier as a favor for a friend who needed a schedule change. As he looked at his watch, he realized he would normally be in bed by this time. Not yet adjusted to the new hours, he yawned as he got ready for the day.

Well over six feet tall and lean, Flocco had the classic build of a baseball pitcher, with a hawk-eyed gaze and the ability to forget himself on the mound and become one with the team. But it was not athletic ability that had made him a valued member of so many championship ball teams back in his home state of Delaware. It was heart. As a young man living in the Brookside community of Newark, Flocco had once saved the life of a friend who suddenly went into diabetic shock without his parents or anyone else around. His friends often noticed him giving food or money to the homeless. But this was typical of Matt Flocco. He was a man who put others first.

An admiral who noticed Flocco's forecasting skills had assigned him to the Meteorology Office of the Navy Command Center. Weather had always fascinated Flocco, and he was glad to be doing what he loved. Recently, he had traveled to the Great Lakes naval training facility in Illinois, where he had successfully completed the standard firefighting course required of all navy personnel. As he yawned and busied himself with work, he had no idea how much of that training he would soon be putting to use. Working alongside Flocco was Petty Officer First Class Edward Thomas Earhart of Salt Lick, Kentucky, whose boyish face looked as if it came straight out of a World War II navy recruitment poster. Earhart, the senior forecaster, was a specialist in predicting the location of icebergs at sea based on historical data that tracked their movements and thickness levels at different times of the year. He had spent a year on a coast guard cutter, studying the ice, and regularly gave briefings to the Joint Chiefs of Staff regarding any threats from oceanic ice to their ships, particularly aircraft carriers. He was considered one of the best weathermen in the service and, along with Flocco, was responsible for operating the "Wall of Thunder," an assemblage of huge classified computer mainframes that could determine weather patterns instantly for US naval vessels operating across the globe. Over time, Flocco and Earhart had become close friends and regularly bowled and played golf together.

NAVY COMMAND CENTER, D RING, FIRST FLOOR—0825 HOURS

Twenty-nine-year-old Lieutenant Kevin Shaeffer swiped his card and limped through the seven-foot-high doors that led into the new Navy

Command Center. After injuries sustained in a motorcycle accident, he had only recently been able to walk around without crutches.

Shaeffer hobbled to his desk in the N513 branch of the Office of Strategies and Concepts in the Navy Command Center, down the hallway from Meteorology and bordering the offices of Intelligence, Technical Services, and Communications. The Command Center was where the navy tracked all of its ships at sea, monitored events around the globe, and kept an eye on naval intelligence matters, watching all seaports, sea lanes, and anything that would be of concern to American maritime security. Directly above Shaeffer's desk was the vast Army Personnel office, and like the army's area, the navy's space was an assemblage of cubicles within a single suite.

Shaeffer greeted his coworkers, as he normally did every morning. Standing nearby was Commander Pat Dunn, a Naval Academy graduate from Boston, Massachusetts. Behind his desk was a photo of him shaking hands with President Reagan at his Annapolis graduation ceremony. Dunn loved the culture and comradeship of the navy and was always telling jokes or just trying to have fun whenever he found time. He had been assigned to the Pentagon after completing an overseas tour in Italy, and his wife, Stephanie, was now pregnant with their first child. Earlier this morning, before leaving his house, he had kissed Stephanie goodbye and then leaned over and kissed her stomach—the first time he had ever done so.

Around Shaeffer and Dunn sat people like forty-eight-year-old Rick Sandelli, a civilian who worked for the navy's counterdrug unit; sixty-four-year-old Jarrell Henson, Sandelli's boss, whom everyone called "Jerry"; fifty-one-year-old Captain Jack Punches, a former anti-submarine pilot who shared an office with Henson; Petty Officer First Class Joe Pycior and Petty Officer Mike Noeth, who worked in the naval graphics shop; as well as many others. The group was a mishmash of youngsters who had never seen service on a ship and veterans with long naval careers who had gotten their "sea legs" many years before. They had all recently moved to this freshly painted command center and were happy to finally be out of their old, obsolete offices— except for Sandelli, who this morning seemed to be irritated by a malfunctioning wall clock.

SUBOFFICE OF SECRETARY OF DEFENSE,
A RING, FOURTH FLOOR—0830 HOURS

Commander Dave Tarantino was in a good mood. As he drove to work on this beautiful morning, he felt thankful to be back home after spending nine months in Iraq. So did his wife.

Tarantino was born on the Guantanamo Bay Naval Base in Cuba. His grandfather, an Italian immigrant, had served with the Judge Advocate General's Office as a lawyer during the Second World War, and his father had served at sea during the Vietnam War. The young Tarantino had lived on various bases from Rhode Island to Sigonella, Sicily, and was a navy man practically from birth.

When Tarantino rowed crew for Stanford University in the late 1980s, he would perform an exercise called a "hip sledge" for which he would lie on his back while a platform loaded with free weights was placed on the pads of his feet. Tarantino spent hours pressing the heavy board toward the sky, strengthening the muscles in his legs. The exercise made him a formidable crewman. At the time, he had no way of knowing that these painful, repetitive movements would one day mean the difference between life and death.

After graduation from Stanford, Tarantino had backpacked around the world before attending Georgetown University School of Medicine, from which he graduated in 1992. This was followed by flight surgery school at Naval Air Station Pensacola in Florida, where he flew in fighter jets to study the reactions of pilots to various types of stress.

ARMY PERSONNEL CENTER, E RING,
SECOND FLOOR—0830 HOURS

As Marilyn Wills changed into her uniform in the Pentagon dressing room, she glanced at the clock. It was 8:30 a.m. Her meeting with her boss, Colonel Phil McNair, was at 9:00 a.m., and she was due to give a presentation. A woman at a nearby locker noticed she was missing a pair of socks, so Marilyn loaned her some. Checking herself in the mirror, Wills then rushed upstairs.

When Marilyn was a child, growing up in Monroe, Louisiana, her greatest fear was that her oldest sister, Sandra, would leave her behind as they walked to school. She remembered running after her, yelling for her to slow down, and her sister continuing on because she was older and bigger and didn't want to acknowledge her kid sister in the presence of her friends. Wills was the daughter of Fanny Toombs, a teacher who had taught at both Little Rock's Central High School, famous for its role in the integration crisis of 1957, and at Grambling State University in Louisiana. Toombs imbued Marilyn and her sisters with a sense of self-discipline and self-respect as well as a desire to get out of tiny Monroe and explore what life had to offer.

When Marilyn graduated from high school, she attended Grambling, where she joined the army's ROTC, thus beginning a career that would span twenty-one years prior to September 11. In the years since joining the army, she had served as a military police officer in Germany, attained the rank of lieutenant colonel, and had been stationed at many posts around the country, ending up at the Pentagon, working for Lieutenant General Maude. More important, she had married and had two daughters, Portia and Priscilla, who meant the world to her.

Wills's job at the Pentagon was basically that of a congressional liaison. She was charged with keeping Lieutenant General Maude apprised of any dealings on Capitol Hill concerning the army and its personnel, with a primary focus on funding. She was also required to answer any questions Congress might have about Army Personnel policy. Like the other officers in the command, Wills both liked and respected Lieutenant General Maude, a man who seemed to have a vision of where he wanted to take the department and the unique ability to make others follow his lead.

Wills began the day like any other, rushing to get her daughters out of bed and ready for school, speaking briefly with her husband, Kirk, and then jumping into her car to head to the Pentagon and slipping her favorite gospel CD by Hezekiah Walker into the player. There was one song in particular that was like a prayer for her, something she sang to ask God to watch over her and her family.

As she rushed to her 9:00 a.m. meeting, she sang the chorus to herself, "Jesus be a fence around me every day."

FOREIGN MATERIAL PROGRAM OFFICE, UNITED STATES AIR FORCE, D RING, FIRST FLOOR—0830 HOURS

Blair Bozek, a defense analyst with the US Air Force, arrived at his office this morning and set his briefcase down near his desk, then said hello to Melody Johnson, one of his coworkers.

In the 1980s, Bozek was known in the air force as a "wizzo" or weapons systems officer. What made him stand out among other such officers was that he served aboard the top-secret SR-71 Blackbird. At the time, the Blackbird was used for strategic high-altitude reconnaissance in a high-threat environment at a ceiling of eighty thousand feet and a speed of Mach 3. Bozek remembered going from New York to California in about sixty minutes, traveling at over two thousand miles per hour. Once in a while, he would reflect back on the thrill of those days, working aboard such an aircraft, the missions of which were tasked directly from the White House and are still largely classified to this day.

After leaving the Blackbird program, Bozek served as a diplomat in Germany with a short staff tour at Ramstein Air Base. Thereafter he attended the United States Air Force Academy in Colorado Springs and after an exemplary career, formally retired in 1998. In May 2001, he returned to service at the Pentagon, again with the air force, working with its foreign material program, a good portion of which was highly classified.

WALTER REED ARMY MEDICAL CENTER—0830 HOURS

Jim Goff took a sip of coffee and prepared himself for his usual Tuesday in the vascular clinic—women convinced they were dying from their varicose veins and old soldiers who just wanted somebody to talk to. Of all the surgeons at Walter Reed, Goff was perhaps the most outspoken. He always cut straight to the heart of the matter, even if he was standing in a roomful of generals who tolerated him only because he understood military procedure. In other words, he knew when to push and when to back off.

Goff had the respect of his residents, all of whom he referred to as "sugar," a word used to keep all of their egos in check and teach them a little humility. Everyone knew that you always heard Goff before you saw him. He had a loud voice that seemed to cut through any kind of din, the result of a lot of time spent in beer joints in the days when he was a medical student at Tulane.

These qualities, along with a natural ability to lead, made him valuable in the hospital on days like this when there was a heavy docket. Sixty patients were scheduled for the clinic on September 11, an unusually large workload. He checked the roster and saw that he would be working with an old friend of his, Major Benjamin Starnes. Goff and Starnes had known each other for over a decade. He knew that Starnes, a vascular surgeon in training, liked a challenge, and he suspected that at least one or two good surgical cases today might give him a workout.

AMERICAN AIRLINES FLIGHT 77, SOMEWHERE OVER NORTHERN VIRGINIA—0840 HOURS

Near the cockpit door, flight attendant Renee May stood talking to Jennifer and Ken Lewis, married flight attendants from Culpeper, Virginia. A quiet professional with blond hair and blue eyes, May had been serving on commercial aircraft for over fifteen years but had recently been thinking of quitting. Flying for a living no longer held the attraction it once had. Her boyfriend had recently asked her to marry him, and she had said yes. She knew that this was going to change her life, and she was ready to settle down and have children.

Jennifer and Ken Lewis had met at an American Airlines party in the early 1990s and wed shortly thereafter. Friends jokingly called them "Kennifer" because they seemed to go everywhere together. The flight attendants talked for a moment and then began preparing the rolling trays for the cabin service that would begin shortly.

Walking down the aisle was fifty-two-year-old Michele Heidenberger, an experienced flight attendant who had recently received training in aircraft hijack scenarios. There was no doubt that she occasionally thought about what she would do if ever confronted by such a situation. She remembered the instructor telling the students that cooperation with the hijackers was their best chance of surviving.

A few feet away from May and the Lewises, an inconspicuous Hani Hanjour sat in his seat, watching their every gesture and movement. Hanjour had made many visits to the US in the years prior to September 11 in an attempt to secure a pilot's license. It had been a troublesome experience. His first trip was in 1991 when his brother, a car salesman, had brought him to Arizona. His brother was older than he was and possessed a love of "Western ways." He liked to drink and party, which was against strict Islamic law, and he had a stronger personality, eventually prodding his younger brother to take English lessons that went nowhere. The whole experience had been a bad one, and Hanjour went home after only a few months. By 1996, he had returned to America to study at the University of Arizona in Tucson, which had a strong community of fundamentalist Muslims. In this orthodox setting, he felt comfortable, and the desert conditions reminded him of home. He decided he wanted to become a pilot. Legally residing in the US on a student visa, Hanjour found an apartment in Scottsdale and took lessons at a flight school called Cockpit Resource Management, Inc. or CRM. The training lasted about three months and cost nearly five thousand dollars, but he still didn't understand English that well and had trouble reading the texts. He remembered asking one of the instructors, a man named Hastie, if he could train on a simulator for a Boeing 757. He would always remember what Hastie had said to him: "Forget it. You're wasting your time. You'll never make it through this school." Hanjour considered this an insult and promptly quit.

Hanjour glanced at the flight attendants and then looked over his shoulder in the direction of the Hazmi brothers. All around them, people were sleeping, reading, or listening to music. He turned back around, trying not to seem nervous. His mind was racing fast, reliving the memories of his short life now that he was so close to death.

ROSSLYN, VIRGINIA, THREE MILES NORTH
OF THE PENTAGON—0845 HOURS

Major Dan Pantaleo, USMC, gazed out of the car window at the Pentagon, the Washington Monument, and the Capitol Building, all of them stark white against the blue sky. He counted himself lucky to be working in the most powerful city in the world. For a blue-collar kid of Lebanese Italian extraction from Mount Clemens, Michigan, he had come a long way.

Pantaleo was sixth in a family of nine children, and his father had always impressed upon him the value of hard work and the fact that freedom wasn't free—that it had to be defended. These words followed the young Pantaleo through college on a wrestling scholarship and straight into the Marine Corps, where he went through Officer Candidate School and into Communications. His first encounter with terrorists was in the jungles of the Philippines in the early 1990s, where one of his units suddenly found itself in a gunfight with insurgents. Pantaleo was in a rear area and rushed to the scene only after the guerillas had vanished into the woods. He thought nothing about it at the time, but he would later come to realize that his unit had come face to face with an offshoot of what would become America's number one enemy: al-Qaeda.

AMERICAN AIRLINES FLIGHT 77—0845 HOURS

Nawaf al-Hazmi looked out the window and could tell that American Airlines Flight 77 would soon reach its cruising altitude. He had learned to determine this through numerous flights across the country in practice for the real event. He turned and watched the flight attendants preparing the rolling trays for service. There would be two of them manning the cart, and they would move all the way to the rear over the next several minutes, a good time to rush the cockpit.

In the front, Hani Hanjour eased back in his seat. His target would be the Pentagon, but he also had the option of crashing the plane into the White House. He had flown light planes over both of them so that he would be better prepared to identify them when the time came.

He remembered recently being stopped for speeding in Arlington, Virginia, as he drove around doing research. He had shown the cop his Florida license and was worried because the van he was driving sported New Jersey plates. As he tried his best to remain calm, the cop simply issued him a ticket and let him go. Hanjour threw the little piece of paper down on the floorboard and ignored it. What good was it? By the time they got around to coming after him, he would be in paradise.

Now, as Hanjour gazed out the window at the clouds, he thought about the instructor at the CRM flight school telling him he was "wasting his time" and would "never make it." He remembered joining the simulator club at Sawyer Aviation Flight Academy in Phoenix after being so rudely turned away at CRM. Sawyer was universally known as a "last chance" flight school for students who had flunked out everywhere else. Friends told Hanjour that the school had good instructors and that he was certain to get a license there. After a few days at Sawyer, though, he had become frustrated with his inability to understand the complex instrumentation. He dropped out and tried two more schools, flunking out of both. After this, he crisscrossed the country until April 1999, when the FAA finally granted him a commercial pilot's certificate. During all this time, he worked endlessly on computer simulators for passenger jets and in actual simulators rented with money provided by al-Qaeda.

After training on the simulator, Hanjour flew three times with instructors in small planes, but he really didn't like being at the controls. It scared him, and when he made a mistake, these American instructors had no patience. After a third, "hair-raising" flight, they refused to let him rent a plane, but at this point, he had already acquired the knowledge he needed. Hanjour looked at his watch again, then glanced back at the Hazmi brothers. It was almost time.

ARMY PERSONNEL ADMINISTRATIVE CENTER, E RING, FIRST FLOOR—0849 HOURS

Inside the Personnel Administrative Center, Sergeant Roxane Cruz-Cortez readied herself for the day. Over the years, Cruz-Cortez had built up a reputation of being antisocial. At four feet eleven and 102 pounds, the proud Puerto Rican American seemed to be constantly on the defensive, as if she had a classic "little person" complex. Some considered her downright mean. She was loud, fearless, and didn't take any sass, but this was an outer shield that protected a shy, easygoing personality and strong character.

Cruz-Cortez was born in El Paso, Texas, where her father, Rafael A. Cruz, Sr., had been stationed in the army. She had moved around like a typical army brat, being stationed in many different places with her family, including Alaska, which she loved and where she had wanted to move at one time. In July 1998, she joined the army and was eventually assigned to the Pentagon.

Arriving at work at 7:30 a.m., Cruz-Cortez headed to her office, which was on the first floor in Corridor Five of E Ring. This morning, there were only three of a normal complement of five soldiers at work in the area. They were Cruz-Cortez, Sergeant Savage, and Corporal Eduardo Brunoporto, known to everyone as "Bruno." Savage had left the office to attend a meeting, leaving Cruz-Cortez and Bruno by themselves.

Arriving before the others as he normally did, Bruno had turned on the small radio that sat on his desk. The news at that hour was mostly a rehash of the previous day's events. At eight o'clock, Specialist April Gallop arrived with her two-month-old son, Elisha. She asked to use one of the computers to type a memo for the first sergeant. Cruz-Cortez told her to go ahead. The first sergeant was in a meeting with Sergeant Savage and would be gone for a while. Gallop sat down at the computer and began typing, holding little Elisha, who looked around the room, wide-eyed at his new environment.

GENERAL OFFICERS' MESS, C RING, THIRD FLOOR—0850 HOURS

In the kitchen of the General Officers' Dining Room on the south side of Wedge Two, Staff Sergeant Christopher Braman had just returned from purchasing groceries at Fort Myer. Breakfast was well underway in the cafeteria, and he had needed some last-minute supplies in order to prepare for a special luncheon that afternoon between army brass

people in New York City. Goff put her on hold and walked into the waiting room, where he looked at the monitor and saw one of the World Trade Center towers on fire. What was he or any of his staff going to do from two hundred miles away with a large building now engulfed in flames and hundreds of people dead or dying? How would anyone get in there to help?

For now, Goff thought it best to keep his feelings to himself. "Yes ma'am, I'll be there in a minute," he said, and ended the call.

AMERICAN AIRLINES FLIGHT 77, SOMEWHERE OVER THE OHIO-KENTUCKY BORDER—0852 HOURS

Charles Burlingame didn't even have time to react. Three men were on him before he could turn around, one of them holding a small knife to his throat. Speaking in broken English, the man told Burlingame to turn the plane east toward Washington, DC. As Burlingame glanced to one side, he saw the skinny, hollow-eyed Hanjour staring at him. He looked over at his first officer, Dave Charlebois, who was covered by one of the other hijackers and wasn't moving.

All his life, Burlingame had been a problem solver. The three terrorists appeared small but determined, and they had no pistols, only knives. Burlingame was not one to back down from a fight, but he wasn't stupid either. As captain, he now held the lives of fifty-eight passengers and crew in his hands, among them five schoolchildren. It was not in his nature to go peacefully, but he knew that resisting now could result in one of the passengers or even one of the children being killed.

The terrorists ushered Charlebois out of the cabin. Hanjour now began looking for the transponder beacon, the piece of equipment that identifies an aircraft and relays its altitude and position to air traffic controllers as it travels through the sky. Burlingame remained still, thinking about the training he had received, instruction that if hijacked, they should cooperate, land the plane, and then let the military deal with the situation. They had been told that if they did this, the odds of surviving were good. This ran counter to Burlingame's nature, but, unaware of the New York attacks and concerned for his passengers, he decided that it was best to cooperate for the moment.

He reluctantly turned the big aircraft to the east in a wide arc and headed for Washington, DC.

AIR TRAFFIC CONTROL, INDIANAPOLIS INTERNATIONAL AIRPORT—0854 HOURS

An air traffic controller in the Indianapolis sector looked at his screen and noticed that American Airlines Flight 77 had abruptly turned southeast without receiving permission to do so. He immediately attempted to contact the pilot.

"American 77, this is Indy. I need a radio check, over."

There was silence.

The controller repeated his request.

"American 77, Indy, radio check, how do you read?"

Again, there was no response.

The last transmission from American Airlines Flight 77 had been at 8:51 a.m., when the pilot had requested permission to increase altitude. The controller had advised him to turn south toward a radio beacon at Falmouth, Kentucky. Everything had been going smoothly, but now, the aircraft was deviating from its flight path, and the pilot wasn't responding. The controller felt a cold sweat on his brow. It was the kind of thing that gave him nightmares. As he attempted to reach the pilot a second time, he suddenly noticed that someone had turned off the transponder beacon. American Airlines Flight 77 was gone.

PENTAGON FIRE STATION—0855 HOURS

In an easy chair in the fire station lounge, Alan Wallace sat reading a book about opera. He felt a hand touch him on the shoulder. It was Mark Skipper.

"Hey, Alan," he said, a concerned expression on his face. "You'd better come look at the TV; an airplane just hit the World Trade Center." Wallace dropped the book and walked over to the television. As he stared at the screen, something just didn't seem right. Maybe a pilot had suffered a heart attack and lost control. This was certainly

possible, but to him it looked deliberate. The acute situational awareness he had developed in Vietnam took hold of him now and brought
back that old sick feeling in his gut.

ARMY PERSONNEL CENTER, E RING,
SECOND FLOOR—0855 HOURS

In the little time she had before her nine o'clock meeting, Marilyn
Wills chatted with her friend and supervisor, Marian Serva. The two
women had worked together for several years and had become as close
as sisters. Serva, with over fifteen years' experience in the Adjutant
General's Office, had taught Wills most of what she knew. They talked
often about their daughters. Serva had only one daughter, who had just
started her senior year in high school. Wills always marveled at how
close the two of them were; they did everything together, and she knew
Marian was very proud of her daughter.

As Wills and Serva talked, John Yates walked by. A former soldier,
Yates always seemed to have luck on his side. He sometimes told a story
about his enlistment during the Vietnam War. He had been issued a
low lottery number and decided to join up and choose where he was
going instead of waiting for the military to do it for him. When he went
to the row of recruiting stations in Perth Amboy, New Jersey, he was
intending to join the navy. The navy recruiter was out to lunch, so he
listened to the pitch of an old "brown shoe" army sergeant. If he would
join the Army Intelligence unit and enlist for an additional year, the
sergeant told him, he would not go to Vietnam. No sooner had Yates
signed on the dotted line than a brash Marine Corps sergeant walked
into the room and proceeded down the row of frightened youngsters
until he came to the smiling Yates.

The grizzled leatherneck punched his finger into Yates's chest and
said, "*You* are in the Marine Corps now."

Yates looked into the man's hard eyes and said, "No sir, I've got a
contract." And that was the story of his life.

Now, some thirty years later and long retired from a produc-
tive career in the army, the bespectacled Yates worked security for
Lieutenant General Maude and his staff. This morning, he had just

finished his breakfast in the cafeteria, his usual bowl of grits with brown sugar, and was on his way to his cubicle, where his job was to make sure his coworkers had the proper security clearances for their work. He was known in the office as "the Grim Reaper" and "the Prince of Darkness" for his eagle eyes when it came to security matters. Staffers knew not to accidentally leave secure documents lying around or in the copier. If they did, they would soon find Yates standing over them with that stare of his.

Yates, Wills, and others now gathered around Serva's TV as footage of the World Trade Center appeared on the screen. Black smoke poured out of one of the top floors, and in the background, they could hear the slow, measured voice of the reporter, unsure of what was really happening. The footage was distressing to Wills, but like the others, she figured it was an accident. She glanced at her watch. She knew she would much rather sit and talk with Marian than give a long, drawn-out speech, but time was getting short. She said goodbye to her friend, then picked up her things and headed for the conference room. As she looked back, Marian was smiling at her.

WALTER REED ARMY MEDICAL CENTER—0858 HOURS

As Major Benjamin Starnes stood at the call desk drinking his coffee, one of his colleagues told him that a plane had hit the north tower of the World Trade Center. Starnes went into the waiting room to see the coverage on television. The sight of the burning tower initially shocked him, but he figured it to be a freak accident. The pilot must have passed out at the controls or something.

Before that moment, Major Starnes had been preoccupied with thoughts about his father, who had recently endured a round of chemotherapy and radiation for a dangerous form of esophageal cancer. His father was due for surgery the next week at Memorial Sloan Kettering Cancer Center in Manhattan, where they were going to remove most of his esophagus. Starnes had worried night and day about his father's prognosis, but it looked as if, miraculously, he was going to pull through.

Starnes turned away from the horrific sight in front of him and set his mind on the tasks of the day. He had seen the enormous caseload, and he had no time to stand around watching television.

ARMY PERSONNEL CENTER, C RING,
SECOND FLOOR—0900 HOURS

As Lieutenant Colonel Victor Correa walked through the secure fire doors into the Army Personnel Center, he greeted his coworkers and then proceeded to his cubicle. Correa was in good spirits because of his morning commute. It generally took him fifteen minutes to walk from his home in Crystal City to the Pentagon, but the beauty of the day slowed his steps and made him reflect on how lucky he was. His lovely wife, Oretta, and their four children had stayed home today rather than come with him to the Pentagon day care center as usual.

ARMY PERSONNEL CENTER, E RING,
SECOND FLOOR—0900 HOURS

Inside a small conference room, Lieutenant General Timothy Maude, Army Personnel chief, prepared to conduct a meeting with his staff. Commissioned as an officer in 1967, Maude had served with the 199th Light Infantry Brigade in Vietnam, where he earned the Bronze Star in combat. Thereafter, he served with the Second Infantry Division in Korea, followed by a stint as commander of the Enlisted Records and Evaluation Center in Indianapolis, chief of PERSCOM's enlisted directorate, and then as personnel chief for the army in Europe, ending up at the Pentagon as the DCSPER. Maude's primary concern was the well-being of the rank-and-file American soldier. He was once quoted as saying, "If a soldier's in a foxhole worried about his wife and kids, then he's not focused on taking care of his buddy." When the "Be All You Can Be" army promotion lost its attraction with young people, Maude helped develop the "Army of One" program, which empha-sized individual accomplishment within the team. It did well. He also worked hard on a plan to link military records and files with the internet. Because of his efforts, US soldiers can now access and audit their official files at home on their personal computers.

Seated next to Maude this morning was Sergeant Major Larry Strickland, his senior enlisted assistant. Strickland's greatest contribution was in the development of a brand-new program for noncommissioned officers. He was considered the top enlisted advisor on all human resources matters for the army and was known to everyone as "the enlisted man's champion." Strickland was getting ready to retire within the next few weeks and had already begun taking the pictures down in his office.

Gary F. Smith and Max Beilke were also in this section of the building. Both were retired from the army but had returned to work with Lieutenant General Maude in the Adjutant General's Office. As a soldier in Vietnam, Smith once risked his life by running back into the wreckage of a burning helicopter to rescue his fellow comrades. Beilke held the distinction of being the last American soldier to leave Vietnamese soil in 1973. Now, Smith was the chief of Army Retirement Services, and Beilke served as his deputy. Both men worked hard to arrange benefits for veterans. This morning, they were at the Pentagon to muster support for special retirement legislation for survivors of military personnel killed in the line of duty. Both were low-key individuals who didn't call attention to their military service.

WALTER REED ARMY MEDICAL CENTER—0900 HOURS

Lieutenant Colonel Ed Lucci sat at his desk in the emergency room, listening to the radio and silently bemoaning the fact that the station it was tuned to never reported any news—just talk or advertisements. Lucci was a laid-back character with a slow, deliberate way of speaking and a dry sense of humor that occasionally caught people off guard. He had grown up in West Aliquippa, Pennsylvania, a small steel town about twenty miles northwest of Pittsburgh, and had earned a reputation for keeping a cool head in a bad situation. A graduate of West Point, he had been stationed in many countries around the world, including some third world locales such as Haiti and Peru. He was trained in a multitude of specialties, including counternarcotics tactical operations, tropical medicine, and chemical/biological warfare.

Whenever the FBI, the Drug Enforcement Administration (DEA), or the US Marshals Service needed a highly trained doctor to accompany them on a clandestine mission, he got the call, oftentimes being summoned to some obscure airfield in the middle of the night.

As Lucci sat listening to the radio, a news report came through that one of the World Trade Center towers in New York had been hit by an airplane. Lucci listened for a moment and, like most other people, figured it to be an accident. He walked out of his office and approached one of the nurses.

"Hey, Monica, a plane just flew into one of the World Trade Center towers."

"Yeah, right," the nurse responded, not giving it a second thought.

"No," Lucci insisted, "that's what they said on the radio."

The nurse just walked away, thinking she was finally becoming wise to Lucci's incessant practical jokes.

NEW CASTLE COUNTY COURTHOUSE WORK SITE, NEW CASTLE, DELAWARE—0900 HOURS

For the past several months, Mike Flocco had been installing ductwork for the New Castle County Courthouse. Working on the tenth floor this morning, he was just getting ready to go downstairs for supplies when another worker approached him.

"Hey, Mike, I heard one of the World Trade Center towers got hit by an airplane."

Flocco raised his eyebrows at the news, but for some reason figured it was probably a light Beechcraft plane that had somehow gone off course. The only response he offered was his signature grimace, one that reminded people of the actor Robert De Niro.

Even when Flocco smiled, his face bore a world-weary grin, a kind of reverse grimace that let you know this man had seen hard times in his life but hadn't let anything get the best of him. Flocco came from a time, long past, when sons followed their fathers into the trades as a matter of course. His father and his uncle had been sheet metal workers, so he in turn became what they called a "tin knocker." Looking down at his right pinky that was fused, leaving him unable to bend it, he would laugh and say that he was supposed to go to college, but he just loved his father's tools too much.

Trying to put the morning's news aside, he called to his apprentice, Chris Oberhausen, and they both took the elevator down to the first floor to get more supplies. As the two men reached the "boneyard," the staging area where the supplies were kept, Mike thought about his son, Matt. He was so proud of the boy that he sometimes had no words to express it. The elder Flocco was deeply religious and old-fashioned; he remembered telling his son that it was alright for his friends to hang out at the house, but if any of them ever showed up with a tattoo, he would kick them out. He always looked forward to weekends when "Matty," as he and his wife, Sheila, called their only child, came home on leave from the Pentagon. He was relieved that his son was nowhere near that terrible tragedy in New York.

B RING, FIRST FLOOR—0900 HOURS

Four rings in from the west wall on the other side of A/E Drive, John Driscoll, a colonel in the Montana Army National Guard assigned to the Joint Chiefs of Staff, busied himself with a report he was to deliver this morning to the Defense Supply Service, outlining a plan to better train and educate army, navy, marine, and coast guard officers; both active and reserve. It was a big project that he had been working on for the past twenty-two months. As he was getting his papers together, a fellow staff officer spoke to him in a solemn voice.

"Sir, something's happened in New York. We'd better turn on the television."

As Driscoll headed for a conference room, army major Stephen V. Long was attending a meeting. Like Chris Braman, Long was also an airborne ranger attached to the Second Battalion of the Seventy-Fifth Ranger Regiment. During the invasion of Grenada in 1983, Long had been part of an assault force charged with taking out a Cuban military installation on the island. During the insertion, the CH-47 Chinook helicopter carrying his unit collided with three other helicopters.

Many of his comrades, including his roommate and best friend, were killed in the ensuing crash. As the chopper came to ground, Long found himself pinned under a piece of the tail section with a broken back. He had no idea whether the helicopter would burst into flames at any moment. Suddenly and for no apparent reason, the tail shifted and released him from its grip. Long remembered lying on the ground and feeling as if he had cheated death. It was something that would haunt him for many years afterward. He always wondered why fate had spared him and taken his friends.

NAVY COMMAND CENTER, D RING, FIRST FLOOR—0903 HOURS

As Lieutenant Kevin Shaeffer stood listening to the other officers talk about the first plane crash, he heard a collective gasp and looked at the TV just as the dark silhouette of a passenger jet came out of nowhere and hit the second World Trade Center. The sight raised the hairs on the back of his neck. He checked the time. It was a little after 9:03 a.m.

ARMY PERSONNEL CENTER, E RING, SECOND FLOOR—0903 HOURS

Marian Serva had averted her gaze for only a second when she saw the black wing of the second plane suddenly appear in one corner of the screen. She tried to catch her breath as a huge fireball shot out one end of the south tower. No one in the room moved, their eyes fixed on the television set. John Yates walked up and stared at the TV. A black hole appeared where the plane had literally disintegrated. Through the smoke, he could see the fires beginning to race through the floors. Yates looked around as more people emerged from their cubicles to watch. One of these was fifty-three-year-old Canfield D. Boone, a former National Guard reserve officer who had gone on active duty in 1986 and had only just been promoted to a "full-bird" colonel. He had a wife at home and three grown sons. All morning, his mind had been occupied with plans for the restoration of an old Chevy Impala convertible that his sons were helping him with, but right now he couldn't think about anything else but the fate of the people in those towers. Deep down, a part of him was also worried about his family and his country.

SUBOFFICE OF SECRETARY OF DEFENSE, A RING, FOURTH FLOOR—0903 HOURS

Commander Dave Tarantino saw the second plane hit and knew instantly that it bore the particular stamp of the al-Qaeda terrorist organization. Working for the Office of the Secretary of Defense, he was aware that al-Qaeda was the primary threat to the United States and had been for some time. Many different organizations had been hard at work for years trying to get the leader of this group, the Saudi millionaire Osama bin Laden. The CIA even had its own "Bin Laden task force," which in the late 1990s had tried to either kidnap or assassinate him. There were many terrorist organizations in the world, but none were more possessed of a hatred for America than this one.

Watching the footage, Tarantino now concluded that it was part of a coordinated attack and was amazed that Washington, DC, had not been hit yet. His senses went into overdrive.

PENTAGON FIRE STATION—0903 HOURS

Alan Wallace, Dennis Young, and Mark Skipper stood silently in the fire station lounge, having just witnessed the second attack. Wallace watched the hot orange fireball explode out of one side of the World Trade Center, engulfing the top half of the tower in smoke. Large pieces of debris fell to the streets below. Being a fireman, he could well imagine the horror of being inside that building. The three men stood in the same place, watching repeats of the footage for nearly ten minutes.

ROSSLYN, VIRGINIA—0903 HOURS

Major Dan Pantaleo, USMC, and his coworkers had heard about the first plane crash into the north tower of the World Trade Center. Everyone assumed that this was a small plane that had flown too close to the great tower, but now news was coming over the radio of a second plane crash into the south tower and that it was a jetliner. Pantaleo instantly thought of Pusan, Korea, where he had been stationed in 1989, and the scene of two horrific plane crashes that took the lives of twenty-one of his fellow marines. He had personally helped with the recovery that day, and the scene had been so gruesome that the memory was still fresh in his mind.

WALTER REED ARMY MEDICAL CENTER—0903 HOURS

Lieutenant Colonel Ed Lucci stared at the horrifying image on his TV. His training and his instincts told him that this was an act of terrorism, but he didn't have the feeling that anything was going to happen in Washington. He looked at his watch. He was due to meet several people within the next half hour. Ironically, they were going to ride downtown together for a meeting on counterterrorism. He left the waiting room and went to get his papers together but thought he might just as well stay where he was. New York City was now the real classroom.

NEW CASTLE COUNTY COURTHOUSE WORK SITE, NEW CASTLE, DELAWARE—0903 HOURS

Mike Flocco and his apprentice took the elevator back up from the "boneyard," where they had assembled the supplies they would need for the afternoon's work. As they stepped off the elevator, someone told them that the other World Trade Center tower had been hit.

"This is war," Mike said flatly. The seriousness of his statement now weighed heavily on everyone in the room.

ARMY PERSONNEL CENTER, SECOND FLOOR—0905 HOURS

Lieutenant Colonel Ted Anderson stood in front of a television set, watching both towers of the World Trade Center burn. Nearby, he could hear someone crying. Anderson quickly broke away and walked out to the mall entrance of the Pentagon to the security desk. He asked the officers there if they had seen the attacks in New York, and they said that they had. Anderson advised them to initiate an immediate security upgrade for the Pentagon. He told them that this was likely organized state-sponsored terrorism and that the Pentagon was an obvious target. The security officers agreed with him and initiated the upgrade. Anderson walked back to his office. As he sat down at his desk, he tried to focus on his emails but couldn't get his mind off the images of those burning towers. His situational awareness, the result of years in the military, was telling him that he was in danger.

FEDERAL CREDIT UNION OFFICE, FAIRFAX, VIRGINIA—0906 HOURS

Arlington County fire chief Ed Plaugher sat at a desk, filling out paperwork to secure a loan for a motor home he and his wife were trying to buy. A few minutes before, the loan officer had told him about a plane flying into the north tower of the World Trade Center. Plaugher instantly remembered an incident during World War II when a bomber had flown into the Empire State Building. He sat there, thinking about all the trouble the FDNY would have getting the thing under control, when the loan officer returned to his desk and informed Plaugher that a second plane had just flown into the south tower of the World Trade Center. Plaugher now knew it was a terrorist attack. The thoughts of the chief of the Arlington Fire Department immediately turned to the Pentagon.

For many years, the Arlington Fire Department had been the designated first responder to any fire at the Pentagon. Plaugher knew that the sheer size of the structure could pose problems for rescue crews and firemen alike. In July 1959, a fire broke out in the basement of the great building and burned for five hours, destroying four thousand square feet of space and doing some $7 million worth of damage. It had taken three whole engine companies, with over three hundred fire fighters and seventy pieces of equipment, to fight it.

Times had changed in terms of both the quality of equipment and technology, but a fire was still a fire. For the past several years, Plaugher had spent a lot of time trying to get the US government to approve upgraded equipment for his people. The money had finally broken through the red tape, but no one had seen any of it yet, most of it being tied up in federal coffers. It made him angry that politicians would risk the lives of his men because of concerns over money.

ARMY PERSONNEL ADMINISTRATIVE CENTER, E RING, FIRST FLOOR—0907 HOURS

Roxane Cruz-Cortez ate breakfast and listened as her coworker Bruno told her about the World Trade Center fire. Cruz-Cortez noticed that he seemed especially nervous. He couldn't take his eyes off the television screen and talked in a voice that seemed calm but was laced with fear.

"I've got a cousin who works in one of those towers," he said. "I tried to call home, but I couldn't get anybody."

"Did they say if it was an accident?" she asked him, trying to downplay the thing. Bruno shrugged his shoulders.

"I don't think they know what it is," he said quietly, the anguish beginning to show on his face.

"Just keep trying them," Cruz-Cortez reassured him. "You'll get through."

All at once, Bruno turned toward her. "You know what," he said. "When I was in New York last time, I remember somebody telling me that the Pentagon would be a good target for a terrorist."

The thought struck Cruz-Cortez, and she froze for a moment, thinking about the possibilities.

"I hope you're wrong," she said, but almost as soon as the words left her mouth, the radio blared that a second plane had just flown straight into the south tower of the World Trade Center. Cruz-Cortez stopped chewing and looked at Bruno, whose face had a sudden, horrified look.

B RING, FIRST FLOOR—0908 HOURS

John Driscoll and several of his coworkers walked into a conference room, where they were immediately confronted with a television screen showing the images from New York City. Driscoll stood lost in thought. He remembered being interviewed by Wall Street financial analysts years before in the Windows on the World restaurant at the top of one of the towers.

Upon viewing the first plane crash, he had been one of the few who had sensed that it wasn't an accident. It looked too deliberate. Now that a second plane had struck the other tower, Driscoll knew instantly that it was the work of terrorists. Without hesitation, he picked up the phone and called his wife, Kathy, at their home in Foggy Bottom some three and a half miles from the Pentagon and told her to stay away from the World Bank Headquarters building. Trouble had been expected there some days before because of meetings held in early September, which usually drew protesters. After speaking with his wife, Driscoll grabbed the package for the Joint Chiefs of Staff and told one of his coworkers that he was going to take it across the Pentagon to the contracting officer.

"We could all be doing something different in a few days," he said prophetically as he walked out the door.

WALTER REED ARMY MEDICAL CENTER—0908 HOURS

Major Ben Starnes stood at the front desk, thinking about family friends who lived in Manhattan. Someone had told him that the plane that hit the north tower of the World Trade Center was a passenger aircraft. He had seen the footage on CNN and was worried. His friends lived only five blocks away from the towers in a small loft in Tribeca Square, very close to everything that was going on. As he watched the TV screen, a frantic patient approached him.

"Hey, Doc, a plane just hit the south tower of the World Trade Center."

"Yes, I know," Starnes replied. "I already saw it."

"No, you don't understand," the patient said. "The first plane hit the north tower. Another plane just flew into the second tower, the south tower, on live television!" Starnes rushed back into the waiting room to see both towers now on fire and burning.

ARMY PERSONNEL CENTER, E RING,
SECOND FLOOR—0909 HOURS

Lieutenant Colonel Kip Taylor, possibly feeling crowded out by all of the people around Marian Serva's TV, walked to his office, which was along the west wall, directly overlooking the helipad. He closed the door and turned the channel on the TV to CNN, then sat down and watched the broadcast. Somewhere inside, like all other people watching the events in New York City this morning, he was glad it wasn't him. His wife, Nancy, was now pregnant with their second son, and he couldn't bear the thought of leaving his young children fatherless.

OFFICE OF THE SECRETARY OF DEFENSE,
E RING, THIRD FLOOR—0909 HOURS

Secretary of Defense Donald Rumsfeld sat in his private dining room on the north side of the Pentagon, conducting a meeting. The Defense Department was trying to secure $18 billion in funding from Congress, $8.3 billion of it earmarked specifically for defending the country against ballistic missile attacks. The sixty-nine-year-old Rumsfeld, a former naval aviator, was an old hand in Washington and experienced in Middle Eastern affairs. As Ronald Reagan's special envoy to the Middle East, he had been one of the last US officials out of Lebanon in 1983 when American troops withdrew. Rumsfeld himself was the man who had personally informed General Tannous, the leader of the Christian militia, that the US was pulling out of the region.

As secretary of defense, Rumsfeld was privy to daily intelligence briefings, which he studied with the diligence of an astronomer looking for a comet. But he also possessed something more: an understanding, born of years of involvement in diplomatic and intelligence matters, of the dangerous forces in the world bent on destroying America and its people. He believed that a strong Defense Department was essential to ensuring peace and stability in both the US and the world, and this would be his guiding light in matters in which he had a direct hand.

This morning, news had come of the first plane crash into the World Trade Center in New York. Rumsfeld, always alert to anything suspicious, was instantly on guard, yet remained reserved. Most people were saying that it was probably an accident, and he knew this was the most likely scenario. Still, he was not a man to ignore even the slightest ripple in the firmament. In the back of his mind, he was not going to relax until he had a satisfactory explanation.

As the meeting continued, US Representative Christopher Cox, R-California, saw Rumsfeld's eyes grow cold as the secretary threw a hard stare at everyone in the room.

"Let me tell ya," he said in what was left of a Chicago accent, "I've been around the block a few times, and there will be another event and it could be us!"

Just as he uttered these words, an aide walked into the room and handed him a note informing him of the second tower hit.

LANGLEY AIR FORCE BASE, HAMPTON ROADS, VIRGINIA—0910 HOURS

Major Dean Eckmann of the 119th Fighter Wing, North Dakota Air National Guard, heard the horn sound and saw the yellow light blink on the control tower, indicating battle stations. Captain Craig Borgstrom and Major Brad Derrig, standing nearby, also heard the alarm. All three pilots ran to the command center for further instructions. Out on the tarmac, air force weapons technicians prepared three F-16 fighter aircraft for battle, loading ammunition into the General Electric M61 20 mm Vulcan cannons mounted near the cockpits. These modern-day Gatling guns could fire 6,600 rounds per minute, enough to quickly destroy any aircraft in their sights. Under the wings of the aircraft, the technicians had loaded AIM-9X Sidewinder missiles, which could destroy a jet in midair by homing in on the heat signature of its engines.

As the F-16s were being prepared at Langley, American Airlines Flight 77 was now high over West Virginia. Controllers in Indianapolis, desperately looking for the lost plane, saw an unidentified aircraft reappear on their screens eight minutes and thirteen seconds after they had lost the transponder beacon. They notified Air Force Search and Rescue based at Langley Air Force Base and asked them to dispatch aircraft to look for a downed plane. They also contacted the West Virginia State Police and notified them of the situation. At about this same time, air traffic controllers in the Washington Center sector picked up an aircraft on their screens as the plane crossed into their airspace. It had no transponder signal. Along isolated roads in the mountains of West Virginia, state troopers searched everywhere for any sign of a downed aircraft, but American Airlines Flight 77 was now many miles to the east, closing in on Washington, DC.

NAVAL SPECIAL WARFARE, C RING,
FIFTH FLOOR—0910 HOURS

As a navy SEAL, Commander Craig Powell once parachuted into the middle of the Pacific Ocean to save a man in a small raft who was dying of blood poisoning. The jump had to be perfectly timed, and he had to land right on top of the raft or be swept out into the rough current of the Pacific. Powell rescued the man, saving his life, but he was a navy SEAL, and this kind of thing was considered routine "mule work."

This morning, however, Powell was not in the middle of the Pacific Ocean. He was sitting at his desk, reading an acquisition report. He had recently been transferred from Kingston, Jamaica, where he had served as a defense attaché for Naval Special Warfare. The capital of Kingston was considered one of the three deadliest cities in the world, with a murder rate of nearly two thousand people a year for a population numbering around eighty thousand citizens. The whole city was divided into gang territories controlled by political and tribal factions. A person could get killed just for being in the wrong place at the wrong time.

Powell had seen his share of violence before Jamaica, though. The six-feet-five, 260-pound SEAL had been born in Des Moines, Iowa, but had grown up in places as diverse as Thailand, the Philippines, and Australia. He had seen action in the Gulf War, and he knew firsthand that mistakes in the field got people killed. Powell's training also provided him with a heightened awareness of the possibility of random violence and how terror was used to gain an objective.

He remembered one incident wherein someone had called in a bomb threat in order to evacuate a building. When the occupants walked outside, they were blown up with a hand grenade.

On September 11, Powell had been in Washington barely four days on his new assignment to the OPNAV staff as deputy branch head for Naval Special Warfare. That morning was the first day of school for his kids in nearby Herndon, Virginia.

Sitting in the office with Powell was Lieutenant Olin Sell, his assistant. As the two men talked, a sailor came into the room.

"Sir, you'd better turn on the TV." When Powell turned on the set, he could not believe his eyes. He rose up slightly in his chair as he watched the replay of a plane striking the south tower, his senses instantly on overload.

Damn, he thought to himself. *We're going to war, and I'll be sitting at a desk.*

ARMY PERSONNEL CENTER, C RING, SECOND FLOOR—0910 HOURS

People from around the town of Gum Neck, North Carolina, will tell you that Tony Rose is as tough as a "lighter knot," that part of the heartwood of an old tree that will burn for hours in a woodstove. When he was a boy, he and an uncle were once clearing fence line in the swamp when his uncle's machete glanced off a vine and cut his knee open to the bone. "I need some help, son," his uncle said calmly as Rose turned to see the older man's leg covered in blood. In a few minutes, Rose had stopped the bleeding, patched the leg up, and carried his uncle through more than a mile of swamp and tangled vines to the porch of his ancestral home, where his mother promptly sewed up the wound.

As he grew older and joined the Eighty-Second Airborne Division, rising to the rank of sergeant major, Rose sustained many injuries, but he was always like those old lighter knots, and you just couldn't burn him up. On one tour, when Rose was stationed in Bosnia, a UN soldier from France threw his machine gun over his shoulder and caught him in the cheek, giving him a nice-sized gash. Rose stopped the bleeding, went to a hotel room in Sarajevo, and called the main desk for a needle and thread.

"Just set your clothing outside the door, and we will take care of it," the hotel manager graciously informed him.

"No, you don't understand," Rose replied. "I need it for my face."

Through perseverance and tenacity, Rose gained a reputation for never allowing his men to be tougher than he was and never asking them to do anything he wouldn't do first. He was a man who led from the front.

On this morning, Rose got up early, fed his dogs, and made the short drive to the Pentagon. His wife was in St. Louis, helping her sister prepare for a nephew's wedding, and he would be going there in a few days to join her.

Rose arrived at the Pentagon and greeted his operations NCO, a man named John Frazier. Both men were lucky in that they had desks that faced a set of huge windows looking down onto A/E Drive between C and B Rings. Rose had been told by someone that these windows were bombproof and cost $10,000 apiece. He and Frazier headed to get coffee as they usually did each morning. Rose wanted to get started early because he had to finalize an agreement with a local hotel for a counselors' conference to be held in two weeks.

As the two men walked together, Rose thought about how the old offices of the Pentagon on the first and second floors had been turned into enormous "cubicle farms" as a result of the recent renovation. Like the high-priced windows, everything was now Kevlar or steel-reinforced. At the far end of the hallway were huge security doors leading into the main hallway, which Rose knew would automatically lock during emergencies, thereby sealing off one section of the building from another to prevent the spread of fire.

Prior to the renovation, Tony and John would have been separated by two walls. Rose looked out over the rows of little hutches everywhere.

People intermingled a lot better without the walls. It felt like a family; to him these people *were* his family. All of the people working in this vast area were involved in Army Personnel, the "people" side of the military, and they were some of the finest men and women Rose had ever worked with, trudging through government red tape and bureaucratic wrangling every day and trying to improve the lives of their fellow soldiers. It wasn't an easy job, but when you succeeded, the end result was far more gratifying than any other type of job.

As Rose and Frazier headed across the cubicle farm to get coffee, Victor Correa was in his office checking his emails. As Correa tried to concentrate, he kept hearing the words "New York" and "towers" and saw a crowd gathering around a nearby TV. Unable to stem his curiosity, he left his cubicle and walked over to watch with the others. He stared in horror as a replay of a plane striking the second tower played over and over.

Correa knew that the army would shortly activate "the cell"—a plan of action to be implemented by the Personnel Command in the event of a major disaster. Activation of the cell would require a large output of human resources, and in his mind, he was already at work preparing for it, thinking about what New York City would need.

US MARINE CORPS OFFICE OF THE GENERAL COUNSEL, E RING, FOURTH FLOOR—0911 HOURS

Marine Corps lawyer Peter Murphy, personal counsel for the commandant of the Marine Corps, stood in his office on the fourth floor of Wedge One's E Ring. From his window, he could see the helipad and the firehouse below with the firemen working on their truck. The day before, he had watched President Bush fly off in Marine One. This morning, he was meeting with two of his lawyers, Major Joe D. Baker and Mr. Robert D. Hogue. Hogue was Murphy's deputy counsel. In one corner of the office was the red flag of the Marine Corps with its eagle globe and anchor and the words "Semper Fidelis" trimmed in gold across the bottom. On the wall near the flag was a clock. Murphy glanced at it. It was almost a quarter after nine. The meeting would begin shortly.

In front of Murphy on the blue carpet was an antique desk presented to him by a former Marine Corps commandant. A Bible sat on
one corner of this desk. In the corner opposite the desk was a television monitor tuned to CNN. For the past ten minutes, Murphy and
the others had been watching the north tower of the World Trade
Center burning. In the middle of the discussion, Murphy saw something that made him stop talking. He paused midsentence, walked to
the TV, and turned up the volume. The second tower was now on fire,
and playbacks showed a jet appearing out of nowhere and exploding
into the building. He immediately asked Hogue to walk into the outer
office and check with the administrative clerk, Corporal Tim Garafola,
on the current security status of the Pentagon. Garafola checked his
emails and found a security status of "Normal."

PENTAGON FIRE STATION—0911 HOURS

In the yard below Wedge One, firefighters Mark Skipper and Alan
Wallace resumed working on Truck 61, engaging in an intense discussion of the New York attacks. There was little else on their minds at
this point.

Truck 61, a Titan 3000, was fully equipped for dealing with the
worst kinds of fires. In its steel belly, it carried fifteen hundred gallons
of water and two hundred gallons of 3 percent foam, used specifically
to fight fires involving jet fuel. It was equipped with a high-powered
water cannon on top that could pump six hundred gallons of water and
foam per minute. Inside was a full equipment kit as well as a breathing apparatus and a high-band radio for communication. As the two
men worked, neither of them could stop thinking about the New York
attacks and the people in those towers.

In the lounge of the Pentagon firehouse, firefighter Dennis Young
stared at the television. Young had been fighting fires for twenty-two
years, starting in the air force when the military still retained active-
duty firemen. As he watched the towers burn, he recalled a C-130
crashing to earth near Fairbanks, Alaska, in 1989. He remembered
the smell of the jet fuel, the fireball, and the incredible destruction.
He was one of the first on the scene and knew how quickly fire could

consume a human body. His unit was only able to save nine out of the thirty passengers on board that day. Now, as he watched this, the memories came flooding back. The Fairbanks incident was the first time Young had seen somebody burn to death right in front of him. He never wanted to see that again.

PENTAGON AIR CONTROL TOWER—0912 HOURS

Sean Boger and Jackie Kidd readied themselves for the arrival of President Bush. Both were active-duty soldiers assigned as air controllers for the helipad, Boger being a former NCO of the year for the Military District of Washington. They, too, had been monitoring events in New York City. After witnessing a second plane fly into the south tower, they both realized that security would immediately be tightened around the Pentagon.

"I guess I'd better get my lunch out of the car," Kidd said as she got up and walked to the exit. Boger stared at the television.

"I'm amazed no one's ever flown an airplane into the Pentagon," he said, "even by accident."

Kidd grinned. "Keep your eyes open!" she said, and left to get her lunch.

CLASSROOM, FORT MYER, VIRGINIA—0912 HOURS

Assistant Fire Chief Russell "Rusty" Dodge, Jr., a six-feet-two, 275-pound firefighter, stood conducting training in airport emergency operations for the Fort Myer crew normally assigned to the Pentagon. Dodge was a member of Virginia's Fort Belvoir Fire Department and a veteran firefighter with many years of experience. Raised in Massachusetts, he had once belonged to the FDNY before moving to the DC metropolitan area. Near Dodge sat Captain Dennis Gilroy, chief of the Fort Myer station and Alan Wallace's boss.

During a break, Dodge heard about the attacks on the World Trade Center and immediately thought of his close friend Joel Kanasky, a firefighter in New York City. Dodge remembered Kanasky's big shaved head and knew that he still worked with RESCUE 1 in Manhattan, only three blocks from the World Trade Center. He would surely be involved in this.

The only form of communication in the room was a radio tuned to an emergency frequency. With no TV in the classroom, Dodge tried to carry on with the training even though he couldn't stop thinking about his friend and about what was happening two hundred miles to the north. It almost seemed useless to continue. All thoughts were on New York City now.

HOME OF NANCY MAY, LAS VEGAS, NEVADA—0912 HOURS

Nancy May picked up the phone. The voice on the other end of the line was that of her daughter Renee, a flight attendant on board American Airlines Flight 77, telling her that six Arab men had hijacked the plane. May felt a sudden coldness in her heart, but she marveled at how her daughter could be so composed in such a situation. It helped calm her down. She listened as Renee told her that the pilots were being taken to the back of the plane with her, and she didn't think any of the crew had been able to inform the airline. The sound of her voice made it clear that she was in deep trouble, but she was levelheaded enough to ask her mother to call the airline and notify them of the situation.

"I love you," Nancy told her, and hung up the phone. It would be the last time she would hear her daughter's voice. Her hands trembling, she immediately made a call to American Airlines.

E RING, THIRD FLOOR, WEDGE ONE,
THE PENTAGON—0915 HOURS

On the third floor of E Ring, the outermost section of the complex, Dan Fraunfelter, a contractor on the Pentagon renovation, was busy finishing up a punch list of last-minute tasks to be done before the new upgrades to the building were considered finished. This was the third phase of a $1.2 billion renovation begun in 1998 and considered the largest effort of its kind in the world. Wedge One alone had taken

Fraunfelter and his crew nearly four years to complete. Many of the new offices were already occupied, and in a few days, the area would be officially turned over to the government.

Fraunfelter, an architecture student, remembered the day he first inspected the Pentagon and how shocked he had been at the condition of a building that he, like most other Americans, had always considered impregnable. His construction crews were astounded to find that the original wiring, piping, and ventilation systems from the 1940s were all still in place—and rapidly deteriorating.

This obsolete infrastructure was creating immense problems. When the Pentagon was first built, telephones were scarce. There were no computers, electric typewriters, or fax machines. There was no such thing as fiber optic cable. The only power outlets were like those of an ordinary house. Illumination came from common ceiling lights. As the years wore on, these ancient systems were never replaced, only added to as new technologies developed. What resulted was a mass of wires, cables, and pipes going in every direction with no guidebook or map to show the engineers where they came from or where they terminated. Insufficient grounding and unsafe routing of the wires overloaded the power grid, causing as many as thirty localized power outages every day. The potential existed for a complete power failure in a building that operated around the clock. Of major concern was the possibility that any outage would cause the Department of Defense computers, which required optimum temperature control in order to function, to shut down within ninety seconds.

Worse yet, Fraunfelter was astounded to learn that the building had failed to pass the national electrical code every single year since 1953. In the winter months, occupants used space heaters for warmth because of the failure of the old heating systems. An additional surprise was the discovery of tinder-dry horsehair in the attic near the roof, a primitive form of insulation.

If all this wasn't enough, Fraunfelter also discovered that the very foundation of the building was not up to modern standards. He had inspected the construction of the walls and found them to be about two feet thick, with the inner wall comprising ten inches of concrete, buttressed by eight inches of brick and six inches of Indiana limestone in layers on the outer wall, but he was amazed to discover that the rebar (or iron reinforcing rods) was only an inch and a half thick.

The Pentagon had been built like a fortress, so why did the government skimp on the steel? Because it had to.

When original construction commenced, America had just entered World War II, and workers were not allowed to use any steel to frame the building, all of it being diverted to shipyards and war production plants. All framing was done with reinforced concrete. Instead of steel elevators, concrete ramps were used to gain elevation from one floor to the next. By sacrificing steel in the construction of the Pentagon, the United States Navy gained enough surplus steel to build one complete battleship. This was deemed a good trade-off at the time, and the absence of steel reinforcement wasn't cause for much concern.

Oklahoma City changed everything. After the terrorist attack on the Murrah Federal Office Building at Oklahoma City in 1995, Fraunfelter's people received the go-ahead from Congress for a full renovation and upgrade of the Pentagon, which commenced in 1998. Floor joists were installed throughout the structural supports for added strength. All of the wiring and piping in Wedge One was replaced, and a new heating and refrigeration plant was created. New power grids were installed, and the floors were double-framed to enable them to withstand an abnormal amount of stress. The vertical supports were replaced with spiral steel-reinforced concrete columns. In addition, a special mesh had been installed in the section parallel to the helipad to protect the sensitive new Navy Command Center in the event of a helicopter crash and/or bomb attack. The rebar in the new concrete walls had been increased an inch in thickness. In fact, everything was increased in size proportionately. Blast-resistant windows two inches thick and weighing 2,500 pounds each had been installed on the outer ring with double-paned insulation to save on heating costs in the winter. Vertical steel beams flanked each of these windows, with a Kevlar-like material stretched between them to catch debris in the event of an explosion.

These new features made Wedge One far safer, though the rest of the building was much the same as it had been in 1943. Even so,

Fraunfelter was confident that Wedge One could now withstand the effects of a truck bomb like that at Oklahoma City. But what about some other kind of attack?

ARMY PERSONNEL CENTER, E RING, SECOND FLOOR—0915 HOURS

Inside the large conference room, Phil McNair's meeting was now in progress, and Marilyn Wills was speaking. The room had a raised platform at one end where a person could stand to give a presentation. The usual people were in attendance, including Max Beilke, who, midway through Wills's speech, left the room to go over to the small conference room and sit in on Maude's session. It would be the last time anyone there would see the old warrior alive.

At 9:20 a.m., just as Beilke was leaving the conference room, Lieutenant General Maude's secretary, Deborah Ramsaur, received a call from McNair's wife, Nancy, who was worried about the attacks in New York.

"Deborah, there are funny things going on right now. You all need to be careful," she said.

"Want me to get Phil?" Ramsaur asked.

There was silence for a moment. "No, don't bother him," Nancy McNair said. "It can wait."

SOUTH PARKING LOT, PENTAGON—0920 HOURS

Frank Probst, a defense contractor on the Pentagon renovation, got out of his car and began walking toward a construction trailer located just south of the helipad. As he walked toward the construction trailer near Washington Boulevard, he glanced at the large olive-drab-green diesel backup generator, surrounded by concrete poles and a chain-link fence. Anything olive drab took his mind right back to Vietnam.

In January 1967, Probst had been a platoon leader with the 173rd Airborne Brigade, patrolling in a place called the "Iron Triangle" near

Bien Hoa, Vietnam. The Iron Triangle was a Viet Cong stronghold with a vast network of underground tunnels leading in every direction.

Probst would never forget the day he actually went into one of these tunnels where VC guerillas were making "pie-pan" mines, explosives sandwiched between two tin plates and then lacquered to keep them waterproof. He had gone inside with a gas mask on his face and was crawling through the tunnel, when one of his men set off a booby trap that ignited the lacquer fumes on some of the pie-pan mines, causing them to explode. The next thing Probst knew, he was lying in the grass with burns all over his back, hands, and arms. He was taken away by helicopter, but that day would never be far from his memory.

BOLLING AIR FORCE BASE, WASHINGTON, DC—0920 HOURS

Reserve Senior Master Sergeant Noel Sepulveda, USAF, rode his motorcycle through the gate at Bolling Air Force Base, headed for the Pentagon, where he was due to take a test at 9:30 a.m. The fifty-three-year-old Sepulveda was a reserve medical inspector with the air force but was currently assigned to an office within the Pentagon even though his home base was Kirtland Air Force Base, New Mexico, where he worked for the Air Force Inspection Agency. Today, as he did every Tuesday, he had gone to Bolling for a first sergeants' meeting. Like everyone else, he grumbled as he got caught up in traffic coming into the Pentagon, but heavy traffic was a fact of life in the morning in Washington, DC.

In the back of his mind, though, Sepulveda was grateful for the quiet monotony of office work. In 1970, he had been a medic with the First Cavalry Division working on board a Huey helicopter when an enemy soldier, posing as wounded, tried to sneak onto the helicopter with a weapon. Sepulveda released the winch and dropped the man on the ground, at which point the tail rotor was hit by a mortar round, the resulting shock wave throwing Sepulveda out of the helicopter and dropping him through tree branches to the ground. The fall broke his lower leg, his right hand, and two of his ribs.

Squinting through the pain, the tough Puerto Rican American from Passaic, New Jersey, saw a bright orange fireball as the Huey exploded and crashed. He was the only survivor.

NORTHEAST AIR DEFENSE SECTOR COMMAND, ROME, NEW YORK—0921 HOURS

A controller for the Northeast Air Defense Sector (NEADS) now took a call from an FAA controller in the Boston sector who had an urgent message. The Boston controller informed the NEADS controller that American Airlines Flight 11 was apparently still in the air and on its way toward Washington, DC. To the NEADS controller, this was confirmation of the whereabouts of Flight 11, a missing aircraft for which they had been looking for more than an hour.

Both controllers continued to talk, unaware that American Airlines Flight 11 had crashed into the north tower of the World Trade Center over thirty minutes before. The FAA controller proceeded to plan a reaction.

"I'm going to try and confirm an ID for you, but I would assume he's somewhere over, uh, either New Jersey or somewhere farther south," he said.

The NEADS controller tried to confirm the information. "So American 11 isn't the hijack at all then, right?"

"No, he is a hijack," the FAA controller shot back.

The NEADS controller sat up straight in his chair. "American 11 is a hijack?"

"Yes," came the shocking reply.

"And he's heading into Washington?" the NEADS controller asked, shaken.

"Yes," the FAA controller replied. "This could be a third aircraft."

OFFICE OF SOLICITOR GENERAL
THEODORE OLSON—0925 HOURS

Theodore Olson heard his cell phone ring and hit the Talk button. It was his wife, Barbara. He knew right away from her voice that something was wrong. She told him that some hijackers had taken over the plane and moved everyone to the back. From what she could see, they were armed with knives and box cutters. Hearing this, Olson knew that his wife was a fighter and would do anything to help resolve the situation. After watching the footage from New York City, he was also aware that her chances of getting out of this thing alive were slim. He tried his best to remain calm. He continued to talk to her, and then the phone went dead. A few minutes passed, and the phone rang again. It was Barbara, who must have seen one of the terrorists approaching and quickly cut the phone off and hid it, redialing when she figured it was safe.

Theo Olson told his wife about the attacks on the World Trade Center. There was silence on the line for a few seconds as husband and wife somehow knew this was the last time they would ever talk to each other. "Everything will be alright," Olson told his wife, knowing the only thing to do now was pray.

"What do I tell the pilot to do?" she asked her husband. Before he could reply, the phone went dead.

Theodore Olson didn't know whether his wife had been discovered talking on the phone and killed, or whether the plane had crashed. He didn't know anything. The ensuing seconds were like a hundred years as he waited for his wife to call back, but a third call never came. As calmly as he could, he picked up the phone and called the office of Attorney General John Ashcroft but could not reach him.

Failing this, he immediately dialed the command center at the Justice Department and informed them of his wife's call.

SOUTH PARKING LOT, PENTAGON—0927 HOURS

Senior Master Sergeant Noel Sepulveda sat on his motorcycle, talking to a Department of Defense policeman. Sepulveda wanted to park in the huge south lot, but the policeman advised him to park it against one of the light poles next to Washington Boulevard. This was going to make him late, but he followed the instructions, running toward the building with his cell phone in his hand. He called the testing station to keep them from locking him out, but the voice on the other end told him the test had been canceled. "Didn't you hear?" a woman said. "The World Trade Center towers in New York were hit by passenger jets. They think we're under a terrorist attack."

Sepulveda looked around at the calm of the morning and the blue sky. He had heard earlier about a crash in New York but had understood that it was an accident, that it was a light aircraft or something. Reaching Corridor Two at the south wall, he immediately turned around and began running back toward his motorcycle.

At 9:25 a.m., in response to the attacks on the World Trade Center, the FAA Command Center gave the order for "full ground stop." This command, which had never before been issued in the history of the country, effectively grounded all private and commercial aircraft in the continental United States. Within an hour, all international flights currently inbound to the US would be diverted to other countries, primarily Canada. Air traffic controllers in the major Canadian cities grew concerned as their flight loads increased dramatically with jets headed into Canadian airspace from every direction. There were 3,949 flights in the air at this moment, and over the next hour, 75 percent of them would come to ground. Many of these flights were forced to circle continuously with Canadian controllers denying them permission to land. Within the next two hours, the skies over the US would be virtually empty, with the exception of military aircraft.

AMERICAN AIRLINES FLIGHT 77—0929 HOURS

In the cockpit of American Airlines Flight 77, pilot Charles Burlingame was removed from his seat and taken to the rear with the other passengers as Hani Hanjour sat down and took control of the aircraft. Flight 77 was now less than forty miles from the Pentagon.

In the months leading up to September 11, Hanjour's specified target had been the subject of much debate among the al-Qaeda hierarchy.

Bin Laden continually insisted that they strike the White House. He seemed to be completely obsessed with it. Others among the inner circle argued for the Pentagon. This debate raged back and forth until a rumor began to circulate that the United States Secret Service actually had a battery of surface-to-air missiles protecting the White House. Upon learning this, the decision was made to have Hanjour strike the Pentagon and Ziad Jarrah, the pilot of United Airlines Flight 93, strike the Capitol Building. Bin Laden's insistence on the White House never waned, however, as Hanjour was undoubtedly aware.

In the cockpit, Hanjour pushed forward slightly on the controls and began his descent into Washington, DC. Now, less than fifteen minutes from impact, Hanjour was still unsure which target he would attack. At one point, he must have indicated that he was going to dive toward the White House, since one of the terrorists walked to the back of the plane and announced to the passengers, "Call your family and tell them you are going to die. We are going to hit your White House."

Huddled at the back of the plane were the passengers and crew of American Airlines Flight 77, frightened and wondering what was going to happen next. Fifty-nine-year-old Robert Ploger III and his wife, Zandra, were on their honeymoon. Today, they were on their dream trip to Hawaii. Staring at the terrorists, Robert thought of his father, retired Major General Robert Ploger, who had helped take the Normandy beaches in World War II. *What would the old man do in this situation?* he asked himself.

He had heard his father's heroic stories many times, but when danger and the certainty of death were present, it was a different thing altogether. He was worried for his wife.

Standing silently off to one side were Wilson "Bud" Flagg and his wife, Darlene. The couple had driven to Dulles International Airport this morning from their cattle farm in Clarke County, Virginia. They were on their way to a family reunion in California. Flagg was a retired navy admiral who had piloted F-8 Crusader jets in Vietnam. He held the distinction of logging over three thousand hours in a jet fighter, more than any other pilot of that era. In the early 1990s, he had become embroiled in the navy's infamous Tailhook scandal, but the resulting fallout had never dulled his love of his country or the military.

Standing out among the other passengers was a tall, formidable-looking man with a black patch over his left eye. His name was John D. Yamnicky, Sr., a seventy-one-year-old defense contractor for Veridian Corporation and a retired navy pilot whose accomplishments in life would fill volumes. During the landings at Inchon, Korea, in 1950, he had served as an assault-wave leader on the beach, following this up with a tour of duty in Vietnam. His service as a test pilot bordered on the legendary. In one incident, both engines of his aircraft failed, forcing him to crash-land. He hit the runway so hard that it tore his landing gear off, causing the jet to slide down the runway and crash into a volleyball game being played by a group of marines. The marines ran in all directions as Yamnicky's jet cut its way through them, finally colliding with a wall of fifty-five-gallon drums that shot up into the air and fell directly onto his canopy, the plexiglass bubble saving his life.

The Pole's big arms were still rock hard even in his twilight years; Jennifer, his daughter, recalled him doing one-arm push-ups on a dare. Like Flagg and Burlingame, Yamnicky was a warrior, and with his one good eye he watched every movement of Moqed and al-Mihdhar, looking for any chance to get the drop on them, but his actions were undoubtedly tempered by the fact that a large number of children were standing close by. Seated near Yamnicky were Leslie Whittington and her husband, Charles Falkenberg, and their two daughters, eight-year-old Zoe and little Dana, just three years old, an innocent toddler who would be the youngest victim this day. The Falkenbergs were on the first leg of a two-and-a-half-month trip to Australia. Whittington was an economist and associate professor at Georgetown's Public Policy Institute and an expert on the impact of taxation on families, especially poor ones. Falkenberg worked for the Ecologic Corporation in Lanham, Maryland, and was involved in data delivery systems dealing with oceanography, ecology, and space science and had also worked on a study of the *Exxon Valdez* oil spill in Alaska. Their daughters had been excited about going to Australia, where Zoe couldn't wait to see kangaroos and koala bears.

Also present were several young students and their teachers from local DC middle schools, accompanied by two staff members of the National Geographic Society. One of them was Ann Judge, the head of National Geographic's travel department. Judge was known for her ability to arrange transport for personnel to difficult destinations and locations in backwater areas, including places in Africa and China that had no roads or limited access. This trip was special to her and more exciting than most of her former assignments because she was helping to introduce young children to the world of National Geographic. One of the children in Judge's group was eleven-year-old Bernard Curtis Brown, Jr., the son of navy Chief Petty Officer Bernard Curtis Brown, Sr., who worked in the new Navy Command Center at the Pentagon. Bernard was a quick-witted, assertive little boy who loved basketball and played as much as he could even though he was afflicted with chronic asthma. He and the other children had been selected by National Geographic to participate in their Sustainable Seas Expedition, a marine research project at the Channel Islands National Marine Sanctuary near Santa Barbara, California. Teacher Hilda Taylor was escorting Bernard, who was representing Leckie Elementary School. This morning, Bernard's mother, Sinita, had driven Taylor and her son from their home in the naval housing section at Bolling Air Force Base to Dulles for the trip to the West Coast. She remembered him smiling and waving goodbye to her as he walked proudly through the turnstile, wearing his National Geographic cap. His father would have normally been at work in the graphics shop of the Navy Command Center but had taken the day off. Bernard, frightened, sat on the floor of the plane, thinking about his mom and dad, wondering what was happening, and knowing that something had gone terribly wrong.

Standing near the front of the crowd, pilot Charles Burlingame pondered what to do. In all the hijackings he had ever heard about, the terrorists left the pilot in control of the plane. Now he had been removed from the cockpit. This worried him deeply. These men acted as if they knew how to fly a 757! Something far more sinister was at hand.

Burlingame had thought many times about the possibility of his airplane being hijacked and knew that the captain rarely survived a crash. He was a navy man and didn't yield easily to fear. Burlingame looked at Flagg and Yamnicky and some of the others and then at Charlebois. There was no way for them to get together and plot anything. Al-Mihdhar and Moqed were watching them all the time. And the women and children were too close. It was too risky. Even though the hijackers had taken complete control of the flight, Burlingame figured they would surely fly the plane somewhere, then land it and negotiate. This had been hijackers' modus operandi for decades. He tried to stay calm and let this thing play itself out. He still knew nothing of the New York attacks.

Huddled near Burlingame and Charlebois and partially hidden by them was Barbara Olson, well known to Americans as a commentator for CNN. Upon completing her law degree, she had worked as an assistant US Attorney and then as chief investigative counsel for the House Reform and Oversight Committee leading investigations into the Clinton administration. Over the years, she had been a Hollywood producer, a ballet dancer, and a lobbyist, but had recently become famous in political circles as a voice for the conservative right. She had been due to fly to Los Angeles the day before to appear on the television show *Politically Incorrect* but decided to stay at home to help her husband, Theodore, celebrate his sixty-first birthday. In one hand, she concealed a cell phone. As she watched the movements of the terrorists, without arousing suspicion, she quietly dialed a number.

LANGLEY AIR FORCE BASE, HAMPTON ROADS, VIRGINIA—0929 HOURS

Three fully armed F-16s lined up on the tarmac, awaiting the launch signal. Sitting in the cockpit of one of the planes, Major Dean Eckmann heard the words "Active air scramble, zero one, zero, max speed, zero nine zero for sixty." At this command, he and pilots Craig Borgstrom and Brad Derrig taxied onto the runway. In less than a minute, they were all launched and airborne, heading east. According to the standard flight plan, they would plot a trajectory of ninety degrees for sixty miles, heading straight out over the Atlantic Ocean. Eckmann knew this was done as a matter of routine because of civilian concerns over noise. It allowed them to gain altitude before coming back in over land.

At Dulles Airport, air traffic controllers spotted a blip on the radar screen. American Airlines Flight 77 was now between twelve and fourteen miles away from Washington, DC.

PENTAGON FIRE STATION—0930 HOURS

The phone rang like it was going to jump off the wall. Dennis Young picked it up. It was Fort Myer chief Charlie Campbell. His voice was deadly serious.

"Dennis, I'm getting a lot of information that the Pentagon might be targeted. You all need to be aware of everything that's going on around you right now, understand?"

"Yes sir," Young replied. He called outside to Alan Wallace and Mark Skipper, who were standing near the fire truck. Both firefighters came inside and spoke to Campbell individually. After hearing Campbell's advice, Wallace looked at Truck 61 and wondered whether he should move it back inside. He decided not to. This decision would save the lives of most of his friends.

AIR TRAFFIC CONTROL, REAGAN NATIONAL
AIRPORT—0930 HOURS

Air controller Chris Stephenson watched as an unidentified object entered his radar screen. It had no transponder signal and was traveling at over several hundred miles per hour. In addition to this, it had penetrated Prohibited Airspace 56, a highly restricted area surrounding the White House and the Capitol. Its altitude was well below the minimum ceiling of eighteen thousand feet required for this area.

Stephenson turned and looked through the windows of the tower. In the distance, he could see a jet, several miles out, turning to the right and descending. Aside from this plane, the skies were clear. His eyes followed the aircraft as it descended and then disappeared behind a building in nearby Crystal City, Virginia. He looked back at the radar screen to see the object still descending, the White House right in its path.

At Dulles International Airport, air traffic controllers were also watching the blip of the unidentified aircraft on their radar screen. "My God, it's headed straight for the White House!" Tom Howell shouted. It was now only five miles west/southwest of the Pentagon and closing fast. Realizing the situation was dire, the air control supervisor picked up the phone and called a Secret Service hotline number for the White House desk, speaking directly to the first agent who came on the line. "An aircraft is coming straight at you, and they're not talking to us," he said.

The agent signaled a general alert ordering the immediate evacuation of the vice president and most of the cabinet. While this was happening, Dulles controllers began counting down until the plane reached four miles' distance from the White House. Each of them sat helpless in their chairs, awaiting the inevitable. Then suddenly the aircraft made a sharp turn and veered away.

As Vice President Dick Cheney sat in his chamber in the West Wing of the White House, the door suddenly burst open, and several Secret Service agents entered the room. They grabbed him by his arms, shoulders, and belt and rushed him to a subterranean bunker. A few moments later, National Security Advisor Condoleezza Rice was escorted into the bunker as well. Several other agents went to get Cheney's wife. Reports from air traffic controllers at Dulles and Reagan, along with the events in New York City, led to an immediate evacuation of the White House and Congress.

On the streets surrounding the White House, government workers emerged to see military police carrying automatic weapons guarding every conceivable avenue of approach, their eyes focused intently on all movement. Secret Service and security guards hurried people away from the building and directed them down side streets. Some shouted orders to keep the crowd moving as they held submachine guns in their hands. Many of the people, their heads darting back and forth, gazed at the sky. Scared and confused, they carried briefcases and pocketbooks that almost appeared to be useless appendages weighing them down and slowing their escape.

ANDREWS AIR FORCE BASE, MARYLAND—0933 HOURS

Lieutenant Colonel Steve O'Brien, call sign "Gofer 06," had spent the night at Andrews Air Force Base after returning from a supply run to the Virgin Islands. This morning, he had taken off in his big C-130 Hercules en route to Minnesota, when he received an urgent request from controllers at Reagan National Airport via NEADS to break off and vector toward Washington, DC, to get a visual confirmation on a civilian jetliner. To O'Brien, this was a highly unusual request, but an order was an order. He immediately turned the C-130 around and began looking.

NORTHEAST AIR DEFENSE SECTOR COMMAND, ROME, NEW YORK—0933 HOURS

NEADS mission commander Kevin Nasypany now listened in shock as an FAA controller told him about another flight that had gone missing over Ohio nearly forty minutes earlier. All this time, they had been planning to deal with a threat from a plane flying in from the north. *Where in the hell did this other one come from?* he asked himself. He checked with nearby controllers for the approximate position of the unidentified flight and found that it was now less than six miles west-southwest of Washington and headed straight for the White House. For the past three-quarters of an hour, they had been chasing the wrong plane! His rush was intensified when it was reported that the fighters from Langley were currently two hundred miles from Washington, out over the Atlantic Ocean.

Nasypany demanded to know why the fighters had not gone directly to Washington as ordered and discovered that the FAA controller relaying the information hadn't realized that the order was to take precedence over the standard command to go zero nine zero for sixty out over the Atlantic first, which was based on civilian complaints about noise and shattered windows. In a cold sweat, Nasypany took control of the airspace personally, ordering the F-16s straight to Washington at the maximum speed of fifteen hundred miles per hour, yelling into the mic, "We need to get those back up there, now! . . . I don't care how many windows they break, goddamn it! . . . Push 'em back!" As he said these words, he knew it was too late.

At the Pentagon, on the second floor of the Army Personnel Center, John Yates was on the phone with his wife, Ellen, who had heard about the New York attacks but hadn't seen them on television.

"Please just work under your desk for the rest of the day," she pleaded with him.

"OK, honey, I will," Yates said as he hung up the phone and walked back to the television near Serva's cubicle, where he stood watching the footage from New York with Colonel Canfield Boone.

AMERICAN AIRLINES FLIGHT 77—0935 HOURS

Hani Hanjour now searched the landscape for the Pentagon. He was having trouble telling one building from the other. In the simulator, it had been easy to tell the different buildings apart, but now, up in the air, it wasn't so easy. He had been given alternate plans in case something went wrong. If he couldn't hit the Pentagon, he would go for the White House. He had been told that Bin Laden favored the White House above all other targets. He also remembered Mohamed Atta saying that if worse came to worst, he was just going to crash his plane into the streets of New York. Hanjour circled for a few moments, making erratic turns back and forth.

Air traffic controllers at Dulles and Reagan Airports were now watching Hanjour's irregular movements on their radar screens. American Airlines Flight 77 had been four miles from the White House when it abruptly turned away. This had put them into a panic. Where was it headed? The collective pressure in the room became almost too much to bear as they tried to pinpoint the exact location of the aircraft. They were soon put in contact with controllers in the Boston sector, who continued to maintain that the unidentified aircraft was probably American Airlines Flight 11, which had disappeared from their screens at 8:21 a.m. The last known communication from this aircraft had come at 8:14 a.m. It had now been nearly an hour since American

Airlines Flight 11 had crashed into the World Trade Center, yet they continued to look for it.

Near Terminal B of Reagan National Airport, a mile to the southeast of the Pentagon, a man driving his car suddenly grasped his side and blacked out, his hands falling from the wheel and the car crashing headlong into several other vehicles. Mike Defina, shift commander of the Aircraft Rescue Firefighting Unit, took the call as he sat in the fire station, watching the images from New York. He immediately activated both a paramedic unit and Rescue Engine 335, commanded by his friend Captain John Durrer, to respond to the incident.

SOUTH PARKING LOT, PENTAGON—0935 HOURS

Navy lieutenant Evelyn Gibbs, assigned to the Navy Annex, had just dropped her children off at the Pentagon day care center before she headed to work. Like all mothers, she hated to be away from them, but at least she was close by. As she neared the Pentagon, she looked up at the blue sky, the white stone graves of Arlington National Cemetery on the hill in the distance, the sunlight gleaming off the windshields of the cars. All seemed quiet and peaceful.

NAVY ANNEX, ONE MILE SOUTH OF THE PENTAGON—0935 HOURS

In a secure conference room of the Ballistic Missile Defense Organization inside the Navy Annex, Bruce Warner was just walking through the door when he heard breaking news on CNN. His friend Deborah Vinson, on temporary duty from the Joint National Test Facility, met him in the hall and asked if he'd heard about the New York attacks. Warner walked to the TV and stared at the images of the burning towers. Most of the staff members were watching the screen and talking about the events in New York until Lieutenant General Ron Kadish entered and they quickly scattered.

Kadish was ready to get started with the day's activities. He acknowledged that the CNN reports were terrible, but they had work to do. Warner and Vinson left the room, but Warner kept thinking about New York as he walked into the office of Gary Ramos.

Warner thought Ramos's office was one of the nicest in the Annex for its view of the west wall of the Pentagon. Across Washington Boulevard, he could see the heliport and the fire station. There didn't seem to be anything going on.

B RING, CORRIDOR FOUR, FIRST FLOOR—0935 HOURS

Near the courtyard of the Pentagon, John Driscoll, on his way to deliver his package to the Joint Chiefs, noticed that the hallways and corridors were unusually quiet. Looking out on the courtyard, he could see the famous hot dog stand, which looked abandoned. He went down into the basement and handed the package to an officer, then climbed the stairs to level two. He stopped at a Starbucks stand in the cafeteria and noticed there was no line for coffee. Then it struck him that something wasn't right: there had always been a line for coffee, every morning as long as he could remember. The whole place was like a ghost town.

Grabbing a white Starbucks paper cup full of coffee, Driscoll continued back to his office, taking a newly completed escalator down to level one. As he walked, he noticed that the corridor was almost empty. He sensed a strange stillness. Normally at this time of the morning, the place was hopping with activity and a considerable amount of noise, but today the place had the aura of a graveyard. He assumed everyone was in front of a monitor somewhere watching the events in New York.

WALTER REED ARMY MEDICAL CENTER—0935 HOURS

Lieutenant Colonel Ed Lucci and several other physicians climbed into the WRAMC commander's van and headed downtown for a conference. As the van moved along the street, Lucci thought about what was happening in New York and about his many experiences overseas, some in the Middle East. He had known for a long time that America had many deadly enemies whose attacks had grown more serious through the decades. Perhaps this time, he feared, it was finally going to come home.

PENTAGON FIRE STATION—0935 HOURS

Mark Skipper called Alan Wallace to the rear of Truck 61, parked outside the firehouse. Wallace walked around to see his friend looking at the foam-metering valves for the water cannon, used to mix the foam with the water. "You know you can get a lot more foam out of this roof turret through these discharges," Skipper said, indicating that the metering valve could be set to produce a whole lot more foam than was needed. Wallace smiled, knowing they weren't supposed to waste foam like this, but it was comforting knowing they would have the extra if they ever needed it. Even though both of them appeared relaxed, the New York attacks had seriously unnerved them.

SOUTH PARKING LOT, PENTAGON—0935 HOURS

Arriving at the Pentagon, Major Lincoln Leibner found that someone had taken his usual parking space, so he drove to the south parking lot, parked his truck, and headed for the entrance.

Leibner had been at home talking to his girlfriend when he saw the second tower collision. After completing several tours as a Green Beret in Grenada, Panama, and Bosnia, Leibner knew what death looked like, what it smelled like. When he saw the second plane strike, he had no doubts about what was happening.

"I've got to go," he told his girlfriend, rushing outside to his pickup truck and heading to the Pentagon.

Leibner was an executive support officer in the Office of the Secretary of Defense. His job was like that of a high-level telephone operator, connecting calls between Secretary of Defense Rumsfeld and the top tier of government officials—people such as National Security Advisor Condoleezza Rice and even President Bush. Leibner wasn't scheduled to report to work until later in the day, but after watching the broadcasts from New York, he figured he'd be needed at the office. The image of the plane, the south tower, and the fireball in New York had him worried. As he looked around, everything seemed bright and beautiful, one of those calm, comfortable days when it felt good to be alive, but as a former combat soldier, Leibner possessed "situational awareness." After seeing those towers burning in New York, he felt anything but comfortable.

South of the helipad, Frank Probst stood inside a construction trailer, watching CNN. He glanced at his watch. He needed to be in the Penren building at the north end of the Pentagon by 10:00 a.m. for a meeting, so he walked through the trailer, gathering what he needed. As he turned to leave, he overheard someone say that the Pentagon would make a good target. The thought glued itself to his mind as he grabbed his notebook and stepped down out of the trailer. As he walked along, he couldn't get those words out of his head.

GOFER 06, C-130 HERCULES OVER POTOMAC RIVER, WASHINGTON, DC—0935 HOURS

In the sky far above, C-130 pilot Steve O'Brien suddenly spotted American Airlines Flight 77. The big jet was very close, a time distance of about two minutes, he figured, and the plane seemed almost to stand still in the sky. Reagan air control came over the radio. "Do you have him in sight?"

O'Brien looked at the huge plane taking up most of his windscreen. "That's an understatement," he replied.

"What kind of plane is it?" Reagan asked. The question stunned O'Brien. *The air traffic controller should be the first person to know what kind of a plane it is,* he thought to himself as he listened to the instructions.

"We want you to turn and follow this aircraft and identify it," the controller told him. The air controller's telling a pilot to get a visual on a plane didn't make sense to O'Brien. He could not recall ever receiving such an order, but he did as he was told, putting the big airplane into a turn and coming back around.

"Roger, that is a Boeing 757," he said as he passed by. On the side of the plane, he could see the silver sheen of the fuselage and the words "American Airlines."

At Reagan National Airport, Mike Defina and his firefighters, now arriving at Terminal B, saw several damaged vehicles littering the area. At one end, they found the driver of the car responsible for the crash. He had gone into diabetic shock and needed to be evacuated to the hospital as quickly as possible. As paramedics and firefighters pulled the man out and helped the others, Defina turned around and looked in the direction of the Pentagon. After seeing the New York towers burning, he had an awful feeling inside, an ominous premonition that Washington would be next.

OFFICE OF THE SECRETARY OF THE ARMY, SECOND FLOOR—0935 HOURS

As Lieutenant Colonel Ted Anderson sat at his desk, thinking about the New York attacks, the phone rang. It was his wife, calling him from her middle school in Fayetteville, North Carolina. She was watching the images on TV with her students and was worried about it. Anderson tried to calm her. He told her that he didn't know exactly what was happening, but not to rush to judgment and assume that it was the work of foreigners as they had in Oklahoma City.

AMERICAN AIRLINES FLIGHT 77—0935 HOURS

The time had come. Khalid al-Mihdhar and Majed Moqed now joined the Hazmi brothers and Hani Hanjour in the cockpit to deliver the final vengeance into the Pentagon, the home of the "great Satan," the very heart of the infidel. They gave thanks to Allah as Hanjour brought the aircraft around one last time and pushed the controls of the big 757 forward into a steep dive.

NAVY ANNEX, ONE MILE SOUTH OF THE PENTAGON—0935 HOURS

Vice Admiral Darb Ryan held the phone receiver in a tight grip, frantically dialing phone numbers and trying to get the great building evacuated. He was absolutely convinced that the attacks in New York were part of a coordinated attack on the country and that the Pentagon was going to be next, but he was now like a man sitting high on a mountaintop, watching two trains drive head-on into each other. He could yell as loud as he wanted, but it would do no good.

II

TERROR STEW

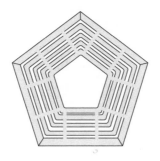

GENERAL OFFICERS' MESS, C RING,
THIRD FLOOR—0935 HOURS

Staff Sergeant Chris Braman stood in his office near the kitchen, talking to his wife, Samaria, on the phone.

"Did you hear what happened in New York?" she said, her voice tense.

"No, sweetheart," he said.

"An airplane hit one of the World Trade Center towers," she said, sounding frantic. Braman listened as his wife told him what she was seeing on TV. He quickly punched the keys on his computer to bring up the CNN website, but it wouldn't load.

"Your father just called and said the Pentagon could be next," she said, her voice beginning to break.

"Don't worry about this, OK?" he said, trying to comfort her. As he said this, he recalled an article he had read in the newspaper earlier this morning about an Afghan general who had been assassinated just a few days before. Maybe this had something to do with the attacks in New York.

PARKING LOT NEAR PENTAGON—0936 HOURS

Thirty-eight-year-old Isaac Ho'opi'i, a K-9 cop with the Pentagon police, fiddled with the radio dial in his car as he was driving back from a Fort Myer veterinary clinic where he had taken his bomb-sniffing German shepherd, Vito, for his regular checkup. Ho'opi'i had been listening to the reports from New York and thought it was some kind of joke—the kind of thing these radio stations did from time to time. In the back seat of the car sat Vito, quietly watching his handler as he listened to the broadcasts.

The six-feet-three, 260-pound Ho'opi'i had grown up in Wai'anae on the west coast of Oahu and had spent his early years spearfishing in the coastal waters. The art of spearfishing required slowing one's breathing to stay underwater longer, and Isaac excelled at it. Even though he had left Hawaii many years before, moving to the mainland and starting a family, Ho'opi'i's heart was never far from home, and in his spare time, he continued to perform in a popular DC wedding band called the Aloha Boys, in which he was known for his big voice. Growing up with many brothers and sisters and a pack of dogs, Isaac always put family first, and in the Hawaiian tradition, all human beings were part of this family.

E RING, THIRD FLOOR—0936 HOURS

Daniel Pfeilstucker, Jr., a commissioning agent for the John Kirlin mechanical contracting firm, was searching for a leaky pipe among all the building's ancient plumbing and heating systems. The work order he was holding stated that the leak was coming from a hot water pipe. Pfeilstucker decided to go downstairs to the second floor to take a look at that section of the plumbing. He boarded the service elevator and glanced at his watch. It was 9:36 a.m.

NAVY COMMAND CENTER, D RING,
FIRST FLOOR—0936 HOURS

In the Meteorology Office of the Navy Command Center in D Ring, Matt Flocco and Ed Earhart prepared weather reports as they monitored the massive Wall of Thunder, over a ton of computer equipment all around them and concentrated directly in front of Earhart. Flocco sat at his computer, facing away from his friend, who was looking in the direction of the west wall. Their supervisor, Nancy McKeown, started to walk through the door into the outer office.

ARMY PERSONNEL CENTER, C RING,
SECOND FLOOR—0936 HOURS

Sergeant Major Tony Rose stared through the windows for a moment, then all at once looked at his colleague John Frazier.

"Something's going to happen, John," he said. "I can feel it."

Thirty feet west of Rose, Lieutenant Colonel Victor Correa stood talking to Major John Jessup. Jessup looked at another replay of the second attack on the World Trade Center and then turned to Correa. "You know, sir, they could do that here, and we wouldn't know it until it happened."

AMERICAN AIRLINES FLIGHT 77—0936 HOURS

Hani Hanjour was now convinced that his short, pitiful life was finally going to mean something. He pushed the controls forward to full throttle and bore down on the handles. The engines screamed as a hundred tons of steel and aluminum dove toward the Pentagon at over five hundred miles per hour.

In the back of the plane, little Bernard Brown closed his eyes for the last time. Dana Falkenberg, just three years old, hugged her mother's arm.

SOUTH PARKING LOT, PENTAGON—0936 HOURS

Halfway to the south entrance, Lincoln Leibner heard the jet engines throttle up. He had been raised nearby, so the sounds of aircraft flying in this area were as common to him as bird noises. He knew the flight paths for Reagan National took planes very near the Pentagon, but at this moment, he suddenly remembered that such sounds never came from the southwest. It was then that he turned his head and looked into the small windows of American Airlines Flight 77, now only a few hundred yards from the west wall of the Pentagon. Leibner didn't want to believe what was happening even though his instincts told him to get moving. Still, the veteran soldier could not move for several seconds due to the sheer horror of it. This wasn't supposed to happen. Not here. Time seemed to slow down with his thoughts, and then he was suddenly running as fast as he could.

PENTAGON FIRE STATION—0937 HOURS

After speaking with Campbell, Wallace and Skipper finished setting the metering valves on Truck 61 and started walking toward the helipad. They were both walking side by side talking, when Wallace suddenly turned his head and saw the plane. It just appeared out of nowhere, low to the ground, and headed straight for the west wall.

Wallace and Skipper watched as the belly of the plane caught a green highway sign and knocked it down onto the roadway, barely missing a passing car as the sign bounced off the asphalt. The plane passed the two oak trees next to Washington Boulevard and tipped its left wing slightly. Wallace could clearly read the words "American Airlines" as the plane came closer.

"Get the hell out of here!" Wallace yelled at the top of his lungs. Skipper froze and looked at his friend, then turned and ran. For Wallace, it was a gut reaction, sudden and quick, born of reflexes developed in Vietnam. His body reacted to the situation without his mind having time to think about it. He turned and ran north, away from the plane, as fast as he could. Skipper ran to the northeast, but Wallace would not remember seeing him.

SOUTH PARKING LOT, PENTAGON—0937 HOURS

Frank Probst had just left the construction trailer south of the helipad and was walking along the sidewalk when he turned his head and saw American Airlines Flight 77 skim the hoods of cars stalled in traffic on Washington Boulevard.

One of the people sitting in this gridlocked mess was Don Mason, an employee of the Pentagon Renovation team. Mason saw the jet come right over him, cutting three light poles in half and snapping the antennae off a Jeep Cherokee immediately to his rear. Nearby, a piece of one of the light poles fell onto a taxi, smashing the windshield and wounding the driver.

As Mason looked in the direction of the west wall, he could see a man standing right under the plane, almost directly in its path. As he looked closer, he realized it was his friend Frank Probst. Mason heard a noise and saw a woman jump out of her car and begin screaming at the top of her lungs, flailing her arms in the air at the ghastly sight. A man quickly hugged her and calmed her down. Mason, mortified at what he was seeing, was sure that Probst was going to be killed.

Probst looked at the big jet in horror. It was coming straight at him. In that instant, he thought to himself, *I'm dead. My wife has to go to another funeral, and I'll never see my boys again.* He dove to the ground as the aircraft passed less than five feet over the top of his head, the right wing striking the big olive-drab 750-kilowatt generator, swatting it off its base and whipping it around at a forty-five-degree angle. The right wing bent the concrete pillars surrounding it in half, then ripped up the chain-link fence protecting it and dragged the whole tangled mess into the wall. Probst glanced up and saw the right engine of the aircraft cut through a low concrete wall a foot in thickness, instantly pulverizing it.

Contractor Mickey Bell was just leaving his construction trailer when he heard the earsplitting whine of the jet engines. He looked up as the right wing of American Airlines Flight 77 came within inches of his face. Reaching his pickup truck, he fired up the engine just as he felt the concussion rock the vehicle. He heard a sound like hail striking the hood and door, but in the adrenaline rush that followed, he would only remember leaping into the driver's seat and stomping his foot on the accelerator, unable to move the truck fast enough to get away from the scene.

PENTAGON CONTROL TOWER—0937 HOURS

In the control tower, Sean Boger had just watched Jackie Kidd leave the room to walk downstairs, when he happened to look toward the helipad as the left wing of American Airlines Flight 77 passed by him, its nose nearly at the wall. Down on the ground, he could see Alan Wallace running. The image would be forever frozen in Boger's memory. He dropped to the floor and covered his head with his hands, the roar growing louder and louder until it became deafening. Then came the awful whine of the engines as they struck the west wall, the turbines screaming and exploding, tearing into the fuel tanks in the wings. The fuel spewed forth, unleashing a fireball that arched some two hundred feet into the sky, reaching one thousand degrees Fahrenheit in seconds with a force equivalent to approximately three hundred tons of TNT, the blast shaking the ground and filling the air with debris.

WASHINGTON BOULEVARD—0937 HOURS

As Isaac Ho'opi'i drove along, he received a police call alerting him to the attack on the Pentagon. He glanced at the building and saw a large, steadily rising column of black smoke. He hit the gas, putting all the weight of his big frame into the accelerator, nearly pushing his foot through the firewall. It seemed he could not move the car fast enough.

GENERAL OFFICERS' MESS—0937 HOURS

In the kitchen of the Officers' Mess, Christopher Braman had just hung up the phone after talking with his wife, when he was rocked forward by a massive vibration that seemed to come from beneath the floor.

The initial shaking reminded him of the earthquakes he had experienced as a boy growing up near Los Angeles. As the building heaved and shook, he was thrown forward into a liquor cabinet, and the window in his office shattered. As Braman stood up, he thought of what his wife had told him about New York.

One of the cooks ran into the kitchen and looked at Braman. "What do we do now?" he said.

Braman knew the man's wife worked down the hall. "You need to go get your wife," he said. The man just looked at him. "Go get your wife," Braman said, again. The man turned and ran away. Braman instinctively rushed to the gas stoves and shut them off.

WASHINGTON BOULEVARD—0937 HOURS

Sitting in his car, Alfred Regnery, CEO of Regnery Publishing, watched as American Airlines Flight 77 was blown to pieces. Tony Terronez, nearby, jumped out of his car. As the fireball rose into the sky, he could see debris swirling at the outer edge of its head, beginning to drop rapidly to earth and seeming to come straight at him. He began yelling at the other drivers as pieces of metal and concrete began raining down on the highway.

"Get the fuck out of here!" he yelled. "Move!"

Other people began panicking, trying to get away but finding themselves trapped by the surrounding cars. Some people, seeing that the southbound lane of Washington Boulevard was empty, crossed the median into the path of oncoming traffic, trying to escape. Many people jumped out of their cars and began screaming and pointing. One man leaped out of his car and pounded on the window of the car in front of him.

"Move, goddamn it!" he yelled at the driver, who was in such shock that he was simply unable to move any part of his body.

Donald Bouchoux, a fifty-three-year-old retired navy pilot, saw an emergency oxygen bottle shoot across the hood of his Ford Explorer. James Cissell, in another car, saw a tire rim pass his window. He sat in his car, terrified. As the plane passed by him, he had actually seen the faces of some of the passengers looking helplessly through the windows.

Reaching the light pole, Noel Sepulveda saw pieces of metal from American Airlines Flight 77 strike his motorcycle and bounce off the ground. Looking back, he saw the mushroom head of the fireball as it quickly swallowed what was left of the aircraft. Then a sudden hot wind lifted him up and slammed his head back hard into the light pole. He collapsed next to his motorcycle and lost consciousness.

E RING, FOURTH FLOOR—0937 HOURS

Robert Hogue could clearly see marine counsel Peter Murphy standing next to the window overlooking the helipad. Corporal Tim Garafola had told him that the security level at the Pentagon was normal, when a terrific blast sent Murphy hurtling across the room and knocked Hogue to the floor. Joe Baker was hurled out of his chair by the pressure wave, and in the outer office, Garafola's desk was thrown straight up in the air and slammed down onto the floor. Then the floor split in two at the expansion joint that ran between the two offices, leaving one office floor a full step up from the other. The ceilings in both offices crumbled, and a tremendous flame shot upward through the window at an angle. The floor rumbled and shook, and a cloud of dust filled the area. The door leading out of the suite containing both offices was magnetic, and the explosion jammed it.

"Corporal, get us out of here!" Murphy yelled.

As the counselor and Hogue got to their feet, Garafola yanked at the heavy door but couldn't budge it; then Murphy saw the marine in him come alive. He concentrated and took one hard pull. The door opened, allowing the men to escape into the hallway.

The enormous mushroom head of the fireball, fed by thousands of gallons of jet fuel in the wings and fuselage of the plane, now covered most of the south corner of the west wall, producing incredible heat. In less than a second, the internal temperature of the fire reached two thousand degrees Fahrenheit, vaporizing anything it touched.

Deborah Ramsaur felt a violent shock to her body and sudden heat as a wall of fire enveloped her and ended her life. The quickness of it all made her one of the lucky ones.

E RING, THIRD FLOOR—0937 HOURS

On the third floor above the Army Personnel Center, contractor Dan Fraunfelter heard a loud sucking noise. He glanced at his subcontractor.

"You hear that?" he said.

Neither man moved a muscle as they both watched and listened. In a few moments, the walls and floors began to shake violently, the movement steadily increasing in intensity. The lights went out, and darkness descended on the area.

Fraunfelter grabbed his flashlight and dashed down the hall. He passed a blown-out window and ran over to it. Peering through it, he could see an old electric generator in flames, the same one Frank Probst had seen earlier. He could feel the heat coming up through the floor through the soles of his shoes. He turned and ran back down the hallway, twisting his ankle as he tried to get away.

E RING, SECOND FLOOR—0937 HOURS

With a ladder in his hand, Dan Pfeilstucker was on his way to look for a leak on the second floor of E Ring. As he stepped out of the elevator into Corridor Four, he saw a bright flash of light that went from orange to red to black in seconds. He felt a swell of pressure as the ceiling and walls caved in around him; then his left leg began to twitch uncontrollably. A second later, he felt his chest tighten as if it were in a vise. A tornado-like wind lifted him off the floor, and he felt his body being carried away into the blackness. The powerful wind hurled him eighty feet down Corridor Four. His hard hat, goggles, and the ladder he had been holding were sucked off him and swept away into the vortex. A few seconds passed, and his back hit something hard. As he looked up, the smoke cleared, and he could tell he was inside a telephone closet.

The pressure wave had thrown him against the wall of the closet and then slammed the door shut.

The pressure wave that held Pfeilstucker in its grip also threw Lieutenant Colonel Brian Birdwell, who was exiting a nearby bathroom at the time, onto his back and doused him with jet fuel. The fireball instantly set him ablaze, his polyester slacks melting into his knees, the fire enveloping his head, neck, and upper torso and burning the tops of his ears off. He managed to stand up, and it was then that he felt his skin shrinking as it peeled away from his body. He tried to move but couldn't. Fire was coming from every direction, trying to consume him. His body was literally melting away. At this moment, Brian Birdwell knew that he was standing at the threshold of life and death. He felt his own voice cry out to heaven. This was not his normal voice that came from his throat but one that came from deep within his soul, like the shrill cry of a baby being taken from the womb of its mother. "Jesus, I'm coming to see you!" he shouted through the din. He fell to the floor and waited to die.

Farther down the hallway in the DCSPER, Kip Taylor, watching replays of the World Trade Center attacks, suddenly saw an enormous silver mass and then a blinding flash of light. He was instantly burned to death as American Airlines Flight 77 came into the west wall, his office simply disappearing. Everyone in the small conference room meeting with Lieutenant General Maude and his staff was incinerated within the first few seconds after impact.

In the large conference room directly across the hall, Colonel Phil McNair sat listening to Marilyn Wills speak. Suddenly, he heard a loud bang from behind the wall where Wills was standing. "What the hell was that?" he shouted as Wills stopped speaking. Everyone froze and looked around the room. McNair knew nothing about the New York attacks and instantly thought that a construction crane had dropped something. In a few moments, the lights went out, and the ceiling tiles started to fall. Along the walls and across the ceiling, McNair now noticed a creeping flame, which seemed to grow and move faster with each passing second. Marilyn Wills saw the walls bulge and shake and a tongue of fire lick the walls and ceiling. She looked up as the whole conference room began to implode.

"Hit the floor!" McNair yelled as he saw Rob Grunewald lunge across the table and throw Martha Carden to the floor. Wills fell down in the fetal position. Over her right shoulder, she saw fire race along the wall, the flames singeing her hair. Next to Wills, McNair watched as a thick oily smoke filled the room quickly, seeming to come from the ceiling tiles down to the floor. No one in the room had any idea that a fuel-laden jet had just passed beneath them.

Marian Serva, who had been watching the images from New York, was in the direct path of the fireball, which killed her and leveled everything in the surrounding area. John Yates, standing next to Lieutenant Colonel Canfield Boone watching TV, was blown through the air and hurled thirty feet backward into a large metal filing cabinet. Boone and everyone else standing in the immediate area were killed almost instantly.

As the aircraft disintegrated beneath the unconscious Yates, the floor behind him buckled and cracked, creating a fissure that soon became a hole, a large chunk of the ceiling falling to the floor below, the filing cabinet sitting on the edge of a precipice. Smoke filled the area, turning everything black. The temperature of the room went from seventy-four degrees Fahrenheit to over eighteen hundred degrees in less than a second.

Out in the cubicle farm on the other side of the wall from McNair and Wills, Lieutenant Colonel Victor Correa stood talking to John Jessup when both of them heard a dull but very loud thud on the other side of the wall. "Sounds like somebody hit a gas line," Correa remarked. No sooner had he said this than he was picked up and thrown into the air by the same pressure wave that had grabbed Pfeilstucker. As Correa was flying through the air, he saw the bright orange head of the fireball coming toward him with a powerful hot gush of wind before it.

In an office near Corridor Four, Sergeant Roxane Cruz-Cortez sat silently, thinking about the people in New York, when she heard a loud rumbling like a freight train passing right next to the office wall. Ed Bruno looked up and around at the sudden noise and vibration. The roar got louder and louder until the office itself began to shake, all of this happening in seconds. Cruz-Cortez now watched as the ceiling fell through, knocking Bruno to the floor and burying him under a pile of debris. She covered her face with her hands as she watched the wall cave in. The pressure wave hit her and knocked her sideways, still seated in her chair. She immediately passed out.

Sitting at his desk near Corridor Five, Blair Bozek had heard the initial explosion and then felt the building vibrate with a succession of loud tearing and chopping sounds as if giant dominoes were collapsing nearby, the sounds growing louder and getting closer. Having already seen the New York attacks, he immediately figured that it was a plane and that it was now cutting its way through the building toward him. He listened as the walls of the surrounding offices began to collapse. Within seconds, the walls to the right and left of him and the very floor he was standing on began to vibrate, the ceiling tiles falling to the floor. The sound increased; then all at once the wall in front of him began to move.

Ted Anderson had been speaking with his wife and her grade school class over the telephone. He had just told his wife not to jump to conclusions as they had at Oklahoma City. His wife turned to her class and said, "Yes, we remember Oklahoma City." With these words, Anderson suddenly heard an explosion down the hallway. His office began to fall in on itself.

"Everyone get out," he yelled. "Now!"

As a former combat soldier, Anderson reacted to the first explosion by anticipating a second. His first priority was to get everyone out of the immediate area. In the next few moments, his actions would save countless lives.

C RING, FIFTH FLOOR—0937 HOURS

Commander Craig Powell, USN, and his assistant, Lieutenant Olin Sell, sat watching President Bush give a speech on television live from an elementary school in Sarasota, Florida. "May God bless the victims, their families, and America," Bush said as he turned to the right and started to walk away.

The president had taken only a few steps when Powell felt the shockwave come from below and to his left. He and Sell jumped up and ran to the door. Opening it, they looked down the hallway to see a cloud of black smoke quickly filling the hall. People came running out into the corridor. Powell looked at Sell. "Get everybody out," he said. Then he turned and went back inside the office to get a tool bag. Sell started moving people off the fifth floor. When Powell returned, everyone was gone. He ran toward the fire door as a deafening cacophony of emergency beacons wailed through the hallways and corridors. Pulling hard on the door, he found that it was locked tight.

B RING, FIFTH FLOOR—0937 HOURS

Natalie Ogletree turned and looked toward C Ring. It was a wall of flame. She knew that the wedge was under renovation and figured one of the construction workers had hit a gas line, but then someone yelled, "Bomb! . . . Everyone out!" and she joined a crowd of workers as they desperately tried to get out of the building.

As they left their offices, they blindly headed toward the site of the crash, unaware that they were moving straight into the maelstrom. They soon found their way blocked by a large piece of the ceiling in the middle of the hallway. Ogletree, being on assignment, was unfamiliar with the layout of the Pentagon, so she followed the crowd into the stairwell. They would all soon discover that there was no easy way out. Every door they came to was locked.

OFFICE OF INFORMATION MANAGEMENT, D RING, FIRST FLOOR—0938 HOURS

Along the west wall, the flames quickly spread into the left wing of the aircraft, igniting the fuel cells there and releasing a second fireball that superheated the concrete walls and sent small pieces of debris flying in every direction. In less time than it takes to tell, each bladder of fuel was ripped or burst open, spilling its contents into the building. Some of the fuel in the wings penetrated the building without igniting and was splashed forward into the interior, where it doused people in ultraflammable liquid.

Janice Ann Jackson found herself splashed with jet fuel and then immediately engulfed in flames. She screamed and started running, trying to put the fire out. Coworker Stuart Fluke saw this, tore off his shirt, and put it over her head to smother the flames.

Moments earlier, marine lance corporal Dustin P. Schuetz, assigned to Lieutenant General William Nyland's office, had been using his hands to describe the crash of the second plane into the south tower of the World Trade Center. He had been explaining the crash to Lance Corporal Vera, making a motion with his right hand into his left hand, when the building quivered and shook, and he heard a loud thud in the background. Schuetz stopped what he was doing and dropped his hands, startled. At first, both men thought it was an old boiler exploding. Vera didn't hear anything, just an abrupt vibration of the office; then the pressure wave hit both of them, and they were knocked to the floor, their offices barely a hundred feet from the crash.

SOUTH PARKING LOT, PENTAGON—0938 HOURS

For Frank Probst, time now slowed to a crawl, everything around him except the plane seemingly in slow motion. He felt as if someone had flipped a switch and turned off his hearing. Everything was muffled. The motion of the plane was like a silent movie from another place and time. He watched as the fireball surged away from him at high speed, heading north toward the firehouse.

PENTAGON FIRE STATION—0938 HOURS

Alan Wallace ran as fast as his legs would carry him. He knew the fireball was behind him; he could feel his back getting hotter by the second. He turned and headed for the truck bay at the south end of the firehouse toward the place where Dennis Young had just been sitting, but Young was nowhere to be found. Where in the hell was Dennis? Was he alive? Questions raced through Wallace's mind, but his instinct kept him moving.

As he looked over his shoulder, he could see an immense wall of fire over a hundred feet high right behind him. He looked ahead. If he went into the firehouse, he would be trapped, so he ran north and west of it. As he did, he thought he saw a piece of the airplane's tail skid sideways and slam into his fire truck, breaking into pieces.

The fireball now rolled across the ground, approaching the firehouse and tower, igniting the blacktop, catching the trees on fire, and covering the side and rear of Truck 61 in flames. Next to the firehouse, the grass in the surrounding field began to burn.

Wallace looked up at the sky, that beautiful blue sky. As long as he could see it, the fire had not taken him. His back now felt like it was pressed to hot iron, his lungs being squeezed hard, a very powerful force pushing him from behind like a giant picking him up and throwing him forward. His legs left the ground for a moment. His heart climbed up into his head, his ears pounding with each beat like he remembered from combat. He thought he could feel the skin peeling from his left shoulder. *God, please don't let me burn,* he prayed as he ran. Three more steps and he had done all he could do. The fireball was upon him. He had to get down. He saw the Ford passenger van and headed for it, diving for cover at the last second, the fireball rolling up and over him. He crawled underneath the van at the left rear wheel, then made his way to the front, but it was like climbing into an oven and shutting the door.

PENTAGON CONTROL TOWER—0938 HOURS

Jackie Kidd had just come down the stairs and was heading for her Jeep Cherokee in the parking lot to get her lunch when she decided to go to the bathroom before going outside. As she entered the stall, the ceiling caved in on her and everything turned dark. She fell on the floor. "They got us!" she said as she pulled herself up and clawed through the debris, trying to get back into the tower to get to Sean Boger. As she tried to climb the stairs, she found the way blocked by concrete and fallen ceiling tiles.

Suddenly, from above, Boger sprinted down the stairs, his head covered in blood. He grabbed her, and they both fell to the floor, the fireball headed right for Boger's 3000GT sports car. He looked on as it was incinerated into a burning hulk. Next to it, Kidd's Jeep Cherokee met the same fate.

SOUTH PARKING LOT, PENTAGON—0938 HOURS

Noel Sepulveda had regained consciousness and, seeing the tragedy unfolding before him, began running toward the west wall for all he was worth. Reaching the impact site, he suddenly felt a searing heat that stopped him in his tracks. He peered into the blackness.

"Is there anybody in there?" he yelled. Near one of the windows, a severely burned man emerged and staggered toward him. Sepulveda helped him away, then ran back to retrieve more survivors.

GOFER 06, C-130 HERCULES OVER POTOMAC RIVER, WASHINGTON, DC—0938 HOURS

In the sky above Washington, C-130 pilot Steve O'Brien could hardly believe what he had just seen. One moment, the big jet was flying next to him; the next, it just dropped from the sky like a stone, swooping down in an arc and exploding straight into the west wall of the Pentagon. Over his radio came the frantic voice of an air traffic controller at Reagan, asking repeatedly for a report on the unidentified aircraft. O'Brien's response masked his shock and disbelief.

"Looks like that aircraft just crashed into the Pentagon, sir."

The nose of the plane now gone, the pressure wave forced shards of steel and aluminum forward into the interior of Wedge One at terrific speed. The tail, engines, landing gear, and other debris were propelled forward into the interior of D Ring as the aircraft disintegrated, the offices and cubicles of the Navy Command Center and the Army Personnel Center squarely in its path. Fires erupted sporadically, with some areas being incinerated and others left unburned with only structural damage. But everywhere, everything was saturated with jet fuel.

D RING, FIRST FLOOR—0938 HOURS

Sitting in his cubicle in D Ring of the Navy Command Center, directly in the path of the disintegrating right wing of American Airlines Flight 77, Matt Flocco heard a sound like a tidal wave coming toward him. He didn't have time to turn around; a tremendous gush of hot wind fell on him like a hammer and knocked him to the floor.

Flocco pulled himself up as smoke began to rapidly fill the room. He looked back to see his friend Ed Earhart lying facedown, his head turned to the left, blood running out from underneath his head and chest, surrounded by pieces of furniture and computer equipment. Through all corners of the room, Flocco could see smoke flowing inside as if it were being blown by a machine. To his left, he could barely make out the doorway.

"Nancy," he cried to his supervisor. There was no answer.

Unaware that his friend Earhart was dead, Flocco crawled toward him and straddled him from behind, hovering over him, pulling at his arm, trying to get him to wake up. He turned and looked into the blackness.

"Nancy!" he cried in a weak voice, but he couldn't see in front of his own face. Again, there was no answer.

In a few moments, it became very hard to breathe, but he couldn't leave Ed behind. He had to get him up so they could both get out. As he pulled at the lifeless body, he could feel himself losing consciousness. He couldn't breathe anymore. All his life he had been a fighter, full of raw determination, but now his strength was gone. He gasped and fell sideways to his left, his body coming to rest next to his friend, his left foot crossed over his right and his right hand over his heart.

In the outer office, Nancy McKeown heard her name being called but couldn't see anything. She knew it was either Matt or Ed, but she was blind to everything around her, even her own hands. Black smoke filled the room that had become a maze of debris, chairs, and the hulls of heavy computer equipment, what had once been the Wall of Thunder. She attempted to move toward the voice, but debris blocked her way. She had lost her sense of direction and was sure she was going to die. It was impossible to see anything, so she kept crawling, her head close to the floor. She moved to the right, toward what she could sense was a pocket of cooler air, trying to get away from the smoke.

The hulk of the doomed airliner plowed forward through the columns on the first and second floor, taking out over fifty of them in a matter of seconds. Penetrating some three hundred feet into the building and carving a wide swath clear to C Ring, it left a large slice of the third and fourth floors suspended in midair. Strips of the aircraft were sheared off and propelled ahead like razor blades. The Kevlar mesh in the E Ring windows had caught much of the concrete and chunks of metal, throwing them back out into the parking lot and onto Washington Boulevard, thereby preventing the interior of Wedge One from turning into a hailstorm of hot metal.

In the Navy Command Center, Lieutenant Kevin Shaeffer saw the fireball come through the wall, a bright orange fist consuming everyone and everything in its path. The pressure wave threw him across the room and slammed him to the floor. He rose up and put his hand to his head. The whole top of his head was slick with jet fuel. In seconds, the flames ignited the fuel, and he discovered to his horror that his hair was on fire. He desperately tried to pat it out. His lungs burned and stung, like he had swallowed a hive of bees. When he tried to get up, he discovered that his whole body was burning. He immediately fell to the floor and rolled as he had been trained, smothering the flames. The damage to his upper body, his arms, hands, back, and much of his lower face had already been done, however. As he lay there, he thought of an old photo he had once seen from the Vietnam War, of a little Vietnamese girl running naked, her arms outstretched as she cried in pain from being burned by napalm.

I'm as helpless as that little girl, he thought to himself.

SUBOFFICE OF SECRETARY OF DEFENSE, A RING, FOURTH FLOOR—0938 HOURS

Commander Dave Tarantino, watching television in a suboffice of the secretary of defense on the fourth floor of A Ring near Corridor Five, felt the initial shock wave but did not see the flames. Having seen the two towers hit in New York, he knew that this could be the beginning of an all-out attack on the country, but a part of him was in denial, not wanting to believe someone would have the audacity to attack the Pentagon. Hearing sirens blare, he rushed out into the hall, where he immediately came upon victims of the attack, wandering the hallways in a state of confusion. Smoke was rapidly overtaking the area, and some sections were completely blocked by rubble.

ARMY PERSONNEL CENTER, E RING, SECOND FLOOR—0938 HOURS

Seconds after impact, Specialist Mike Petrovich, US Army, felt the whole room begin to cave in on top of him, the air rippling as if he were in a paper bag being crumpled by a giant hand. Directly beneath him, what remained of the airliner was ripping the floor joists apart, the pressure blowing holes in the floor. As he looked over his shoulder, he saw an orange glow that soared over his head. Then the lights faded, and black clouds of smoke began to fill the cubicle farm. All at once, the floor cracked open, producing large fissures that split the room from end to end.

Lying on the floor, Victor Correa stared across the cubicle farm at the Kevlar windows overlooking A/E Drive and saw Tony Rose standing near them as they began to swell and then come back in, not breaking but simply expanding like a bubble with the pressure. He heard fire alarms go off. Then the sprinklers activated, raining water down on everything. As he lay there, he saw smoke, fire, debris, jet fuel, and pieces of the building swirling around him with screams, yelling, moaning, and general chaos—a "terror stew."

C RING, SECOND FLOOR—0938 HOURS

Near the windows overlooking A/E Drive, Tony Rose saw a blinding light come over his left shoulder and then felt a gut-wrenching wallop that seemed to go right through his chest. He looked down at John Frazier just in time to see his friend blown under his desk, before he himself was thrown ten feet backward. As he hit the floor, he suddenly lost his hearing. The unexpected shock of the experience numbed the pain in his right shoulder, which had been completely dislocated. Looking up, he saw a red and black fireball shoot across the room, burning as it moved.

Rose now put his head against the floor just in time to see a second fireball blow a hole straight up through the center of the room, igniting the jet fuel and rising into the ceiling—a vertical chimney of fire. He kept his head down and watched as the fireball fanned out and headed for the windows.

Rose knew that as soon as a fire was born, it quickly began to die from starvation. It was now looking for oxygen anywhere it could find it. He knew that once the fire reached those windows, it would blow them out, and the air rushing in would turn the entire cubicle farm into an inferno. He had to get his people out before they all burned to death.

In Corridor Four on the first floor of the Army Resources Center, Sheila Moody felt a sudden blast of hot air that smacked her hard in the face. She shut her eyes and then opened them to see a red fireball passing within inches of her cubicle. In that instant, she became mesmerized, thinking that she could almost reach out and touch the deadly fire; it was so close. Moody then felt pieces of the ceiling strike her hands. As fire shot through the room, she momentarily heard the screams of dozens of people at once, and then all was quiet. Then she felt something collapse onto her. When she got up, the room was dark, the only light coming from nearby fires. This was only her second day on the job, and she had no idea how to get out.

In every office and hallway now were the dead bodies of people who had suffocated from lack of oxygen caused by the pressure and the sudden, overwhelming approach of the fireball. They lay slumped on the floor against walls and doors or seated at their desks, their faces frozen in their death gasps, the fires burning some and going around others in what firefighters referred to as a "flashover," when the fire creeps along the ceilings and walls as it moves ahead, bypassing the center of the room. In other areas, the oxygen level fell to almost nothing, the fire waiting for someone to open a door so that it could suck in the fresh oxygen and explode in a backdraft of violent fury.

Parts of the shattered hull of the aircraft together with bits of wood, glass, and other debris were scattered from one end of the wedge to the other. Ceiling tiles and drywall turned to dust. Power lines were ripped out of walls and severed, the electricity still running through them creating a gauntlet of deadly electrical snakes hanging from the walls and ceilings. Water pipes burst, turning many hallways into rivers. Unignited jet fuel thrown clear of the explosion, some of it as far as A Ring, created small ponds lying dormant while the sputtering power lines threatened to ignite them. Near Ground Zero, the fire was approaching two thousand degrees Fahrenheit, and the steel of the support columns was beginning to warp, writhing and moaning like an elephant in its death throes.

D RING, FIRST FLOOR—0939 HOURS

Pinned against the wall by his desk, Blair Bozek watched as the wall in front of him was thrust forward into the center of the room. It was closing in on him fast. He was sure the nose of the jet was right behind this wall and about to crush him. He tried to reach his briefcase, which was only inches away, but he couldn't get to it. Then the sound moved off to his left and faded, and the wall suddenly stopped moving.

Bozek used all his strength to push and squeeze out from behind his desk, then ran to Melody Johnson, his coworker. The two decided not to go through C Ring, which was directly in the path of the fire, agreeing that a better plan was to try and get out through E Ring and onto the lawn. They climbed over a large pile of debris that had once been offices and heard the voice of Lieutenant Colonel Jim Edge calling to them to follow. They soon became part of a general daisy chain formed by the personnel in this section of the building.

Bozek waited until everyone had been evacuated, then tried to sweep the area for classified material, but the smoke was down to chest level, and pieces of the aircraft lay burning everywhere. He quickly abandoned this plan and focused on getting out alive.

ARMY PERSONNEL CENTER, E RING,
SECOND FLOOR—0939 HOURS

Slumped against a metal filing cabinet, John Yates opened his eyes. The scene around him now was like a burning mine shaft a mile deep in the ground, black and stifling with unbearable heat and no air to breathe. It was the darkest place he had ever been in. Since childhood, Yates had harbored a fear of dying in a fire. He never understood where this fear came from, only that it had been with him as long as he could remember. Now, his nightmare was coming true. He tried to pull himself together as he fought the fear inside him.

He tried to take a breath, but it burned his lungs as if he were inhaling fire. He felt something wet running down his face, covering his glasses. He reached up in the darkness and felt the liquid. He was sure it was blood, but in reality, it was jet fuel.

He thought about his wife, Ellen. Would he ever see her again? He loved her so much. There was no way he was going to give up; he had to get out. He put his hands out and groped in the darkness, then rose up and began moving forward with his arms outstretched, not knowing there was a massive hole in the floor right behind him, the filing cabinet sitting on the edge of it. Everything Yates touched now burned him, but he kept moving forward, away from the hole in the floor.

A few yards from where John Yates wandered in the darkness, General Glenn Webster and some of his staff tried to think of a way out. Some of his people saw the hole in the floor and jumped through it, right onto the top of the burning fuselage of American Airlines Flight 77.

Ron Schexnayder, a retired sergeant major and contract employee working for Webster, returned with a flashlight and helped guide the rest of the office outside, moving debris out of the way so people could pass through. Webster stayed outside, performing first aid on many of the victims and preventing several of them from going into shock in the first moments after the attack.

Stuck inside a telephone closet after having been thrown through the air by the pressure wave, Dan Pfeilstucker pulled himself up and grabbed the doorknob, then lurched back as it burned his hand. He covered his palm with his shirttail and carefully twisted the hot knob.

The door opened, and he stuck his head out. The entire area, which had been brand new just minutes before, was now a mass of blackened wreckage. All Pfeilstucker could smell was jet fuel.

It had all happened so fast. He couldn't believe he was still alive. He moved out of the closet now and yelled for help. Suddenly, he felt someone grab his arm and pull him toward the courtyard and safety.

TWENTY THOUSAND FEET ABOVE WASHINGTON, DC—0940 HOURS

F-16 pilot Craig Borgstrom of the 119th Fighter Wing North Dakota Air National Guard had been advised to report on any smoke coming from the ground. Borgstrom looked to his left. Some forty miles in the distance, he could see a column of black smoke rising into the sky. He checked his flight path and could see that he and the other two pilots were closing in fast on Washington. He now received a command from NORAD:

"Can you confirm that the Pentagon is burning?"

As he neared the DC metropolitan area, Borgstrom could see the Potomac River, the white stones of Arlington National Cemetery, and then the distinctive five-sided shape of the famous building below, burning from one end.

"Roger that," Borgstrom relayed.

NEADS now advised the three fighters to set up a defensive perimeter around Washington to protect it from any incoming aircraft. Rumors were persistent that as many as eleven planes might be in the air and headed for Washington. Borgstrom, Eckmann, and Derrig began patrolling.

C RING, SECOND FLOOR—0940 HOURS

After destroying the Navy Command Center and most of the first floor of Wedge One, what was left of the nose of American Airlines Flight 77 finally came to rest just east of the Navy Command Center and directly underneath the desk of Tony Rose in the Army Personnel Center above it. The fuel in the right wing of the aircraft surged through the floor under the desk of Louise Kurtz. She had been standing at the copier with her back to the wall when the pressure wave knocked her to the floor. Jet fuel covered her head, face, and arms. It didn't ignite at first. Then, suddenly, a wall of fire hit her broadside and burned over 70 percent of her body, searing the skin away from the lower half of her face and all of her fingers from her hands, burning her ears off, and knocking her unconscious. Kurtz's supervisor, Juan Cruz-Santiago, a twenty-year army veteran, was burned over half his body, losing all but three fingers. One side of his face and both of his ears were nearly burned off.

B RING, FIRST FLOOR—0940 HOURS

John Driscoll looked to his left down Corridor Four. Beyond a pair of glass doors, which closed off B Ring from A/E Drive, everything had turned black. He watched as two men with military haircuts wearing backpacks and civilian clothes slammed the glass doors inward from the other side. The doors were heavy, but the two men popped them open as if they were made of balsa wood. The men were both running with their heads down. One of them screamed, "Get out of the building! All hell's broke loose back there!"

Driscoll watched as a cloud of dust and debris began to fill the air. He looked to his right, down B Ring toward his office. Several doors opened. One officer emerged. "What the hell was that?"

"I think we've been bombed," Driscoll replied.

Another officer emerged. "What do we do now?" he said. Driscoll, by now convinced the disturbance was a terrorist attack and remembering the plane flying into the second World Trade Center, looked at the officers.

"Get behind a wall!" he shouted, his eyes intently focused on the dark hallway. "We've got to wait," he said. "There might be another explosion." Just then, they all heard a dull noise like the sound a furnace makes when it ignites in a home in winter.

An air force sergeant yelled, "There it is!" The men emerged from cover and began moving into the corridor.

B Ring was blocked by a wall, so people began coming out of their offices and moving down the hallway toward Driscoll, then left and directly out into the inner courtyard. What they didn't know was that the secondary explosion they had heard was a pool of unburned jet fuel igniting somewhere in the interior. These pools were now scattered in various places all the way from the west wall to A/E Drive and beyond, creating a sort of liquid minefield waiting for heat and flame to ignite it. The situation was dire for anyone still trapped on the inside.

Along the wall bordering A/E Drive, a black hole now appeared near the eastern part of what had once been the Navy Command Center. A mass of debris had been blown through a cagelike structure and out into the service road. Hovering above all this was a thick haze of dust and water mist from the activated sprinklers mixed with the smoke-filled air. Inside this black hole or "tunnel" as it would later be called, beneath a sagging ceiling, was a deadly maze of broken desks, computer terminals, smashed chairs and filing cabinets, and twisted metal. In pockets everywhere lay the dead and dying. In one corner sat a charred and twisted piece of landing gear and a wheel without a tire. American Airlines Flight 77 had come to an end.

III

A VOICE IN THE DARKNESS

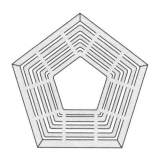

SOUTH PARKING LOT, PENTAGON—0941 HOURS

Near the west wall, Frank Probst lay on the ground, looking back over his shoulder. He was amazed that he was still alive. The right wing of the plane had almost taken his head off. His first thought was that maybe the aircraft had been stolen from one of the airports before any passengers had a chance to board it. His sense of humanity wouldn't let him think that another human being would willingly sacrifice innocent lives like this.

He pulled himself up and instinctively ran toward the south parking lot. Reaching it, he realized he had to go back to help, but now he was faced with police and firefighters suddenly coming onto the scene from all directions. He tried to go back, but they formed a small phalanx and blocked his way.

As the fires died away inside the Pentagon, the silent, black smoke eased its way into every room and corridor, suffocating anything that needed air to live. This was the real murderer; the thing that would account for most of the dead this day.

INTERIOR OF WEDGE TWO, C RING, THIRD
FLOOR, PENTAGON—0941 HOURS

Staff Sergeant Christopher Braman crawled out of the mess kitchen and made his way toward the stairwell. On the first floor, he found an emergency door and broke through it. Reaching the west wall, he beheld what could only be described as controlled chaos—fire, smoke, and people running back and forth.

Ahead, he saw a Pentagon police officer with a woman and a baby. The woman, covered in ashes, was frantic. The officer was holding the baby, who was playful but not making any noise. Braman took the baby in his arms, and the three of them ran into an open area, where Braman placed the baby back in the mother's arms.

"My baby! Where's my baby?" the woman cried. Braman knew that she was in shock and wasn't even aware that her baby was safe in her own arms. He looked at her as she continued to plead for someone to find her baby.

Near Corridor Five of C Ring, a pall of black smoke was coming rapidly toward Commander David Tarantino. All around him lay victims of smoke inhalation, some of them on their hands and knees feeling the walls, their eyes closed due to smoke burn. A military policeman approached Tarantino and told him to get out, but he protested.

"I'm a doctor. I can help," he said.

"Alright, but be careful," the MP said, and left.

Tarantino began helping some of the victims down Corridor Five toward the inner courtyard, stopping in a bathroom to wet paper towels that he then put over his mouth. These wet towels acted like a crude filter to block the smoke.

As Tarantino moved down the hallway, he began to have trouble seeing. Exit signs above the doors and entrances were not visible through the haze. Many people were in a panic, not knowing how to get out.

In Corridor Four on the first floor, Sheila Moody lay in the darkness, thinking about her husband and her children and wondering if she would ever see them again. From the cubicle behind her, she could hear the voice of Antoinette Sherman, one of her coworkers.

"What's going on? What's happening?" Antoinette cried out. "Is anybody there?"

Moody answered her. "Yes, it's me . . . I'm here!"

"Who is it?" Sherman replied.

"It's me, honey; it's Sheila."

"My skin is on fire," Antoinette said. "I feel like I'm burning."

"I know it hurts, baby, but we gotta find a way to get out of here," Sheila said as she extended her hand up toward a window above her, trying to gain leverage to reach it. In a few minutes, she was able to strike the window with her hand, but it was plexiglass and too thick to break. In desperation, Moody looked for something to smash the window with and grabbed what looked like a pipe nearby, but it was in reality part of the sprinkler system. As Moody grabbed it, the hot pipe burned her hand, forcing her to withdraw back into the darkness.

CLASSROOM, FORT MYER—0941 HOURS

Rusty Dodge had been thinking about his friend in New York when he heard an explosion in the distance. One of the Fort Myer firemen stood up.

"What was that?" he said as they all looked wide-eyed at each other.

Simultaneously, all of them jumped up and ran out the door. Outside, in the distance, they could see black smoke rising in the direction of the river. Dodge jumped into a truck with Dennis Gilroy, the Fort Myer battalion commander. The others followed. Once inside the truck, Dodge heard that it was a plane crash and that it was near the Pentagon helipad. Dodge knew this was serious. It meant that their people had been hit.

INTERIOR OF WEDGE ONE, E RING, PENTAGON—0941 HOURS

Back in the large conference room, Phil McNair began to have trouble breathing. He now knew that whatever had happened, it was bad. He had to get his people away from the danger quickly.

It was hard to see because of the smoke, but he knew he was at the head of the table that was farthest away from the E Ring corridor. He could hear screaming and moaning but couldn't see anyone. He tried to keep his mind calm, but he realized if he led people the wrong way, they would get stuck in a maze of cubicles and debris.

Marilyn Wills, lying on the floor and blind to everything around her now, heard a voice cry out. "Somebody help me!" It was Martha Carden.

"Martha, I got ya!" came a reply from someone nearby. Wills recognized the voice as that of Robert Grunewald, who, in the first moments of the attack, had pulled Carden to the floor, probably saving her life. These were the last words Wills remembered hearing before she passed out.

Nearby, John Yates continued to wander through the darkness. In the distance, he could hear occasional cries and moans. As he passed through one area, he heard a voice call out to him in the darkness. "Who is that?" The authoritative Texas twang was unmistakable. It could only be Phil McNair.

"It's John," he said. "John Yates."

He couldn't see McNair, and McNair couldn't see him even though they were very close to each other. Yates continued to move forward. He could hear McNair's voice and the voices of the others but couldn't see anything. The darkness was total. As he moved through the area, he heard another voice.

"Go through the DMPM door; it's clear down there!"

Yates knew that DMPM stood for Directorate of Military Personnel Management and that the door to this area led out onto A/E Drive, so he started moving in this direction.

Marilyn Wills regained consciousness on the other side of the small conference room; only now she was somehow closer to a door along

E Ring. She didn't know how long she had been out or how she had moved to this position. She saw the doorknob and reached up and pulled on it, but it was stuck. She knew there was another door that entered into an office, so she crawled around the conference room. She tried to reach the stage of the conference room with the idea that if she could reach the stage, she could find a way out. As she moved along the floor, she felt someone grab her pant leg.

"Who's there?" she asked.

"It's Lois," came a weak reply.

"OK, Lois," Wills said. "You hold on to me. Wherever I go, you go. We're going to get out of here," Wills reassured the badly shaken woman even though she doubted her own survival. Marilyn knew that she had to keep her head in order to get Lois out alive. In forgetting her own predicament and concentrating on another person, she gained the strength and confidence to continue on. She remembered her mother's toughness through hard times. No daughter of Fanny Toombs was going to give up when the going got rough.

Not far away from Wills, Mike Petrovich got down on the floor and crawled. He knew that the next cubicle was occupied by Dalisay Olaes. He called to Dalisay and told her to grab hold of him, then began yelling at the top of his lungs.

"Everyone get down! Get down on the floor now!"

Olaes fell to the floor and moved toward Petrovich. Petrovich took in a big mouthful of air, then directed everyone to crawl behind the sound of his voice toward the door. As he reached the door, he touched it, and it burned his finger. He flinched and withdrew his hand.

WALTER REED ARMY MEDICAL CENTER—0941 HOURS

Jim Goff walked into the WRAMC command suite located in a basement of the Walter Reed hospital complex. When he reached it, he saw Mary Maniscalco, the chief of surgery, and some other hospital officials discussing the situation in New York and already planning to send help. As they stood there, a soldier entered the room.

"A plane just hit the Pentagon," the soldier said flatly.

Goff felt his insides tighten up as he watched the others stare at the messenger in disbelief. They all knew what this meant.

"What kind of plane?" someone asked.

"We think it was an airliner," he said. "The Pentagon is in flames."

Jim Goff looked at the grave expression on the face of the soldier. The two hundred miles between New York and Washington had now shrunk to nothing. Something catastrophic was in the works.

Goff had been around combat before in Desert Storm. He knew there was a difference between clinical death in a hospital and the sudden death blow of combat, where a man was torn to pieces in the time it took to sip coffee. Now the old memories were coming back—not just images in his mind but a certain smell. Goff knew what fire and intense heat did to tankers, caught inside a steel shell with nowhere to go. He had seen Iraqi soldiers burned to death in this manner and had never been able to get that smell out of his head.

There was complete silence in the room as everyone tried to gather their thoughts. The focus now turned to the Pentagon. Walter Reed was the largest hospital in the Department of Defense and therefore had the primary responsibility of responding to this crisis. But there were problems. Several years earlier, the army surgeon general had developed Specialty Medical Augmentation Response Teams (SMART), and the hospital had a Trauma/Critical Care Team, but it was currently leaderless following the recent transfer of the last team leader. The team itself and its supplies were in complete disarray. With these people unavailable, they would have to assemble a unit from scratch.

Goff got on the phone and discovered that there were only four general surgeons at his disposal. Two were presently in the hospital; one was unable to get to the hospital; and one could not be located. He scrambled to think of whom he could send to the Pentagon. Most important, he needed someone with experience in a combat zone. The first name that came to him was Ben Starnes, the man he had left behind in the clinic. Starnes had served in Kosovo during the Balkan Civil War and had experience with mass casualties in a combat zone. Goff knew Starnes could keep a cool head under this kind of pressure.

Sending him to the Pentagon would get the commander off his back. While he regretted having to be in the position of sending people he liked and respected into harm's way, he had no choice. People were dying every second they waited.

Goff told Mary what he planned to do, then walked back toward the emergency room. No sooner had he left than he got a page to come back to her office. When he got there, Mary told him that Site R was being mobilized.

Site R, also known as the Raven Rock Complex, near Blue Ridge Summit, Pennsylvania, is one of several subterranean bases set up for the president in times of national emergency. From the computers located deep within these mountains, the country can be run indefinitely. Most of the time, this complex sits empty, but at this very moment, White House staff and several top senators and congressmen were being taken there by helicopter. Maniscalco had been ordered to depart by noon. Goff did not hide his feelings. "Mary, I don't think it's good for you to be leaving right now," he said.

"I've got my orders, Jim. You're in charge," she said, and walked out of the room, leaving the stunned Goff alone.

Goff stood there for a long time, contemplating what he was being asked to do. He was now the acting chief of surgery of the largest department of surgery in the Department of Defense. He had seen his fair share of crisis situations before, but this time he would not have the luxury of learning from mistakes. There could be more planes on the way in. There was so much he had to know: How many ORs were currently available? Was the blood bank adequately stocked? Had the hospital admitted any casualties yet? What was going on, on the ground? Had the navy or air force responded yet? He had no idea how he was going to organize this thing, and no time to figure it out.

FEDERAL CREDIT UNION, FAIRFAX, VIRGINIA—0941 HOURS

Ed Plaugher looked up from his paperwork as the loan officer rushed out of a back room and told him that something had happened at the Pentagon. Plaugher left the pen and paper on the desk and in seconds was behind the wheel of his squad car. He drove the Crown Victoria through the streets of Fairfax and into Arlington at well over a hundred miles per hour, its flashing light and high-pitched siren clearing a path through the traffic. Plaugher had never driven the car at such speeds and was amazed at how fast a "police special" could go. As he crested a hill, his eyes beheld a gargantuan cloud of black smoke rising above the Pentagon. Approaching the west wall, he could see that fire units were already on the scene and going about their business. He was proud of his people, who displayed a high level of calm professionalism in the face of such a tragedy.

Plaugher knew that the reason for the fast response was a Comprehensive Emergency Management Plan (CEMP) established by Arlington County in 1956 to provide for the rapid mobilization of police, fire, and medical units to a scene without interrupting the actions of first responders. Looking down at his people, he could see that the forty-five-year-old plan was in fact working. They were keeping bystanders away from the fires and beginning to secure the area. His only concern now was for the people still trapped alive inside the building.

INTERIOR, C RING, SECOND FLOOR, PENTAGON—0942 HOURS

Tony Rose and John Frazier, near the windows overlooking A/E Drive, could see people crawling beneath the smoke, which hovered just above their heads. The air was a haze of dust and debris. People were grabbing belts, shoes, socks, any part of another person they could get their hands on, trying to become part of the chain that was now inching toward the door. Rose could see people completely drenched in jet fuel as if they had taken a shower in it. All at once, he saw Phil McNair and thought he had been scalped; blood covered his head, and his face appeared as if it were falling down around his eyes.

Near the west wall, Victor Correa came out of a daze and realized he was still alive. A second fireball had come up through the floor close to him and shot through the ceiling. He turned to see the entire cubicle farm on fire. Nearby, he saw a civilian partially buried beneath some rubble and, getting to his feet, cleared the debris and helped the stunned worker to get out. A few yards away, he could see Major Jessup pulling himself off the floor. Correa helped the civilian toward Jessup.

"Make sure he gets out, John," he said. Then he started looking for other survivors, but the room was fast filling up with smoke. He came to a lady who was in shock, a blank stare on her face. He put his arm around her and took her over to Jessup.

All around and above him now, Correa could see flashes of fire. In the background, he could hear people screaming and the alarms wailing. A mechanical voice sounded out over the intercom system. "A fire has been detected in your area," it said, repeating its dead, lifeless voice over and over again, part of the din of chaotic noise that filled the area. Correa knew that the smoke would soon force him to the floor. He was beginning to have trouble breathing.

He got down on the floor and began yelling in his loud, strong voice, "If you can hear me, move toward my voice! I know a way out!"

OFFICE OF THE SECRETARY OF DEFENSE—0942 HOURS

Descending quickly from the third to the first floor, Secretary of Defense Donald Rumsfeld ran along the northwest wall at full sprint toward the black cloud, which now reached into the sky above him. Rounding the corner, he came upon a scene that he knew was certainly happening but that a part of him could not believe: a young woman who sat on the ground bleeding.

She asked him to hold an IV above her arm, so Rumsfeld took hold of the IV and held it above her head.

All around were wounded people tending to the injured—people who had responded to this awful thing in seconds, people who were badly wounded themselves but whose primary concern was for their fellow soldiers. Today, Rumsfeld was just another American coming to help. He would continue to act as a litter bearer, helping to bring survivors to safety for well over thirty minutes after the attack.

Farther down the west wall nearer the blast site, Rumsfeld's "operator," Lincoln Leibner, called to people trapped in the darkness, using the sound of their cries to locate their positions. "We're over here!" he heard a small group exclaim. Then he heard sobbing and moaning, cries for help, and some very weak murmurs. Leibner headed inside and found two people pinned to the floor by debris. He got them out quickly, then went back in, but the smoke was beginning to make him weak. There were wounded people everywhere, blinded by the smoke, some of them standing in line, trying to get out. It was a sad, helpless sight.

INSIDE WRAMC COMMANDER'S VAN, NEAR FOURTEENTH STREET, WASHINGTON, DC—0942 HOURS

Ed Lucci sat inside a Ford van, drinking coffee and listening to the radio. As the van moved down the street, he looked out the window and marveled at the blue sky and the sunshine. He always looked forward to fall with its cool mornings and warm afternoons, and this was one of the most beautiful days he'd ever seen.

Lucci and eight other people were on their way to a meeting of the DC Hospital Association. The World Trade Organization meetings were due to be held at the end of September, and this meeting was to help plan for a mass casualty scenario. The WTO had met in Italy some months previously, where nearly a hundred policemen and four hundred citizens had been injured in a riot. The government was expecting a repeat of this fiasco when protesters arrived in Washington for the conference. The scenario was being based on the incident in Italy, and they were expected to prepare for a similar number of casualties.

Fifteen minutes earlier, Lucci had watched the World Trade Center towers burning on CNN in one of the lounges at Walter Reed, and here he was on his way to a conference dealing with mass casualties as a result of terrorism. He had done a lot of research on this subject and had also worked in Saudi Arabia, so he knew a little bit about the Islamic world. It didn't escape him that something terrible was happening and he was about to be swept up in it. He had a sense of what the German philosopher Jung called synchronicity, disparate events all connected to one another and coming together like several storms converging on the same point all at once.

As the van neared the intersection with Fourteenth Street, a call came in, and Lucci was ordered to report to Walter Reed. "They say we've got to bring you back," the driver told him.

"What's up?" Lucci asked the person holding the phone, in his typically nondescript manner.

"They won't say."

Lucci rolled his eyes. He had the driver turn the van around and head back to Walter Reed.

When he arrived back at the ER, several emergency room technicians told Lucci that smoke had been reported coming from the Pentagon and also from the *USA Today* building and the Harry S Truman Federal Building, home to the United States Department of State. Someone else told him that there had been reports of a plane actually hitting the Pentagon. Lucci walked into his office, and the phone rang. It was Major General Harold Timboe, the commander of the Army Medical Corps. Timboe ordered Lucci to the Pentagon immediately with whatever and whomever he could take with him.

Lucci walked out into the ER and told the officer in charge, Sergeant First Class Myers, to find three medics and two ambulances for the response team. Then he grabbed an ER charge nurse named Rod Barlowe.

"You're coming with us," he said. "You can monitor patients in the back of the ambulance."

Barlowe didn't want to leave his current patients. Lucci checked and found that none of the man's cases were urgent. He also made sure that one ambulance would be left on post for any unforeseen emergencies. He looked at Barlowe. "You're coming with us," he said again, reassuring him that the staff they were leaving behind could handle everything. Lucci then noticed Captain Michelle Williams standing by the drug cabinet and ordered her to come along also. This was Williams's first day in the ER. She was undergoing orientation and had clocked in only five minutes before.

As Lucci walked outside, he received another call telling him to wait for buses that were bringing additional physicians to the site. The idea was for these buses to follow behind his ambulance with its sirens blaring and lights flashing to make it easier to get through the streets that, according to reports, were impassable at this moment. He waited a few moments and then grew impatient.

"Where the hell are they?" he asked. He looked around. "We're not waiting. We're leaving now," he said as he walked back inside and told the ER doctors to clear out as many of their beds as possible and to expect casualties. At this point, he figured that by the time he reached the Pentagon, most of the patients would have been evacuated. He was wrong.

Lucci's newly assembled team all climbed into an ambulance driven by one Sergeant Goodwill and left for the Pentagon. As the van moved down the street, Sergeant Goodwill told Lucci that she had a sister who worked in one of the World Trade Center towers. "I don't know if she's dead or alive," she told him. Throughout the day, Lucci would marvel at Goodwill's professionalism as she kept her composure in the face of such anguish.

The ambulance proceeded down the street, headed for the Fourteenth Street Bridge that led to the Pentagon. It was a straight shot from Walter Reed, so Lucci didn't figure they would have the added pressure and delay of making any turns or taking side streets. As they got out onto Fourteenth Street, though, they were shocked by what they saw. Cars and vehicles were everywhere, stretching all the way to the bridge across the Potomac with the black smoke in the distance.

Lucci could see Metro DC cops just standing there out on the street, unable to control the chaos. As the van passed the intersection of Fourteenth Street and Pennsylvania Avenue, one of the officers made eye contact with Lucci. The man just shrugged his shoulders as the drivers ignored his commands. The ambulance continued to move up the street. As it passed the Commerce Department, a woman driving a Volvo blocked the ambulance and wouldn't move. Lucci rolled down the window. "Get your ass out of the way, lady!" he yelled. The woman ignored him. Lucci jumped out of the van and walked up to the car. He was going to pound on her windshield to get her moving, but the thought occurred to him that this could end up on the front page of the *Washington Post*, so he got back inside. In a few moments, Sergeant Goodwill negotiated around the woman and got through the bottleneck to the Fourteenth Street Bridge. Lucci understood that many of these people were just panicking, trying to get someplace safe.

INTERIOR E RING, SECOND FLOOR, PENTAGON—0942 HOURS

Inside what was left of the Army Personnel Center, Marilyn Wills continued to crawl through the black smoke. All at once, her head bumped into something. As she looked up, she could see that it was Regina Grant's rear end. As she looked around, she saw John Yates walking by. Yates had heard a voice directing him toward A/E Drive and was moving toward it.

"Get down, John!" Wills yelled at him.

"Follow me," Yates replied.

Wills could hear his voice, but now the smoke had again enveloped everything, and she couldn't see where he was.

"John, get your butt down, now!" she called out in the darkness, but Yates had disappeared.

Wills and the others continued to move between upturned tables and chairs, office machines, and all manner of debris. Everywhere they turned, they were blocked. The explosion had ripped the cubicle farm apart, scattering the temporary walls all around the area and creating a deadly maze that could trap a person and, in the blindness created by the smoke, so disorient them that they would just lie there and die from smoke inhalation.

Opening her eyes, Wills felt as if the smoke were going to rip her eyeballs out. She had a choice: keep them closed and see nothing or open them into a burning blindness. Either way, she could see nothing and had to rely on the voices around her.

"Marilyn, I can't do it anymore," Lois said as Wills felt the woman's hand begin to lose its grip. Wills's throat began to burn as she heard this. The smoke was now so dense that the pocket of air near the floor was almost gone. The sprinkler system had come on, and Marilyn and the others were doused with water. Marilyn felt one sleeve of her sweater come loose from her arm. She grabbed it and began sucking on it to get the water out. She then handed it back to Lois.

"Take this and suck on it," she told her.

"I can't go on, Colonel," Lois said, now resigned to her fate.

"We've got to keep moving, Lois," Wills said defiantly.

"You've got your girls to take care of. Leave me here," she said.

Wills got angry. "Lois, get on my back, now!" she yelled. The sudden bark of the order from a superior caused Lois to forget everything and just climb on Wills's back. Wills began crawling again with Lois on her back; then she heard Regina Grant cry out in pain.

"My legs are burning!" she shrieked. "My legs are on fire!"

Grant's nylons were melting into her skin from the heat, and the pain was nearly enough to cause her to pass out.

"Stop!" Wills said, and the women stopped moving to allow Regina to sit up on the carpet.

As they did this, Wills looked back and through a break in the smoke saw something that truly shocked her. There behind her was a chain of human beings including Phil McNair and Betty Maxfield, all connected to one another by hands holding on to pant legs and skirts and stretching back toward the wall.

All this time, Wills had thought that it was only Lois and Regina and John with her, but a whole group of people had been linked together almost from the beginning. This scene was being repeated in the darkness throughout the Army Personnel Center. As Wills turned back around, she didn't see Regina.

"Regina?" she called out, but heard nothing. She frantically searched the darkness for a few moments, but Regina Grant was gone.

WALTER REED ARMY MEDICAL CENTER—0942 HOURS

Major Ben Starnes walked into the waiting room and stared at the images of the two towers burning, black smoke pouring out of them. *How will they get those fires to stop?* he thought to himself. In college, many years before, he had traveled to New York City one night with a friend, and they had gone to the top of the north tower of the World Trade Center. Starnes remembered standing there long after midnight, staring out at the lights of the city and feeling the tower move beneath him in the wind. He tried to imagine being on top of that thing with no way to get down, being up that high in the air with everything beneath him on fire. The very thought terrified him. This would be the last time he would see the towers standing.

He turned and walked back into his office. Just as he did, the radio blared that a plane had struck the Pentagon. The initial report said that it might have been a commuter plane, but something was wrong. He knew disasters didn't happen like this. The New York attacks and now this? It was too much of a coincidence to be believed. His gut instinct told him that something terrible was happening to the country. He thought of his family and his parents at home.

A sudden succession of terrible thoughts came into his mind, of nightmare scenarios, but he quickly dismissed them and tried to focus on what needed to be done at the moment.

As Starnes turned to walk out of his office, the phone rang. It was Jim Goff calling from the command suite. "Ben, I need you to stay on the line for thirty seconds," Goff said. Then he put him on hold. Starnes stood at the desk, barely moving. In a few moments, Goff came back. "I need you to go down to the emergency room and get on a bus. You're going to the Pentagon."

"Yes sir," Starnes said as Goff explained further.

"They need a general surgeon down there with experience in dealing with mass casualties." Hearing Goff's words, Starnes had visions of a daunting situation involving thousands of dead and dying, but he didn't hesitate.

"I'm on my way," he said, and hung up the phone.

INTERIOR OF WEDGE TWO, PENTAGON—0942 HOURS

Roxane Cruz-Cortez woke up to the sound of a baby crying nearby. The crying was muffled at first as if she were in a dream. Then it got louder. She lifted her head up and looked around. The office had been destroyed, the far walls gone, the ceiling caved in, and nothing but a pile of junk where the furniture had just been. Everything above her was on fire. She tried to stand up but was pinned between her chair and a wall. She prayed silently. *Please, Lord, I don't want to die like this.* Images of her family began to flash through her mind like the turning pages of an old photo album. "Today is not my day," she said as she desperately tried to pull herself up. She was not going to be afraid. "Bruno!" she called out, but there was no answer. The baby continued to cry. It was a loud shriek that cut through the din. "Sergeant Gallop!" Cruz-Cortez shouted, but again, there was silence.

Lying on the floor in a daze several feet away, April Gallop could see her baby's stroller on fire and burning, but the baby had miraculously been thrown clear and was lying on the floor somewhere nearby, covered in debris. Gallop was half-unconscious and in shock. She tried to scream but couldn't.

Cruz-Cortez could hear voices in the distance, people yelling and calling to each other and, in different places, the moaning of the wounded. After some time, she heard movement nearby. Some debris on the floor began to move, and a hand emerged, then a head. It was Bruno, covered in dirt and bleeding from the forehead. He rose up, shook his head, and tried to focus his eyes. "Bruno!" Cruz-Cortez yelled.

"Is that you, Cruz?"

"Yes," she said in a weak voice. "It's me . . . I need help. I can't move this thing off me."

"Where are you?" he asked.

"I'm on the floor somewhere," she said. "Follow the sound of my voice!"

As Bruno made his way in the darkness toward Cruz-Cortez, she heard another movement nearby and figured this had to be Sergeant Gallop. Meanwhile, the baby continued to cry. The smoke was getting thicker, and if someone didn't get to that baby quickly, it was going to die.

"Sergeant Gallop!" Cruz-Cortez cried again, but Gallop didn't respond. Bruno finally reached Cruz-Cortez and pushed up on the section of the wall that had collapsed and pinned her to the floor. Heaving with all of his strength, he was able to budge it just enough for Cruz-Cortez to look out at him.

The smoke separated for a moment, and Cruz-Cortez could now see Gallop, who had regained consciousness and was screaming at the top of her lungs.

"Where's my baby!" she cried and wailed. "Oh my God, I can't find my baby!"

Cruz-Cortez felt a shock go through her at the pain and anguish in the woman's voice. Knowing she was pinned and couldn't move, she still knew she had to keep Gallop from panicking. "April, calm down!" she called to her. "Listen to the cry. Follow the sound of his cry," she said. Gallop stopped screaming and began moving in the direction of the baby's cry. Cruz-Cortez looked at Bruno, who was struggling to get the section of wall off her. Cruz-Cortez shouted at him. "Don't worry about me," she said. "Help April find her baby."

Bruno ignored her, took a deep breath, and again pushed hard against the wall. Cruz-Cortez reached up and pushed with her hand, and together the two moved the wall just enough for Bruno to grab both of her arms and pull her out. As Cruz-Cortez tried to stand, she found that her knees were so weak that she could hardly get up. Bruno held on to her to keep her from falling.

"I've found him!" Gallop suddenly shouted as she located Elisha. Almost at the same time, the smoke momentarily cleared. From the front of the office, a light shone on all of them, and for a moment they could see the blue sky outside. Cruz-Cortez knew this used to be the window from the office across the hall as she had seen it many times. "Over there!" Cruz-Cortez and Bruno yelled almost simultaneously. As a pocket of blue sky appeared through the haze, all at once they heard a voice shriek, "Oh my God!" and then the muffled sound of sobbing in the distance.

INTERIOR OF WEDGE ONE, PENTAGON—0942 HOURS

Her legs in terrible pain, Regina Grant grabbed hold of the back of John Yates's leg as he moved near the large conference room. In the blackness, she held on to him as hard as she could as he moved forward. But somewhere along the way, she lost her grip, and Yates disappeared. She lay still, just wanting the pain to go away.

Janice Jackson was completely disoriented and in a state of shock until she saw sunshine streaming through a crack in the wall. She heard voices nearby and moved toward them. As she passed a pile of debris, she saw her friend Racquel Kelley pinned to the floor by rubble. She reached down and pulled Kelley up, and the two moved toward the sunlight. When Janice reached the outside air, she began to run and scream. Her hands felt like they were still on fire. Her whole body felt as if it were burning. Rescue workers managed to get to her quickly.

In a smoke-filled hallway, Craig Powell pulled at a fire door, trying to get it open. He finally managed to get it loose. Then with all his might, he pulled it back and stepped into the corridor. He looked around. The ceiling was now falling in, everything beginning to crumble. He got past the door, and it automatically shut behind him. He could see bright lights ahead and to one side, the new escalator down to the first floor. His training and experience had left him with a kind of sharpened sixth sense. He remembered his time in Jamaica years before and paused to consider the possibility that an enemy had attacked the Pentagon from the outside and was trying to draw people into the courtyard so they could be finished off there. He followed his instincts, taking the stairs and sprinting to the first floor, staying aware of his surroundings.

When he came out on the ground floor, he nearly collided with a lady running down the hallway. Her head was covered in blood, and she was running back into the building toward the fire. Powell sensed that she didn't know what she was doing.

"I was in the bathroom," she said, her voice trembling. She mumbled something else, and as Powell turned to look down the corridor for a moment, she broke away from him and disappeared. He found her and ushered her toward the courtyard, where he handed her off to someone else; then he turned and moved toward the fire and smoke.

All around Powell now were crumbled walls and debris, fire, noise, and the screams of injured people. The hallway was filled with water. He went one way, and fire and smoke blew him back into the corridor, at which point he ran into a young female naval officer, a lieutenant junior grade, and grabbed her. She was disoriented and soaking wet. "You alright?" he said. She mumbled something, but he couldn't understand it. The woman seemed to be in shock, so he thrust her into the arms of a passerby and moved toward the courtyard.

Lieutenant Colonel Victor Correa could not see what was going on around him. Smoke filled the entire cubicle farm. All he could hear was moaning and crying, the sound of the mechanical voice on the intercom constantly repeating its message, and people crying for help. Tony Rose soon joined him, and the two men crawled among the cubicles, looking for survivors. The smoke at this point was thick and black and hovered some eighteen inches above the floor with a band of white smoke beneath it. Rose and Correa put their cheeks to the floor as if they were crawling under barbed wire on a firing range.

As they slowly emerged into the hallway, the smoke became overwhelming, but at the far end of the hallway, they could see flames.

Correa again began shouting for people to move toward his voice. It was a strong, loud rant that shocked Carl Mahnken back to consciousness. Mahnken had been hit in the head by a flying computer terminal. He got up out of the rubble and followed the sound of Correa's voice. This eventually led him to the outside, where he began helping other victims by ripping pants open, taking shoes off, and trying to get blood flowing in some of the injured. He would continue to help for hours, disregarding a grapefruit-sized bump on the top of his head. Meanwhile, Rose and Correa continued moving through the corridor, clearing rooms. Correa would hold the fire doors open so Rose could go in and evacuate people. Rose, the smaller of the two, was able to get into tighter spaces.

PENTAGON FIRE STATION—0942 HOURS

Amid the burning grass, Alan Wallace huddled under the front of a passenger van. The fireball had surged forward, burning Sean Boger's Mitsubishi 3000GT sports car and Jackie Kidd's Jeep Cherokee station wagon, leaving nothing but charred hulls before abruptly disappearing. Now Wallace looked up to see Mark Skipper standing alone in a field, staring blankly into space. Wallace had lost track of him for what seemed like hours, though it had only been a few minutes. Skipper looked like he was frozen upright in the ground. Wallace thrust himself out from under the van, ran to his friend, and grabbed him by the arm.

"Mark, you OK?" he said. Skipper said nothing for a moment, then slowly turned and looked at his friend. "Man, am I glad you saw that plane!" he said, managing a slight smile.

BUILDING OPERATIONS COMMAND CENTER (BOCC), FIRST FLOOR, WEDGE ONE, PENTAGON—0942 HOURS

In the main physical plant of the Pentagon, air-handling systems, damaged by the initial blast, now began to shut down and emit carbon monoxide. If they weren't restarted soon, they would fill the wedge with the deadly, odorless gas. Pentagon building inspector Anthony Freeman and electrical engineer Daniel Murphy realized this danger and quickly made their way through smoke-filled and flooded hallways toward the interior of the building and managed to shut down these units, all the while exposing themselves to the carbon monoxide. They also worked to repressurize the chilled-water system that powered the air-conditioning units and kept the computers in undamaged sections from overheating.

On the west side of Wedge One, Matthew Morris, the power generator shop supervisor, realized the danger posed by severed power lines and immediately made his way toward the main electrical vault, where four 13,800-volt circuit breakers were allowing electricity to feed the exposed cables in the hallways.

Morris waded through the water in the hallways caused by burst pipes and kept low to avoid being electrocuted. When he reached the electrical vault, he could see that the heavy metal doors that secured the area had been blown off their hinges. Grabbing the first breaker, Morris pulled with all his might but couldn't budge it. The current surging through these lines was so tremendous that he knew it was at least a two-man job, but there was no time. He grabbed hold of the handle with both hands and tried to force it downward against the flow of power. It took every bit of strength that he had. In his mind, he knew that with all of the fire and water around him, he could be killed in an instant, but he persevered, literally taking his life in his own hands. Using all of his strength and body weight, Morris eventually succeeded in cutting power to the wedge. Everything was now plunged into total darkness.

Scattered throughout the devastated Wedge One, survivors from the initial blast wandered aimlessly through the darkness, trying to find their way out, some of them falling into deep crevices where there had once been floors; others just collapsing and dying, their lungs filled with smoke or poisoned by carbon monoxide. A lucky few made it into B and A Rings and thence into the courtyard, their clothes soaked with dirty water, the flesh on their faces and arms burned black.

After escaping from the office on the fourth floor of E Ring, Peter Murphy and Robert Hogue entered the hallway and made sure everyone in their section was evacuated and then attempted to get out. Murphy began walking toward the offices of Lieutenant General William Nyland, the deputy commandant for Marine Aviation. As the others followed behind, they suddenly heard a loud voice calling in their direction.

"Stay out; there's fire down here!"

Hearing this, they reversed course, moving into a bank of smoke that was getting thicker as the surrounding heat grew in intensity. As they moved forward, it increasingly became harder to breathe.

Murphy looked down through a wide crack in the floor and could see the flames beneath him.

As the group passed this hole, they heard another voice call to them in the darkness.

"Come to my voice!"

The sounds emanated from behind them, so they turned around. In a few moments, they discovered a group of navy personnel who were on the second floor overlooking the Pentagon courtyard. From this vantage point, Murphy could see black smoke pouring over the sides of the building. Peering into A Ring, they could see an army lieutenant colonel pulling bodies out, his uniform almost completely blackened.

Murphy couldn't tell if the people the man was helping were dead or alive. They were completely covered with soot. To Murphy's eyes, the lieutenant colonel himself didn't seem to be living. He was clearly wounded, his clothes torn and his face blackened, but he moved with determination. Murphy figured he was by now completely exhausted and going on pure will alone.

Sergeant Francis W. Pomrink, Jr., USMC, a Classified Materials NCO, was at work in his office at the Department of Marine Aviation when the plane crashed. Most of his department had been moved to the "Butler building" the week before. It was two hundred yards from Ground Zero and not nearly as close as their previous offices, which had been destroyed upon impact. Pomrink felt the building shake and ran outside to see the smoke. He then ran back inside and ordered everyone out, remaining behind until everyone had been evacuated and all classified materials were secure. As he went to leave, he suddenly remembered that not all of the marines in his office had moved to the Butler building. Lance Corporals Schuetz and Vera were still working for Lieutenant General Nyland in the old office near the impact site. He stared at the black smoke. He couldn't just assume they were dead. He had to find out for himself.

Pomrink ran toward the barracks at Henderson Hall, about a half mile away, changed from his service C or "Charlies" into his camo uniform, and then ran back toward the black gash where the plane had hit. He made his way through the building to the fourth floor where the Marine Aviation offices had been, but the smoke was too thick, so he retreated to the outside. He then heard people screaming for help and joined a nearby rescue team that was bringing up litters for the firefighters. When he finally reached Nyland's offices, Schuetz and Vera were gone. He figured they didn't make it. Unbeknownst to him, the two marines were very much alive and at this very moment were trying desperately to rescue survivors throughout the wreckage.

WEST WALL, PENTAGON—0943 HOURS

In a field next to the west wall of the Pentagon, firefighters Wallace and Skipper surveyed the devastation of the attack. Wallace began to see hundreds of pieces of flaming debris floating to earth and realized they were the hard leaves of the bull bay Magnolia tree he had seen earlier, now little more than a black stump. These flaming leaves were everywhere, raining fire down on an already burning landscape. To his left was Truck 61, one whole side of it on fire, flames covering the rear wheels.

He looked at Skipper. "Get your gear," he said. "I've got to get to the truck."

Skipper nodded and headed for the firehouse. Wallace ignored the painful burns that had seared his forearms and back. He knew he had to get Truck 61 turned around and get the water cannon working, but as he approached it, he could see that the entire rear end was on fire. Then he looked at the firehouse and realized that the truck had acted as a firebreak, preventing the firehouse from being completely destroyed. Everything around the fire truck and the firehouse was burning, even the ground. The whole west wall of the Pentagon was aflame all the way up to the fifth floor. The plane had disappeared.

Wallace ran thirty yards to the truck, trying not to slip on any of the debris that blanketed the ground. He reached the right cab door, climbed in, grabbed a radio, and put a headset on. Smoke from the fire filled the cab, making it hard to breathe, but he kept moving. His only thought now was to get water on the blaze. He jumped over the radio and into the driver's seat and pushed the engine ignition button, hoping against hope that it would start. In a few seconds, the engine rumbled to life. Amazed, Wallace put the gearshift in reverse and stepped on the accelerator, but nothing happened. He gave it gas a second time, but still nothing. Suddenly, he heard Skipper yelling at him to cut the engine off. The effects of the blast had severed the fuel line, and whenever Wallace hit the accelerator, flames would shoot out of the back of the truck. He was unwittingly pumping gasoline into the fire.

As Wallace turned to get out, he saw Dennis Young walk by. Young was burned but still alive. Upon impact, he had rushed downstairs, grabbed his gear, and escaped, racing through the truck bay, the fireball right behind him burning everything in sight. He now joined the other firefighters as they struggled to get the fires under control.

Wallace looked at Truck 61. He figured that the transmission and the rear axle had been superheated from the collision with the tail of the plane and destroyed. If they weren't able to move the truck, they couldn't get foam and water on the fire. He picked up the radio receiver and sent a message:

"Foam 61 to Fort Myer: We have had a commercial
airliner crash into the west side of the Pentagon at
the heliport, Washington Boulevard side. We are OK.

With minor injuries. Aircraft was a Boeing 757 or
Airbus 320. Send help immediately."

After sending the emergency message, Wallace jumped out of the
truck with some of the radio gear, including the headset. A Pentagon
cop appeared and asked for breathing equipment, so Wallace handed
one set to him and one to Skipper. Wallace then ran to try to get his
gear out of the firehouse, which was covered with burning material. As
he went to grab his fire suit, he noticed that the elastic suspender strap
he was wearing was also on fire. He pulled at it, then tried to stamp it
out, but the thing kept reigniting. He stomped on it until it went out,
then looked at his gear. It was full of concrete chips.

Wallace retrieved his boots and fire pants along with a lantern and
two fire extinguishers. Then, holding a CO2 extinguisher in one hand,
he walked toward the west wall. He had left behind his gloves, helmet,
and oxygen mask and was wearing only a T-shirt, fire pants, and boots,
with his burned suspender straps holding his pants up.

INTERIOR OF WEDGE ONE, PENTAGON—0943 HOURS

Staring at the ruins of the Navy Command Center, Kevin Shaeffer
knew he was the only survivor. Slumped on the floor all around him
were the dead bodies of his comrades. In one spot, he could see the
body of his friend Pat Dunn. Pat's wife was due to have a baby in a few
weeks. Now the little girl would be fatherless.

Shaeffer tried to breathe in, but it hurt badly. In the initial blast,
he had inhaled aerosolized jet fuel—a mist that emanated from the
pressure wave and filled his lungs. Every breath was a struggle. He was
coldly aware that he still might not make it out, but like every other
soldier this day, he knew deep inside that there would be a terrible
reckoning for the people who had done this. He knew that the primal
need for justice, to see the bastards pay, could keep a man alive when
everything else would not.

Shaeffer ran his fingers through his hair. His head felt wet, but he
didn't know if it was blood or water. He looked at the sprinklers dousing the room and figured it must be water, but he was so miserable, he

didn't care. He heard a few moans and cries but could see no movement. In a few moments, the cries faded. Most of the cubicles had disappeared, replaced by a mountain of jumbled wood, glass, and concrete. Live wires hung from the ceiling, sputtering back and forth.

Shaeffer's mind was all that he had now. Much of the outer layer of his skin had been burned away, destroying the nerve endings. He knew that physically he was going to pay dearly for what had happened to him. He thought about his wife, Blanca. He had to survive for her. He knew that if he didn't get out somehow, he would suffocate from the thick smoke and would never see her again. The thought made him sick to his stomach. The motorcycle crash had already weakened his legs. Nevertheless, he put one foot in front of the other and through sheer will made his way to the main entrance.

When he reached the big seven-foot-high metal door, Shaeffer found that it was locked solid. He turned and headed in the other direction, toward offices he had never seen before. He climbed over debris, trying to stay clear of burst water pipes, which were rapidly pumping water into the hallways. Suddenly in the distance, he saw sunlight and began crawling toward it. He found a large hole where there had once been a solid wall and climbed through it into the panic and confusion of A/E Drive between B and C Rings. Nearby, he saw a piece of the nose cone of an aircraft. Next to it were pieces of the landing gear.

So it was a plane, he thought to himself. He could see people running back and forth. He looked at his hands and arms, which were burned black. He knew he needed help, but he just didn't have the strength in his legs to stand, let alone walk, so he simply sat down in the middle of the service road and waited.

In an abandoned corridor on the second floor of E Ring, Brian Birdwell lay on top of broken glass and splintered wood. Death was waiting for him now, sitting amid the destruction. It was so close, and Birdwell was ready for it to take him; then a cool rain came pouring down. He looked up to see the sprinkler head directly above him, spraying water down onto his body, but strangely, as the water doused him, he didn't feel wet. His skin did not feel the way it normally did when water was poured on it. What Birdwell didn't know was that much of the outer layer of his flesh had been burned away. He tried to breathe, but every gasp was a struggle. His eyes were level with the floor, and he could see pieces of desk and ceiling burning all around. Every once in a while, he could see movement. He thought about his wife and son and what they meant to him. He had to stay alive for them. He tried to scream, but he didn't even have enough strength to make the sound come out, and it stayed down there in his gut, clawing at him.

Now roaming Corridor Four near E Ring and looking for survivors, Victor Correa, Tony Rose, and some others came upon Birdwell. Correa could see that much of his skin had been burned off and knew that they couldn't just touch him with bare hands or even lift him up by his arms.

"Let's make a cradle," he said to the others, and everyone crossed arms and then asked Birdwell to lie down on that. Birdwell stood up and then lay down on the arms. Correa and some of the others carried him up Corridor Four until they ran into a locked fire door. Turning to the left, they made their way into the main corridor of A Ring and walked through the Redskins snack bar at the apex of Corridors Five and Six and then out into a triage area in the middle of A Ring, where they gently laid Birdwell down on a stretcher. They released the grips of their hands and moved away.

Where are they going? Birdwell wondered. His body felt as if it had been placed in a furnace. He just wanted someone to put him back under the cool water. Air force colonel John Baxter and a team of medics then approached the motionless Birdwell, having been sent by the first group of people who had found and moved Birdwell out of the danger zone. Baxter could clearly see that much of the skin on Birdwell's upper body had been baked off. He was obviously in terrible pain. Baxter grabbed one of the trauma packs he had brought from the air force clinic and looked for a vein. Afraid to touch Birdwell and unable to find anywhere on his body to safely insert a needle, he gave him an injection of morphine in his right foot, then inserted an IV in his left. He attached a toe tag listing Birdwell's name and the medications he'd given him. Birdwell now looked up into Baxter's eyes and pleaded with him in a low voice to go back to his office and look for his coworkers. Baxter sent some of his people to look for them, but by now, smoke had overtaken the area, and visibility was limited to just a few inches above the floor. Birdwell would not learn until days later that they had all been killed.

Coming down from the fifth floor, Natalie Ogletree saw Birdwell lying on the stretcher, alone and not moving. As she watched her coworkers move into the light of the courtyard, something told her to stay and pray with this man even though she knew it was dangerous. She walked over to Birdwell and took out a Bible she was carrying with her, opening it to the Twenty-Third Psalm. Birdwell lay there in silence as Ogletree quietly read the soothing words.

"The Lord is my shepherd; I shall not want . . ."

BIRDWELL HOME, LORTON, VIRGINIA—0943 HOURS

Mel Birdwell picked up the phone. It was a neighbor telling her that the Pentagon had been hit. She immediately turned on the TV and saw the firehouse and the tower. She knew at once that the plane had hit right outside the window of her husband's office because she had helped him move in only a few weeks before. Her son, Matt, approached and looked at the screen.

"That's not where Dad's office is," he said. "His office is on the other side of the building."

Mel looked at her son. "Honey, I hope you're right, but let's pray about it anyway," she said, knowing the awful truth but trying to be strong for her son.

DUNN HOME, SPRINGFIELD, VIRGINIA—0943 HOURS

Stephanie Dunn watched the fire and smoke coming from the Pentagon on television.

"No!" she cried out as a terrible feeling came over her. "Oh God, no!"

Somehow she knew that her husband, Pat, was dead. She remembered waving to him many times from the balcony of their home in Italy as his ship sailed out of the Gulf of Gaeta. She remembered him standing on the deck of the ship, waving back to her as he slowly disappeared beyond the horizon. She worried each time that he would not return, but he always did. Now, she suddenly felt as if part of her body had been torn away from her.

HOME OF IDA WESSEL, ST. LOUIS, MISSOURI—0943 HOURS

At the home of her mother, Ida Wessel, in St. Louis, Missouri, Beverly Rose stared at the television. She knew where her husband's office was located and knew from the footage that the plane had struck his work area. As she explained this to her mother, everyone in the room, all of whom had previously been in high spirits getting ready for a wedding, started to cry. "If Tony is dead, then he is in a far better place," Bev Rose said through tears. "If he's alive, he is working on rescue."

Bev Rose knew her husband well. Back amid the destruction and chaos of the Army Personnel Center, Sergeant Major Tony Rose was indeed helping to rescue people, moving from corridor to corridor, searching for survivors.

WEST WALL, PENTAGON—0943 HOURS

Pentagon police officer Isaac Ho'opi'i moved his car at high speed into the parking lot. Through his windshield, he could see a great cloud of black smoke rising into the sky. As he got closer, he suddenly noticed that his car wouldn't go into gear any longer. The car just rolled free, and the smell of burned fluid filled the air. In his frantic dash to get to the scene, he had blown the transmission. He hit the brake, jumped out of the car, and opened the rear door to let out his dog, Vito. Then the two began running at full speed toward the crash site.

Reaching the black hole, Ho'opi'i rushed inside with only his short-sleeved police uniform and little else for protection. He immediately began calling to anyone within earshot, projecting his deep voice through the din. Moving farther inside, he found a woman whose skin was peeling from her back. Ho'opi'i picked her up, put her across his broad shoulders, and carried her outside, then went back in and found a woman in shock and without shoes on her feet. He picked her up and she looked at him, beside herself with fear. The big man smiled at her.

"You're alive!" he said, and carried her out.

Despite pleas from others for him to stay out, Ho'opi'i kept going back, pressing forward through the rubble and the darkness, into D Ring. In front of him, he could hear voices coming from every direction. He was breathing the smoke into his lungs, but it didn't stop him. His years of holding his breath while spearfishing were keeping him upright.

Directly above his head, Ho'opi'i heard a weird twisting and groaning sound. He figured this was probably the steel support beams beginning to crack under the intense heat. Not good. As he drew closer to the voices, he called out again with his deep, mellow baritone knifing through the smoke.

"If you can hear me, head toward my voice!"

Wayne Sinclair, lying on a pile of rubble, heard the big voice but could not see where it was coming from. The voice boomed again, and Sinclair directed people toward it. He felt like he was in a dream with the voice of an angel leading him to the light.

Ho'opi'i now turned and headed toward the outside again, calling back to Sinclair and the others as he moved and using his voice as a beacon to guide them to the opening. In a few moments, Sinclair and his people were safe on the lawn, but they never saw Ho'opi'i. He remained near the opening just long enough to make sure they were OK, then headed back into the darkness.

INTERIOR OF WEDGE ONE, DCSPER, E RING, SECOND FLOOR, PENTAGON—0943 HOURS

In a demolished office of the DCSPER on the second floor, Major Stephen V. Long, the former army ranger who had survived Grenada and the Persian Gulf War, had been knocked to the floor by the blast but was able to recover his senses quickly. His experience and training resulted in an almost instantaneous reaction to the danger. He brushed himself off and took one last look at the sky outside. His family, his future, and safety were only a few feet away, but instead of rushing outside, he turned around and headed back into the abyss to look for survivors. Like the other soldiers, he would rather die than leave a comrade behind. It was a creed that had been burned into his consciousness until it became a reflex action, and today it would cost him his life.

PENTAGON DAY CARE CENTER—0943 HOURS

When navy lieutenant Evelyn Gibbs reached her office in the Navy Annex, someone told her about the attack on the Pentagon. Her immediate fear was that her children, whom she had just dropped off at the day care center, were injured or worse. She turned and ran toward the day care center as fast as she could, covering three miles quickly, her heart pounding in her chest. As she drew closer, she beheld the Pentagon and the awful sight of the fires on the ground. Reaching the day care center, she found it abandoned and her children gone. She was beside herself with grief until her eyes caught sight of them out on a grassy hill, happily playing with their teachers, oblivious to the death and destruction around them.

INTERIOR OF WEDGE ONE, PENTAGON—0943 HOURS

Dan Fraunfelter heard voices all around him. Then slowly, black shapes emerged from the smoke like shadows come alive. In a few moments, he could see it was a group of people, stunned and disoriented. He shone his flashlight at them. "Move toward the light!" he shouted. In a few moments, more than fifty people walked into the glare of the flashlight and rushed past him to safety. As this group escaped, the thought occurred to Fraunfelter that more could be trapped inside some of the rooms, so he took off his shirt, covered his mouth, and crawled along the hot floor, trying to find survivors. As he moved, his hands suddenly felt a large crack right through the middle of the foundation. The discovery shocked him. He knew that the floor was concrete covered with an epoxy compound, an extremely tough material that wasn't supposed to crack. *What kind of force was responsible for this?* he thought to himself. Unknown to him, American Airlines Flight 77 was directly underneath, the fires from a lake of jet fuel superheating the floor.

PENTAGON FIRE STATION, WEST WALL—0943 HOURS

The woman stood pleading for someone to find her baby. "Where's my baby?" she cried. "Somebody help me find my baby!" Christopher Braman looked at her, and then he looked at the baby lying quietly in her arms. It would be a sight forever burned into his memory.

The Pentagon police officer standing next to the woman looked at Braman.

"Go get help," he said. "Go get help!"

Braman turned and ran toward the fire station. Surrounding him were hundreds of people looking toward the impact site. Many appeared to be in shock. He stared at the confluence of I-395 and SR 110 where the Pentagon was situated. Near the 110, he saw a fire truck and an ambulance and moved toward them. He could see the ambulance driver hurriedly unloading his equipment. Braman looked at him. "I need help, man. I have a lady and a baby." The ambulance driver seemed to ignore him, and then Braman watched the man's eyes become fixated on something behind him.

Braman turned around to see three men carrying toward the ambulance a woman who had been burned from the top of her head clear down to her thighs. Her skin was bright pink where her flesh had been burned off. Her face showed neither fear nor pain. She just seemed about to pass out. Braman looked closer at her face and recognized her as a woman who worked in the finance department. He remembered her as the lady who had recently taken his travel orders for approval.

As Braman stared at the woman, three men ran past him, and he just started running with them. As he did, he saw several propane canisters coming at him from the direction of the construction trailer, bouncing and whirling across the ground like giant firecrackers, exploding one at a time, with a section of cage entangled and being dragged along with them. Just as he saw this, his eyes caught sight of a man standing off to one side, holding a coffee cup up to his mouth as if about to take a drink. The man just stood there with that cup at his mouth and a blank stare on his face, frozen in place and not moving.

At this point, Braman was operating on pure adrenaline. He quickly ran between Alan Wallace's burning fire truck and the firehouse, past the burned-out hull of Boger's 3000GT. Closing in on the crash site, he peered into the gaping hole and could feel his skin burning. It was terrifying, but Braman knew that he had to get people to safety. His Military Occupational Specialty, or MOS, in the Rangers had been Combat Search and Rescue, so he was well trained for the task facing him. He reached around and pulled off his undershirt, wrapping it around the lower half of his face, but before he rushed back into the building, he said a prayer to himself: "Lord, give me the strength for what I am about to do."

Inside the burning Army Personnel Center, Lieutenant Colonel Ted Anderson continued to move people out of the area, sometimes having to bark commands at them. Some of them were disoriented and in shock, but his only concern now was getting them outside to safety. At one point, he kicked open an emergency door and ran outside, where he began directing people to move in a northeasterly direction. As he now turned to his left, he could see a vast debris field of gray metal, pieces scattered in every direction. Anderson instantly knew it was a plane. The parking lot, the grass, and the trees were all on fire. He turned around and found himself staring into the eyes of Christopher Braman. No words were said between them. In that instant, there was an understanding, and the two men became a team.

Before they could go back inside, Anderson spotted Alan Wallace's fire truck engulfed in flames. He watched as Wallace, Skipper, and Young attempted to fight the fire. *Just three guys,* he thought to himself, *and they're fighting without protective suits.* Suddenly, Anderson heard a series of loud thud-bangs as more propane canisters began to explode from the heat, popping and shooting across the ground. Nevertheless, he and the others ran toward the crash site and came upon two women who had either been blown out of their offices onto the ground or had jumped out. One lady had a compound fracture in her hip. Anderson told her she was going to be OK, but he knew he had to get her clear of the building. He was certain he was going to cause the lady incredible pain, but he had to get her to safety, so he picked her up and threw her over his shoulder. The woman passed out. Braman picked up the other lady and followed Anderson, and they were able to get the two ladies clear of the impact site. Both men then ran back toward the wall.

Anderson found a window that had been blown out, and the men boosted each other up onto the wall one by one and then climbed through the window into the building. Inside, they got down on the floor and crawled, blinded and nearly suffocated by smoke. Braman had never seen such darkness. He had once heard it referred to as "country dark," a blackness so total, a man could not see his hand in front of his face.

Anderson's objective was to stay low to the ground, beneath the smoke, and move about thirty feet at a time, kicking emergency doors open to move farther into the interior. He felt his way forward until he reached a door. He tried to open it but found it locked. He felt around some more until his hands touched a body. He reached around until he found an arm and then checked for a pulse. It turned out to be a heavyset woman who was in shock and covered in debris. She was pinned against the door and unable to move. Anderson looked at her and knew that the only way to free her was to deliberately break her leg to unpin her from the debris. If they didn't take this drastic measure, she would burn to death. Working together, Anderson and Braman broke the woman's leg free and then dragged her outside, where she was transported to a triage unit. When they got her outside, she was conscious and her vital signs were stable, but six days later she would pass away from internal injuries.

Anderson again went back inside and started yelling into the blackness as he heard a series of explosions coming from behind him, one right after the other. These were more propane canisters, stored in staging areas in the construction zone and used by the renovation pipe fitters, and they, too, were exploding from the heat and flames. In a few moments, a fire department car, parked nearby, burst into flames as its gas tank exploded. These chain-reaction detonations caused a high-pitched whine in Anderson's right eardrum as he was knocked to the ground. He managed to pull himself up but was convinced that his eardrum had been punctured.

Everything now became muffled, the sound of his heartbeat louder than the outside noise. All movement around him was like a TV with the volume turned down. He could see Braman directly across from him looking for survivors. As his eyes scanned this scene, he suddenly caught sight of a brilliant orange flame shooting past him. He thought it was a piece of the burning roof but then, to his horror, saw that it was a man—on fire and running. He was bouncing off walls, trying to put the flames out, spinning around and around like a top. All of a sudden, the man hit the window right in front of Anderson, who could see that the entire front of his body was in flames. All of his muscles were contracting wildly as he burned.

Anderson glanced at Braman for only a split second as the two of them instinctively jumped on top of the man and smothered the flames. They grabbed him, one by the feet and one by the hands. At one point, Braman thought he was pulling on the man's shirtsleeve, but it was his flesh.

Anderson and Braman carried the burning man out of the building. As they carried him away, he began to scream at the top of his lungs. "Get the people out!" he said, struggling to mouth the words. "There're people still in there; you've gotta get 'em out now!" he shouted with all the strength he had left.

When they got the man outside, Anderson could see that everything from the top of his head to the bottom of his feet had been burned black, but the back half of him was untouched. The back of his suit still looked like it did the day it was bought, and the back halves of his shoes still exhibited a spit-shine. The front half, however, was unrecognizable. Anderson and Braman made sure the man was taken to a triage unit; then they headed back inside to find others.

WEST WALL, PENTAGON—0943 HOURS

From the outside, Blair Bozek could now see the extent of the damage to the building. He saw very few survivors in the area but could hear cries and moans coming from inside, past some blackened windows. He ran along the outer wall toward where the aircraft had entered the building, somewhere between the exit from Corridor Five and the control tower of the firehouse. He ran up to one of the broken windows and called inside to one of the first-floor rooms. The windowsills here were four to five feet above the ground, and as he called inside, he heard a shout and saw a firefighter running toward him, telling him to get away. At the same time, he heard a voice call for help from inside. Through a pall of black smoke, he could see a hand waving at him.

Standing near the west wall, Alan Wallace heard a shout, "We need some help over here!" He looked over and saw Bozek, wearing black jeans and a polo shirt with a red logo on it, peering into the window. "There's somebody in there," he said. "Give me a lift." Wallace rushed over and pushed Bozek up onto the windowsill, its edges encrusted with glass. Bozek carefully positioned himself so that he could see inside without getting cut.

As he looked into the darkness, he could see that the room was completely devastated. There was nothing left. He knew that if he jumped through the window, he might not be able to get back out, so he kneeled on a flat section of the windowsill and looked down on two older women just below him, their feet pinned to the floor by heavy debris. As he reached down and tried to pull some of the debris off them, another woman stumbled forward through the smoke. Her entire left arm and her shoulder were severely burned, and she was in shock. She collided with Bozek, who was starting to have trouble catching his breath. He figured the woman had aimed for the light or the sound of his voice. She appeared to be entangled by metal from the ceiling or floor. Bozek worked for over a minute to free the woman, then dragged her over his lap and lowered her down to Wallace. Finishing this, he turned his attention to the pair of women on the floor below. Reaching down with his hand, he was able to pull pieces of brick, furniture, and metal off them and lift them out, over his lap and down to Wallace. As Wallace reached up to help one lady out, she panicked and slapped his arms down onto the windowsill. This produced deep scars on the inside of his forearm, which remain to this day.

After freeing the three women in the office, Bozek knew he had to get to fresh air quickly or he wasn't going to be of use to anyone. As he jumped to the ground and moved back from the building, he wiped his face and looked up to see a man standing nearby with a video camera. The man seemed to be a civilian with no identification and was smiling and looked like he was having fun. Bozek just stood there and stared at the man, not knowing what to make of him. It was a surreal sight: the blackened rescuer risking his life and the smiling, unrepentant voyeur.

SOUTH PARKING LOT, PENTAGON—0952 HOURS

Having heard the sound of the plane crash in his office a mile away, Arlington police detective Don Fortunato turned on the radio and listened to reports about the attack on the Pentagon. When what was happening dawned on him, he quickly ran to his car and drove toward the Pentagon but got stuck in a massive traffic jam. He pulled his car to the shoulder and stopped. As he looked around, Fortunato saw a DC cab, its windshield smashed by parts of a lamppost. Pieces of the wing of the aircraft were all over the road. Near the Pentagon, he could see fire trucks shooting water onto the building, and rescue workers spreading tarps on the ground. He made his way toward the south parking lot, and as he drew closer, he could see people running, some toward the fire but most away from it, and some of them in his direction. He spotted an EMS captain and asked for a pair of rubber gloves so that he could help the victims.

Even though he was a plainclothes detective, Fortunato had received medical training through the police force. He carried stretchers, held IV bags, put pressure on wounds, and handed out bandages. Many people were in shock and some were crying, but the burn victims were the worst because many of them were out of control with panic. All Fortunato and others could do was get them to calm down and lie on the grass until a doctor or nurse could be found to tend to them.

Suddenly, someone ran up to Fortunato and told him that there was a second plane twenty miles out and inbound for the Pentagon. This rumor started a second panic as people got up and started running toward the highway, trying to get away from the building as fast as possible.

Fortunato and the others packed up what they could and headed for an underpass, which had been closed to traffic. It had been decided to establish a triage area in this location because of the protection afforded by the concrete. The supplies proved difficult to move, but Fortunato and the others managed to get everything down to the underpass. Just as they reached it, Fortunato heard a thunderous rumble above and very close. Everyone in the area froze and looked up, thinking it was another terrorist plane. Then Fortunato saw two F-16 fighter jets scream past at low altitude. Looks of despair and panic turned to smiles as everyone realized that the cavalry had arrived.

FOURTEENTH STREET BRIDGE, WASHINGTON, DC—0953 HOURS

Approaching the Fourteenth Street Bridge, Ed Lucci could see the Washington Monument glimmering in the morning sunlight, its beauty stained by a black cloud of smoke rising behind it. The van crossed the Potomac River quickly, and ahead he could see the marina with its boats tied up at the docks and then the west wall of the Pentagon in flames.

As soon as the ambulance reached the entrance to the complex, it was stopped by police and rescue personnel who had set up roadblocks to secure the perimeter. Lucci looked at one of them.

"Where are the patients?" he said.

The officer stared back at him. "You people need to get away from here. There's another plane on the way in," he said, directing Goodwill to turn the ambulance around and leave. For some reason, Lucci had a gut feeling that this was just rumor and refused to believe it.

"Where are the patients?" he asked again, ignoring the officer's previous command. The officer undoubtedly saw the determination in Lucci's eyes. He grimaced and pointed toward the north parking area. Lucci directed Sergeant Goodwill to drive right and north along the river.

When the ambulance reached the north parking lot, Lucci surveyed a scene that would be forever burned into his memory: several hundred people were scattered along the highway and open field along the river, metal junk and trash lying everywhere and small pieces of metal strewn in the grass hundreds of yards from the crash site. Looking around, he couldn't tell patients from rescuers because some of the rescuers were themselves walking wounded. There were burned and bleeding people everywhere, but most of them could move on their own power. To his eyes, there seemed to be very few serious cases.

As soon as the two ambulances stopped, they were surrounded by a crowd almost instantaneously. Lucci knew that everyone wanted medical care immediately, but he had to find the most critical patients first and have them evacuated.

"Move back!" he shouted. "Who's in charge here?"

At once, a young man looking to be no more than sixteen years old walked up with a vest that read "Triage" and a handheld radio. Lucci could tell the boy didn't know what he was doing. He had a dazed look and seemed to be in partial shock.

As he looked past the clearly overwhelmed teenager, though, he was amazed at the restraint and lack of panic on the part of the rescuers and, above all, the cooperation that he saw being displayed. Still, most of the people were not aware of what had actually happened.

Lucci now took control of the situation and asked everyone to move across the field and away from the ambulance. He then requested that those people who were only slightly injured take care of the more critically injured. Following this, Lucci's team triaged the remaining patients to identify the most critical for evacuation.

WEST WALL, PENTAGON—0953 HOURS

Less than twenty minutes after American Airlines Flight 77 struck the Pentagon, Arlington's Emergency Operations Center had been activated, and Arlington Fire had established command and control at the scene, effectively sealing off the area to any further outside interference. This included anyone attempting to get inside the Pentagon. The firefighters would have to contend with two categories of people: FBI agents who were presently walking the grounds collecting evidence, and those first responders still near the west wall or inside the building.

Arlington fire chief Ed Plaugher knew that the FBI wanted to take over the site as a crime scene, but it was within his and Arlington police chief Ed Flynn's discretion as to when that would take place. The first priority was to contain the fires still raging inside. Plaugher also understood that his people would be dealing with soldiers, the majority of whom would willingly sacrifice their lives to save their comrades. This was wholly unlike dealing with civilians, most of whom would run from the scene at the first opportunity. When told to stand down by a civilian police or fire authority, military people were more apt to ignore or even resist if the lives of their fellow soldiers were at risk. It had happened many times throughout history, and today, as before, he knew it would pose a problem.

Plaugher knew from reports that the initial blast had caused spot fires throughout Wedge One. He knew that many areas were surrounded by fire on all sides although they had not yet ignited. He also knew that many areas contained pools of jet fuel, which had been thrown clear of the aircraft during the initial impact but had not yet ignited. He also knew that this type of commercial jet fuel did not have a low flash point, like gasoline. It had a high kerosene component, like diesel fuel, and so you could literally throw a lit match into it and it would not burn. However, under adverse conditions, with intense heat, depleted oxygen, and plenty of tinder, it was dangerous, and there was nothing as adverse as this situation.

One of Plaugher's main concerns at this point was flooding. Thousands of gallons of foam and water were being pumped into the wedge, and there were untold numbers of people still in the building, unable to get out safely. In addition, he was receiving disturbing reports about the roof.

The Pentagon roof was unique in that it was constructed of one layer of concrete with a layer of wood sandwiched between the concrete and a layer of slate on top. The fire had reached the wood filling and was burning uncontrolled across the roofline. Every time the firefighters extinguished it, it would flare up again in short order. Also, the firefighters were wholly unaware that the attic was filled with tinder-dry horsehair, used as the original insulation for the Pentagon in 1942 and forgotten about. The whole roof might as well have been doused in gasoline.

WEST WALL, PENTAGON—0955 HOURS

After rescuing the burning man who told them of more people in a hallway just inside the wall, Ted Anderson and Chris Braman and a few other soldiers prepared to enter a fourth time, but District of Columbia firefighters newly arrived on the scene stopped them.

"Nobody's going back in!" one of them said.

Anderson looked at the city firemen, decked out in all their gear. "They're army; we're army," he said. "We're gonna get 'em out!"

Ignoring the orders of the firefighters, Anderson walked steadily toward the burning chasm. A group of firefighters now moved toward him. When he didn't stop, they grabbed him and held him back. The situation quickly developed into a standoff with Anderson, Braman, and a small cadre of soldiers trying to get in and the firemen not backing away. Time and again these veteran firefighters had seen people rush into burning buildings to save loved ones or a treasured memento only to be burned to death for the effort. They had witnessed so much of this that their official policy was not to allow it under any circumstances, and they were now the ultimate authority on-site. The building had been deemed structurally unsound, and under federal law, even the most veteran of firefighters were forbidden to enter. By now, the firefighters considered Wedge One of the Pentagon little more than a burning crypt.

Ted Anderson and Christopher Braman were soldiers, and they lived by the soldier's code. All they knew was the code of combat: you never left anyone behind, even at the cost of your own life. With the exception of a live firefight, everything happening around them at this second was combat. It had all of the stress, death, and destruction of combat. Anderson didn't want a repeat of the fiasco in Mogadishu, Somalia, in 1993, and it didn't matter to him whether the people were civilians, soldiers, airmen, sailors, or just visitors. They were Americans, and more than that, they were human beings, and it was their duty to at least try to save them.

Anderson and Braman and some other soldiers stood facing the firefighters. Neither side was backing off. At one point, Anderson and his team just went around the firefighters and started moving toward the building. Several of them entered back into the hole they had previously been working in. They began moving forward, keeping low to the ground, but only made it some sixty feet before being pulled out by the firefighters. Tense moments ensued until Anderson found a three-star general and had him speak to the fire chief. The general told the chief that he would take responsibility personally for the men if the chief would allow them to go back inside the building, but the chief didn't budge. "It's too dangerous," he said, staring into the eyes of a man who was not used to having to bargain with anyone below his rank.

The general knew he had no authority here. He had made his plea unsuccessfully. He turned and ordered Anderson and the others to stand down, and for the rest of the afternoon, they had to watch the fires burn, unable to enter the building and rescue the people the burning man had begged them to save. Anderson later learned that rescue workers eventually found the group of people the burning man had been talking about—nearly twenty of them stacked together inside the corridor. They had died less than several yards from the exit.

Racing to the Pentagon from Fort Myer, Rusty Dodge, Dennis Gilroy, Chris Evans, and the rest of the Fort Myer trainees, including all of the regular Fort Myer Pentagon crew, heard Alan Wallace's voice come over the radio, giving details of the attack. They were relieved that he was still alive and already responding to the situation. Through the windows of the vehicle, they could see the smoke and flames. The sound of the blast had reminded Chris Evans of when they used to test big guns at Aberdeen Proving Ground near his home in Joppa, Maryland.

Upon arriving at the west wall, Rusty Dodge could see Wallace and Skipper trying to pull equipment off Foam Truck 61, which was still on fire and burning furiously. Nearby was the construction trailer that Frank Probst had just stepped out of when the plane swept by him. It was now consumed in flames.

Dodge looked closely at the west wall. He couldn't believe it was still standing. The off-white color of the concrete told him that the heat of the blast was so intense that the concrete had turned to packed powder. Its structural integrity was gone, and any steel inside was probably beginning to melt. The heat from the flames was intense even out near the highway. Just stepping out of the truck had been like stepping into an oven. Still, he was impressed with the construction of a building that could withstand such a hit and not collapse. Little did the veteran firefighter know that by some miracle, American Airlines Flight 77 had struck the only place in the entire Pentagon where a Kevlar screen, stretched between the steel beams and designed to counter just such an attack, had been erected.

Standing near the blast site, Alan Wallace began to notice that people of all descriptions were coming in to help. Many of them had seen the crash on the highway, stopped their cars, and started walking toward the Pentagon.

One of these people was Eric Jones, a twenty-five-year-old graduate student from Oakland, California, and a volunteer firefighter and paramedic. Jones had heroism in his blood, his grandfather having been one of the famous Tuskegee Airmen during the Second World War. He had been driving to school when he saw smoke coming from the Pentagon. He was aware of the New York attacks and pulled off the highway and into one of the Pentagon parking lots, bounding from his car and running toward the west wall to help.

Alan Wallace now joined a group of people who were carrying an unconscious man out to the guardrail beside Washington Boulevard to get him away from the fire. As he was helping them, he noticed a four-inch-thick fire hose and recognized it as the hose from Fort Myer Rescue Engine 161. His fellow firefighters were now on the scene. They had received his message and reacted quickly.

HOME OF MIKE AND SHEILA FLOCCO, NEWARK, DELAWARE—0958 HOURS

As Mike Flocco opened the door to his house, he could hear his wife crying. He rushed into the living room, where he saw her sitting on the couch with her head in her hands. Next to her was Adam Grimes, one of his son's closest friends, his arm around her shoulder. In her grief, Sheila Flocco remembered taking her boy to the train station only a few days before like she always did. She remembered giving him one last hug and saying goodbye. She clenched her fists. If only she had stopped him from getting on the train. Mike looked down at Grimes, and the young man stared back at him with a sad look on his face.

Mike had heard about the attack on the Pentagon at the courthouse and simply dropped his tools where he stood and rushed home. He stared at the images of the Pentagon on the television. This was the first he'd seen of it. As he looked closer and heard the reports, he realized the plane had hit very close to where Matt worked. He desperately tried to re-create Matt's movements just before the attack. *9:40 a.m., 9:40 a.m., where would he be at 9:40 a.m.?* He remembered Matt telling him once that he usually delivered a report to the senior naval officers on the fourth floor around a quarter to ten every morning. This was routine, so it meant that surely he was not at his desk at the time of the attack.

He looked at his wife. "Aw, Matt's alright," he said, struggling with the awful feeling he had in his gut and trying to stay strong for his wife; trying to hold on to a sense of hope that was rapidly fading. "He's probably helping fight the fire." He knew his son had just completed the navy firefighting course and would know what to do. But why did all this talk seem so wrong?

He looked at his wife, who was completely distraught. He had always heard that a mother instinctively knows when something bad has happened to her child. Nothing he was saying was having any effect on his wife. But in his heart, Mike Flocco somehow knew the awful truth himself.

FOURTEENTH STREET, WASHINGTON, DC—1000 HOURS

Major Benjamin Starnes sat on a bus loaded with physicians headed for the Pentagon. In front of the bus was a police escort, negotiating the traffic on Fourteenth Street. They were making progress but too slowly to suit Starnes. Upon boarding the bus on orders from Lieutenant Colonel Goff, Starnes had discovered that many of the physicians on the bus had never been in a combat zone or in a situation involving mass casualties. He pulled Colonel Oster, the designated officer in charge, aside and told him that the doctors would have to be organized into four teams in accordance with the standard "IDME" concept for triage: "immediate," "delayed," "minimal," and "expectant." He then assigned individual physicians to groups based on their level of trauma training. Each physician introduced themselves and they began to discuss how to proceed once they were on the scene.

"Have you ever dealt with this kind of thing before?" Starnes asked Oster.

Oster looked at him, realizing the gravity of the statement. "No," he replied.

"The first thing you need to do is have everyone take a few moments to themselves to dig deep and think about why they are here and what we're about to do," Starnes said in a low voice.

Oster turned and addressed the crowd of doctors, telling them in no uncertain terms that they were expecting the situation to be bad. Following this, there was complete silence on the bus, the only sounds coming from the street outside, the honking of car horns and blaring sirens echoing off the walls of the buildings.

As the bus slowly made its way toward the Pentagon, the city of Washington, DC, was in crisis. Streets began to clog as people panicked. Fourteenth Street was jammed with trucks and cars as people tried to get out of the city just as others were trying to get to the Pentagon. News reports and rumors merged to create mass confusion.

Along the major thoroughfares and side streets of the capital, people sat down on the curbs and cried, not knowing whether the nation was under a full-scale attack and not really knowing what to do.

The air was full of noise: sirens, screaming and yelling, and the sharp commands of angry police officers trying to direct traffic. This noise bounced between the tall buildings, creating one continuous, maddening shriek. In a few moments, nearly 340,000 federal employees would be released from work at the same time. The city was in total gridlock.

A/E DRIVE, PENTAGON—1000 HOURS

Kevin Shaeffer sat against a wall in the haze of smoke that filled A/E Drive, his khaki slacks seared into his skin, part of his scalp burned off, blood all over his face, much of his clothing in tatters. As he sat there, trying to force himself to get up and keep moving, he was approached by army sergeant first class Don Workman, called "Steve" by his colleagues, a staff noncom with the G-8 Initiatives Group, who had commandeered one of the Pentagon golf carts that was still operational.

Workman would never forget what he saw when he arrived. He couldn't tell the difference between this man's torn clothing and his skin. It was hanging off him in strips as he sat in the road with his arms outstretched. Workman couldn't believe this was a living human being.

Workman gently picked Shaeffer up and put him in the golf cart. Shaeffer looked up at him.

"Please don't let me die," he pleaded.

Workman looked at him confidently. "You're gonna be OK, you hear?" he said as he stepped on the accelerator and drove through a maze of burning debris toward the Pentagon courtyard.

When Workman reached the clinic area, it had been abandoned. He looked at Shaeffer, whose eyes were glazing over and who was starting to slur his words. He was going into shock. Workman grabbed his legs and held them up, then used small talk to keep him from slipping out of consciousness. Shaeffer talked about his wife, Blanca. She was out of town. He wondered if he would ever see her again.

She was so close to his heart but so far off now, and he was slipping away. He rattled off her cell phone number, which he had memorized. Workman now knew he had to somehow keep Shaeffer from going to sleep.

"What do you like to do in your spare time," Workman said, "away from this place?" Shaeffer suddenly became animated. "Golf, man," he said. "I got a friend. We like to hit the course at five thirty in the morning; get in nine holes before work starts."

Workman looked around, frantically searching the area for a doctor as Shaeffer continued to talk. In a few moments, two medics ran up to them and searched Shaeffer's arm for a place to stick an IV, but the arm was too badly burned. Most of the surface skin had been burned off, and it was hard to find a vein. Finally, one of them found a vein and inserted the needle, but in a few moments, the medication failed to ease the pain. When Shaeffer realized this, he started screaming.

"I've had enough of this damned place!" he shouted. "Who the hell is in charge here? Don't you see I need a doctor!"

As Shaeffer started to lose control, Workman saw an ambulance, and they moved the wounded officer toward it. As they went to load him aboard, a doctor stopped them.

"Hey, you can't put him on here!" he said. "You need to take him to the triage."

"This man's on death's door!" he said. "He's too badly burned! We're not waiting for any triage station; he doesn't have that long!" Workman shoved past the doctor and put Shaeffer on board, then climbed inside with him. In a few minutes, the ambulance was moving fast toward the south entrance.

In Corridor Four, near A/E Drive, John Yates sat on the floor in a pool of water, trying to muster the strength to move on. He no longer felt Regina Grant's hand tugging on his leg. Somewhere in the darkness, she had lost her grip and disappeared. He hadn't even noticed until now.

Up ahead, Yates could see that it was getting lighter, and the smoke was less black and choking than before. He could feel the water from the sprinklers raining down on him as he desperately tried to think of a way out. He remembered a dream he'd had while he and his wife, Ellen, were on their honeymoon in Aruba. Even in such a relaxing place, Yates was still stressed about the floor plan of the Army Personnel Center. He was in charge of the move, and the details occupied his thoughts night and day. As a result, he knew the layout of the suite like the back of his hand. There were a lot of turns to the left and right, but his mind was clear on how to get to where the doors of C Ring used to be. He kept crawling until he reached these doors, which had been blown out into Corridor Four. Just as he moved through them, his strength finally left him, and he fell down.

In Corridor Four on the first floor of the Army Resources Center, Sheila Moody and Antoinette Sherman prayed together, with Moody bowing her head and leading the prayer. "God, please help us . . . Jesus, please help us get out of this . . . Please don't let us die."

Sheila Moody thought about the town she had left to come here, how she loved the people back there and how she wished she were back there with them now. She had never felt comfortable with the transfer. Why had she come here? Had she left such a wonderful place, only to come here to die?

WEST WALL, PENTAGON—1000 HOURS

Cruz-Cortez and Bruno heard someone crying but could not see them. Bruno looked up through the blackness at a patch of bright blue sky peering at him through the window. He got up and moved toward it. As Cruz-Cortez tried to stand up, she felt a painful sting in her lungs but ignored it, standing up amid a demolished cubicle and shouting at the top of her lungs.

"Come toward my voice, there's a way out!"

There was silence for a moment, and then Bruno reappeared with Gallop, her son, Elisha, held tightly under her left arm, her right hand on the floor to keep from falling.

As light from the window suddenly appeared through the smoke, Cruz-Cortez saw shadows moving nearby. As she looked on, these shadows became people, dazed and wounded, wandering aimlessly. Two women appeared together, one of them searching her purse for something.

"I've got to call my husband," she kept saying. Cruz-Cortez thought that she must be in shock, her mind trying to stay focused on a single task until it was accomplished, trying to maintain sanity.

Gallop and Bruno reached Cruz-Cortez, who took the baby from Gallop's arms. Bruno moved a few feet away, and they all got down on the floor to form a daisy chain. At this point, they had to cross a wall of debris that was blocking the path. Bruno went first. Then Cruz-Cortez handed the baby to Gallop, who carefully handed him to Bruno. Then Cruz-Cortez helped Gallop over the wall and turned to help the others. As she looked back, there were at least ten people scattered all around. Cruz-Cortez got these people over the wall, then climbed over herself. As she descended to the other side, she realized that the two women she had seen earlier were still sitting on the floor on the other side, so she climbed back over and made her way to them. The one lady was still searching her pocketbook.

"I've got to call my husband," she kept repeating, now on the verge of screaming.

"Let's go!" Cruz-Cortez shouted at them. "We've gotta get out of here now!"

With this, she reached for the women. One of them followed her, but the one with the pocketbook refused. To Cruz-Cortez, it was as if someone were trying to wake her from a dream and she didn't want to wake up. Reaching out, Cruz-Cortez locked her right arm within the left arm of the screaming woman and pulled her forward. The three moved toward the wall until they came to a seven-foot drop from a window down onto the Pentagon lawn.

While Cruz-Cortez was helping the women out, April Gallop succumbed to shock. All of a sudden, she couldn't see her baby anymore, and she had lost sight of Cruz-Cortez and Bruno. She saw no one familiar, and panic quickly set in. As she looked over the ledge, Cruz-Cortez could see Bruno and another man standing by the window, helping to lower the others down. Cruz-Cortez pushed the two women to Bruno, who in turn lowered them to another rescuer standing below, and they were taken away from the building. Then Bruno pushed Cruz-Cortez up to the window and helped her down.

Looking across the Pentagon lawn, Cruz-Cortez had a panoramic view of the tragedy—people being laid out on the grass everywhere, debris and the burned hulks of cars and trucks scattered around, ambulances and emergency vehicles everywhere. In the distance was a massive traffic jam on the expressway. As she began to lead the women away, a deafening explosion knocked the three of them to the ground. The woman with the purse emitted a manic shriek and began crying and screaming uncontrollably as Cruz-Cortez fell on top of her to shield her from the blast. In the same instant, Bruno threw himself on top of the other woman.

FOURTEENTH STREET, WASHINGTON, DC—1003 HOURS

Ben Starnes stared at the black smoke coming from the Pentagon in the distance. It reminded him of one very long night several years before in Albania, standing inside the operating tent of the 212th MASH, waiting for two wounded pilots from an Apache helicopter that had been hit in a wire strike. Low-hanging power lines were a constant danger in the Balkans because none of them were marked as they were required to be in the United States. They could "decapitate" a helicopter by literally shearing off its rotor, flipping it upside down, and slamming it into the ground.

On that particular night, Starnes heard at least five explosions in the distance, one right after the other, then was told the medevac choppers were at the site but could not locate the pilots. He remembered an interminable silence that lasted for what seemed like hours. They were told to stand down twice before the final report came in: the pilots were dead. It was almost like losing a family member. He had worked alongside these pilots on a daily basis, eating, sleeping, showering, and conversing alongside them, and then all of a sudden, they were both gone. Most of all, he felt an emptiness inside and the knowledge that some poor little child was going to have to grow up without a father. He didn't want to feel that again, and he hoped that this time he could make a difference.

Breaking away from his thoughts now, Starnes realized the bus wasn't moving. The police escort wasn't getting them anywhere, so he turned to the senior NCO.

"You think you can clear a path through this traffic for us?" he said.

"Right on it, sir!" the man said as he jumped off the bus, nine other medics dressed in full camouflage following right behind him. The medics ran through the traffic, pounding on windows and ordering cars to move to the side. This continued for nearly twelve city blocks with the soldiers yelling and screaming, using shock to scare the drivers off the road in the same way special forces troops or SWAT teams would clear a building. Starnes was amazed at the speed with which the cars moved out of the way, the medics moving through the traffic like dogs through a herd of sheep.

As soon as the buses reached the Fourteenth Street Bridge, Starnes saw an armada of police cars blocking the bridge, turning away droves of people who were trying to get to the Pentagon. The soldiers approached the police, and the bus was given the go-ahead to pass over. The medics now got back on the bus as it proceeded over the bridge, the ranks of the police closing behind it.

A little after 10:00 a.m., the bus reached the east side of the Pentagon. Starnes could see hundreds of people coming out of the building, many with blood on their faces. As the bus passed by, he saw Ed Lucci standing in the parking lot. The pall of smoke was so thick that it obscured the building. The driver and the doctors were disoriented, not knowing where they were supposed to be. Starnes looked past Lucci and saw many injured people on a knoll.

"We need to be over there!" he shouted to the driver, who turned the bus around and headed toward the west side.

Reaching the west side of the Pentagon, Starnes could see countless firemen, soldiers, medical corpsmen, paramedics, and nurses converging on the area, many of them on the hillside trying to treat the injured. More than a few were "walking wounded," many of whom were attempting to help treat the more badly injured patients. In some cases, it was hard to tell medical personnel from military and patients from doctors. The sight made him uneasy. Near the site of the crash, he could see FBI agents and DC firefighters in the midst of a heated argument. He would later learn that the exchange was over whether the area was a crime scene or an emergency site. The FBI wanted access to the site yet wanted to keep everyone else away, declaring it a crime scene with valuable evidence to be preserved. The DC fire department had the ultimate jurisdiction and wanted triage areas set up close by for care of the wounded. They also wanted to keep everyone away from the unstable structure and the fires, which were getting worse by the minute.

Colonel Oster and the doctors got off the bus in a group. The first thing that hit Starnes was the smell of JP-4 jet fuel, which took his mind back to the airbase in Kosovo where he had been stationed during the Balkan Civil War. Fighter jets would take off on sorties many times during the day, leaving behind the pungent odor of burned JP-4, a combination of kerosene and gasoline, the smell of which would stay in a man's nostrils all day long.

As he stepped out of the bus, he could feel the heat of the fire and could see fire trucks pouring water onto the west wall. As he watched this, he noticed a small red fire truck near the site of the crash with its left side engulfed in flames, the number "61" on one of its doors. It looked to be just a few feet from where the jet had knifed through the building. He wondered whether it had been hit by the plane or was just too close to the fire. Had there been firemen inside it? If so, he figured they were surely dead. He stared at the truck briefly, then kept moving.

The doctors ran toward a site on the lawn that contained at least a dozen casualties. Starnes could see that most were walking around and had minor injuries but nothing requiring surgery. As they approached the site, Starnes saw Janice Jackson, her hair and scalp badly burned. She was having trouble breathing, so he assisted another doctor in managing her airway. In a moment, she was stabilized and placed in an ambulance.

Starnes looked around and saw the two great oak trees near Washington Boulevard and decided that the doctors would regroup under them and make use of the shade to protect patients from the direct sun. Many of the medical personnel got busy obtaining supplies: backboards, litters, airway supplies, IVs, blankets, and drugs. It wasn't long before he realized that there were more caregivers and rescuers than patients. Equipment was beginning to pile up everywhere. Dozens of aid vehicles crowded the parking lot.

INTERIOR OF WEDGE ONE, PENTAGON—1003 HOURS

Ever since they had carried Brian Birdwell to A Ring, Victor Correa had been worried about the closed fire door they had encountered on Corridor Four. There were a lot of people still trapped inside who wouldn't make it out if they encountered that closed door and just gave up. He quickly ran back inside and up to Corridor Four, where he could hear voices praying and crying, with people coughing and gagging everywhere. Tony Rose was in front of him, and the two men reached inside the groove of the automatic door and used all their might to pull it back against the function of its motor. They both heaved until the door finally began to give way. As it did, a cloud of thick black smoke rushed out in a silken plume from the door. Inside, there was very little air left. Correa went into the G-1 Army Personnel area, calling out for people to follow his voice. The heat and smoke were so intense from being trapped in an enclosed area that Correa had to get down in one of the water puddles and soak his shirt again so that he could wrap it around his face.

When Correa rose up from the water, he saw a man approach. At first, he didn't recognize him, but as the man drew closer, he suddenly realized, to his horror, that it was his friend John Yates, so badly burned that he looked barely human. Correa remembered how white Yates's skin had been. Now he was burned black.

"You alright, John?" Correa said, too shocked at the sight to know what to say.

"No," Yates said, sounding like a man who was freezing to death. Yates took a long time to get the word out as though he had to force it from his lungs.

As Correa looked at his friend, he could see the burns, the raw pink flesh surrounded by blackened skin. Drawing closer, he could literally feel the heat radiating from Yates's body like an iron stove. He was afraid to touch him but managed to nudge him out of the area with only one finger placed firmly in the middle of his back. Yates told Correa that he had been watching the TV when the fireball came at him. There had been two people on his left and two on his right. All four had been burned to death.

While Correa was taking care of Yates, Tony Rose headed back toward the conference room to look for survivors. Correa nudged Yates down the hall to the apex of Corridors Three and Four in A Ring. There he found a navy officer named Paul Anderson.

"Hey, will you get him out?" he said, pointing to Yates. Anderson nodded to Correa, then helped get Yates across the corridor, where he was taken to a triage area in the courtyard by another group of people. Correa now headed back toward A/E Drive.

Lying on the floor inside the smoke-filled Army Personnel Center, Marilyn Wills was now frantic that she couldn't find Regina Grant, but in an instant she got hold of her senses. There were many more people who needed to get out or they were going to succumb to the smoke.

At this point, Wills couldn't see anymore. Open or closed, her eyes beheld nothing but blackness. She put her hand in front of her face and could not see it. With all of the chaos around, Wills bowed her head and prayed silently. *God, you've got to help me get out of here. I can't see.* In a moment she saw a break in the smoke and light coming through a window in the distance. It was one of the windows overlooking A/E Drive. Wills quickly began crawling toward it with the others behind her.

Nearby, Specialist Mike Petrovich was leading his coworkers through the darkness, trying to find a way out and bumping into obstacles at every turn. He could hear voices emanating from hidden corners but couldn't tell where they were coming from. He felt Dalisay Olaes grab his belt.

"Hold on and don't let go of me," Petrovich told her.

In a few moments, he spotted the same window that Marilyn Wills was moving toward through the smoke. The blast had destroyed the frame, leaving broken glass and wood on one side. The gap was too small for a body to slip through, so, reaching the window, Petrovich grabbed a damaged laser printer and started pounding it against the window while someone else tried to kick it through.

Across the hall from them, Phil McNair knew the supply of fresh air was almost gone. He had to get his people out, and he had to get them out now! As he stepped into the cubicle area, he could see the way blocked by smoke, fire, exposed electrical wiring, and water. He could hear the Pentagon voice alarm through the smoke, repeating in its calm, mechanical voice, "There is an emergency in the building. Please evacuate immediately." On and on it droned.

At this point, McNair found himself at the head of the daisy chain, crawling along the floor near the copy machine. He knew that the copy machine was near the corridor door, so he figured they were close. As he approached the copier room, he could see flames near the entrance, so he turned around. He knew that the service road would be due east of this, so he led his people in this direction. The group had only advanced a few feet when McNair realized it would be too much of a trek to reach the service road. The smoke was getting thicker and closer to the floor, sucking up all of their oxygen. As he reversed course, he could hear some people beginning to panic and lose hope.

For the next several minutes, McNair kept branching off, trying to find a way out, but every time he thought he had found a doorway into the corridor, it turned out to be a locked closet. Debris, overturned office furniture, and cubicle walls completely disoriented him. To make matters worse, having just moved into this area, no one knew the layout. Not that it would have made much of a difference; the entire landscape had changed in a matter of seconds anyway. They were essentially crawling blind in a maze. A voice in McNair's mind said, *This is a lousy way to go,* as he, too, began to doubt the chances of surviving. Just then, someone called out that they saw light from a window, and McNair and the rest moved in this direction, soon linking up with Marilyn Wills's party that was just ahead of them.

As Wills reached the window overlooking A/E Drive, she could see Mike Petrovich pounding the laser printer against it, trying to break through. Repeated hits failed to even crack the window, so in desperation he heaved the printer like a shot put against the window. This, too, failed. With the intensity of the smoke growing, her lungs burning, and her eyes unable to see, Wills thought that the end had finally come, but she didn't want to lose faith in front of the others, so she kept quiet and managed to hold herself together and keep from breaking down.

Then Petrovich picked up the printer one last time and threw it with such force that it finally shattered the glass, flying through the window and crashing to the ground, just missing some sailors and soldiers running onto the road below. The force of the initial blast had dislodged the window from its frame, but Petrovich now found he could not bend the frame back. McNair came forward and worked with him to try to pry open enough space for a person to climb through. He knew that this was one of the Kevlar windows from the renovation, and they were very heavy. The two men worked until they created an opening, but Petrovich was now in distress. His efforts at breaking the window had taken most of his breath away, and he was beginning to choke.

"Get the hell out of here, Mike!" McNair shouted, but Petrovich ignored him.

As soon as McNair and Petrovich had created the opening, Dalisay Olaes all at once stood up, in a panic to get oxygen. Seeing this, Marilyn Wills smacked her down to keep her from breathing too much of the deadly smoke. Olaes was in a state of pure terror, her lungs struggling to get fresh air. She was crying and nearly incoherent, and she kept trying to stand up despite Wills's efforts to get her below the smoke.

"Get down!" Wills yelled again, pulling her to the floor and shoving part of the wet sweater into her mouth. Olaes finally calmed down and lay still.

As McNair's and Wills's people struggled to get off the second floor, Craig Powell made his way onto A/E Drive. Looking up, he could see three people, two men and a woman. They were Wills, McNair, and Petrovich, standing in the window with smoke coming out of it like a factory smokestack. Powell figured they had to be at least thirty feet above the ground. As he looked on, a long flame shot out from one of the windows. Powell knew something drastic had to be done fast. Those people could not last much longer. He called out in a loud voice for volunteers to help catch people, then ran up to a point right beneath the window and called up to McNair and Wills.

"Jump into my arms!" he shouted. "Now! Make it quick!"

Through the broken window, Phil McNair, Marilyn Wills, and Mike Petrovich forced their heads out, breathing deep to get fresh air into their lungs and peering down at Powell and others standing below. In response to Powell's directions, McNair and Petrovich began to help people onto the windowsill, racing against time to save people who were dying right behind them.

In the torn corridor of the second floor of C Ring just south of where Petrovich and the others were attempting to escape, the sprinkler system was dousing the hallways and everything else with water. Tony Rose and Victor Correa, their faces covered with wet T-shirts and crawling low to the floor, continued to search rooms for survivors. Around one corner, Rose found Regina Grant, who had become separated from John Yates. She was curled up and in shock but still alive. Sitting next to her was Tracy Webb, the back of her shirt still smoking. The two women had given up hope, lying there waiting for death to come for them. Rose figured they had been searching the walls in the darkness for the fire doors, but the doors had automatically sealed off when the plane hit. He wondered how many others were following the walls right back into the fire over and over again, unable to get out, exhausting all efforts until they simply lay down and died. With Correa's help, Rose led Regina and Tracy to safety.

Ever since the moment of the attack, Tony Rose had been searching for Larry Strickland's office, trying to find his best friend. He had no way of knowing that Strickland had been killed instantly along with Lieutenant General Maude in the first moments of the attack, but even if someone had told him this, Rose would have to verify it for himself. He couldn't contemplate otherwise.

Steadily crawling, Rose finally reached a fire door that was still open and within five feet of where he was sure Strickland's office had been. He moved through it, but the fire was just too hot and he couldn't get close enough. Looking around, he knew that if he stood up, he would be burned alive. Jet fuel mist and puddles of the explosive liquid were causing the very air to ignite above him. As he inched closer to the office, he heard a sudden, mechanical sound. He turned around. The fire door was now slowly closing behind him. If he didn't get back into the corridor, he would be trapped. Without another thought, he turned and started crawling as fast as he could, the door steadily inching closer to the jamb. Rose moved faster than he had ever moved in his life. The door was almost closed now. If he didn't get between it and the wall, he was dead. Reaching it just in time, he wedged himself through the opening, his foot catching in the door. He threw his hand up and pushed hard against the doorjamb. The door held just long enough for him to push his body through the crack and back out into the corridor as it closed behind him. If there was anyone left inside now, they belonged to history.

A/E DRIVE, PENTAGON—1003 HOURS

In the middle of A/E Drive, Commander Craig Powell called up to Mike Petrovich and the others to begin jumping. In the corridor above, Petrovich turned and saw Marilyn Wills, Betty Maxfield, and Lois Stevens crawling toward him. Maxfield was sucking on a wet sweater that Lois Stevens had given to her. First to climb onto the window ledge was Lois Stevens. Petrovich and McNair grabbed her, and she jumped through the window into Powell's arms.

Betty Maxfield, still in her high heels and clutching her checkbook, looked down into the courtyard and could see Powell directly below her with his arms outstretched. She was holding on to the hot windowsill when she just let go and fell into his arms. She was a small woman, and Powell caught her easily. He laid her down on the ground softly, and she was quickly taken away to safety.

As Powell caught each jumper, he would squat to absorb the impact and then roll with it as if he were hitting the ground on a parachute jump. He looked around for help, but most people were in shock or just too terrified to even attempt what he was doing.

Next to go was Dalisay Olaes, who was so terrified that the others had to literally pick her up and carry her to the window. She turned to Marilyn Wills. "Colonel, I can't do it. I can't go!" she screamed. Refusing to listen to her pleas, the others quickly grabbed her and pushed her out of the window. She fell through the air, kicking and screaming, and landed hard on Powell, knocking the big man flat to the ground. Powell broke her fall, but she broke her leg as she came to ground.

Some people rushed up to Powell and pulled Olaes off him. When Powell tried to get up, he felt a nasty pain shoot through his right leg. As the next jumper came down, he found that he couldn't bend his knees, so as each body hit him, he would absorb the impact of the fall and then push the body away just as quickly, trying to make it land horizontally so as to spread the impact of the hit out across the body rather than concentrating on a single point. He figured this would limit injuries. He knew his legs were in bad shape, but he kept on going.

Tony Rose and Vic Correa, emerging onto A/E Drive, now came upon the sight of Powell, all alone and catching jumpers. Rose couldn't believe the height from which these people were jumping and the strength of this man who was breaking their falls. It would not be the last time he would see Craig Powell.

Correa turned and watched the smoke pouring out of the windows of the Army Personnel Center. He knew that, somehow, he had to get back to that conference room and get Lieutenant General Maude and his people out. Like Rose, he had no idea of the true scope of what had happened. On the second floor, he could clearly see Phil McNair, Marilyn Wills, and Mike Petrovich thrusting their heads out of a huge cloud of smoke, straining to get fresh air. The speed and thickness of the smoke finally convinced Correa that any attempt to get back into the Army Personnel Center would be suicide.

WEST WALL, PENTAGON—1005 HOURS

At the west wall, near Corridor Five, Noel Sepulveda, working with DPS Master Patrol Officer George Clodfelter, had helped several people to safety. Clodfelter was inside the building, handing people off to Sepulveda. As Clodfelter looked back into the darkness, his hands took hold of what he thought was a bunch of rags. Then his eyes caught sight of a baby's head within the bundle. He quickly handed it to Sepulveda, who moved away from the building and opened the rags to see an infant who appeared to be dead. A tremendous sadness came over the veteran. It was one thing to see an adult hurt or killed, but when something bad happened to a child, it cut right through a man.

He immediately began CPR as he ran toward a nearby group of paramedics. As he reached them, he slapped the baby gently on the back, and suddenly the little boy started crying.

Nearby, Bruno and Cruz-Cortez pulled themselves up after having been knocked to the ground by an explosion. They tried to lift a screaming woman to her feet, but she just collapsed under them. Bruno, in severe pain, squatted down and lifted the woman up in his arms. "Bruno, don't; I'm a big woman!" she cried, but Bruno managed to get her off the ground and began carrying her away from the scene. Cruz-Cortez looked at Bruno's face and could tell he was really hurting, but he kept on moving toward the sidewalk with the woman in his arms. As he carried her, she started to scream even louder. Cruz-Cortez walked alongside, trying to calm her down, but it was no use. The woman was almost insane with grief. Bruno laid her down on the grass as some aid workers arrived. Then he turned to Cruz-Cortez, and the two hugged each other.

Back at the west wall, Noel Sepulveda and George Clodfelter pulled April Gallop out, unaware that this was the mother of the baby they had just saved. She was lethargic and in shock. Sepulveda carried her away from the building and laid her down on the grass.

Cruz-Cortez now looked back and noticed that April was gone.

"Where's Gallop?" she said, "Where's April?"

Her eyes scanning the area in a panic, she finally saw Gallop lying on the grass, covered in dirt, no sound or movement coming from her. Tears streamed down her face, and her feet were covered in blood. Her eyes were blank and staring at the sky.

"April!" Cruz-Cortez yelled at her, but there was no response, just a hollow stare.

"April, talk to me!" Cruz-Cortez shouted at her, but the woman was in deep shock and didn't answer.

Two aid workers walked up to her. "We have to move away from the building," one of them said. "Now!"

"Please help me get her up," Cruz-Cortez pleaded as she pointed at Gallop. "She can't walk." The two men picked Gallop up carefully by the back and feet and carried her away.

"Where's the baby?" Cruz-Cortez cried, afraid that Gallop's son had been lost in the confusion, perhaps killed by the explosion.

All at once, a calm voice responded. "He's right here." It was Noel Sepulveda, holding Elisha. Cruz-Cortez looked at the boy. His eyes were closed, and he did not appear to be breathing.

"Is he dead?" she asked Sepulveda, tears streaming down her face.

"He's fine," Sepulveda said, comforting her. "He's just sleeping."

Cruz-Cortez wasn't satisfied and carefully placed her hand on the baby's chest. Beneath her palm, she could feel his lungs slowly rise and fall, and a feeling of relief came to her. She pointed at Gallop while looking at Sepulveda, who was holding the baby.

"That's the mother," she said. "Stay with her." Sepulveda nodded and smiled. In a few moments, mother and son were reunited, with Sepulveda escorting them to one of the triage areas.

INTERIOR OF WEDGE ONE, SECOND FLOOR, PENTAGON—1005 HOURS

Inside the corridor in the Army Personnel Center, smoke had now completely overtaken everything. As Phil McNair went to get Marilyn Wills, she abruptly turned and headed back inside.

"Marilyn, where in hell are you going?" he shouted.

"Regina's missing. What am I going to tell her husband?" Wills said, then, turning around, she suddenly realized that Marian Serva was also gone.

"Where's Marian?" she cried.

"I don't know," McNair said. Wills was in a panic. Images of Marian and her daughter flashed across her mind—pictures of the beautiful mother and daughter together, thoughts of the daughter somewhere all alone; scared and wondering if her mother was still alive or worse yet, not knowing what had happened.

"I've got to go back for them!" Wills cried out as she turned to go, but McNair caught her by the hand.

"There's nothing we can do, Marilyn," he said as he saw the hope slowly drain from her face. Down below, Craig Powell had managed to stand back up and was calling for more people to jump. McNair turned to see Wills, out of her mind with grief, headed back into the smoke that had by now formed an impassable barrier to any living thing. McNair grabbed Wills and held her.

"I'll go back for them," he told her as he headed into the smoke. In a few seconds, he returned. "It's no use," he said flatly. "It's suicidal." Unable to accept this, Wills turned and tried to go in again. McNair reached out and grabbed her by the arm. "Marilyn, you've got to jump now, you hear me?"

"I've got to find Regina and Marian," she said, refusing to go.

Powell again called up to Petrovich and McNair. "Send her out!" he shouted.

"She won't jump!" they both yelled in unison.

McNair grabbed Wills firmly. "Get out the window, Marilyn! That's an order!" he said.

"No," she said. "All we have to do is shout loud and they'll hear us!"

At this point, Wills was denying the reality of the situation. She just couldn't accept that Marian and Regina could be dead, but McNair and the others well knew that there was nothing left alive on the other side of that wall of smoke. All that could be heard now was the cracking and sputtering, the sounds of fire in the act of breathing, like some monster waiting for anyone foolish enough to come back into its jaws. There were now no cries for help, no yelling or screaming anymore, just silence. The fires had taken all.

A/E DRIVE, PENTAGON—1005 HOURS

On the ground, Vic Correa could see Wills and McNair arguing and Wills refusing to jump. He knew that they were wasting time they didn't have. He tried desperately to think of a way to get up to Wills. In a few moments, he caught sight of a green dumpster nearby and began pushing it toward the window. Powell joined Correa and others, and they moved the dumpster up against the wall and set a ladder on top of it so that they could get close to Wills and physically grab her in order to get her down and save her life.

By this time, Powell was in tremendous pain. Twenty years of driving high-speed boats and jumping out of planes had taken their toll on his joints, and the impact of the woman's body landing on him had now caused some serious damage. Even though he wasn't sure what had happened, he knew that his mobility was rapidly decreasing. It was becoming harder and harder to squat down each time without terrible pains shooting through his leg like electric shocks. If he didn't give it a rest, he wouldn't be good to anyone. He moved to the side and stopped catching jumpers, allowing Correa and the others to try to get to them with the dumpster.

Presently, a man jumped on top of the dumpster and held the ladder on his back while Correa climbed onto it and began to move toward the badly disoriented Wills. She began to lose consciousness as Petrovich and the others lowered her down to Correa, who carefully embraced her and then lowered her to Powell on the ground. As she reached the ground, she refused to be taken away until she was sure that McNair had escaped, but Powell quickly picked her up in his arms and carried her through A Ring and out into the courtyard, setting her down gently in a triage area. This done, he ran back to the service road, his legs racked with pain. In the courtyard, Wills opened her eyes, but the bright sunlight sent a painful sting through them. She quickly closed them and thought of her friends.

After helping people out of Corridor Five and down into the courtyard, Commander Dave Tarantino descended onto the first floor and out into A/E Drive to get fresh air. In front of him was a scene of true despair: black smoke billowing out of the second floor; debris scattered in the road; burned, cut, and disheveled people all over the place. As he walked forward, he noticed a large black hole blown out of one side of C Ring's wall. Inside this hole, he could see flames. As his eyes scanned the debris-strewn floor, they suddenly caught sight of an intact piece of the landing gear of a jet lying very near the hole, its steel leg mangled and torn. To a counterterrorist like Tarantino, it was the affirmation of a nightmare.

As he stood staring at this piece of landing gear, he heard voices crying to him for help. He rushed through the hole, and the scene that greeted him inside was absolutely horrific. All around were the remains of human beings—a foot here, part of a head there, a knee bone lying amid torn and scattered navigation charts. Bits and pieces of all manner of debris, pieces of flesh with clothing still clinging to them were everywhere. Flames moved along the walls, and the aluminum rib cage that once held ceiling tiles dripped molten metal onto the floor. Burned and charred pieces of furniture and computers lay everywhere, and in the blackness, the voices called to him. Tarantino moved forward into the heat, plowing through the debris, throwing pieces of furniture, electrical grid plates, and parts of the plane to either side of him, cutting a serpentine path through to the survivors. His shoes and uniform began to melt. Above his head, he saw melted white plastic falling to the floor in long gooey strings like taffy, the remains of the PVC piping being liquidated by the heat. Some of the plastic fell onto his body, burning his skin along with the molten metal droplets from the ceiling-tile cage. He looked at his shirt pocket and could see his name tag beginning to melt. In the midst of all of this, he could hear water flowing from burst pipes, mixed with the cries of the wounded.

The first survivors Tarantino came upon were naval personnel Christina Williams and Charles Lewis. Lying beneath collapsed partitions, they were weak from smoke inhalation and beginning to panic. By now, Captain Dave Thomas had joined Tarantino in the hole. Tarantino grabbed both Williams and Lewis and passed them back, one at a time, to Thomas, who took them out. Meanwhile, Tarantino pushed ahead, soon coming to a large room, the interior of which was truly apocalyptic. Everywhere his senses were under full assault. The din was incredible—sounds of water running; fires crackling and spitting; the metal, plastic, and wood burning and sizzling as it hit the water.

A few feet away, Thomas searched for his friend Bob Dolan. He crawled through debris, shouting his name. He knew Dolan's office was in this area somewhere. He crawled inside and located what he thought were the remains of Dolan's desk, but there was no sign of him.

"Bob!" he shouted. "Can you hear me, Bob? It's Dave!"

But there was no answer. Suddenly, close by, he heard a weak voice. "Help me," it said. "I'm trapped." Thomas crawled a little farther and came to a crude lean-to created by the explosion and composed of a heavy desk and a pile of debris, which had collapsed on top of it. Through the smoke, he saw the bloody shoulders, head, and neck of a man. It was Jarrell "Jerry" Henson, a former navy pilot.

Thomas got closer to him and saw his eyes move.

Thomas heard Tarantino call to him. "Is that it?"

"No!" Thomas shouted. "There's another guy in here!" As he said this, he crawled over to the man and tried to lift the desk off him. All around now, the smoke was getting thicker, the fires growing hotter, the space around them closing in. Thomas heaved but could not budge the desk enough to free Henson.

Tarantino now appeared in front of Thomas and Henson. He grabbed Thomas by the arm. "Come on," he said. "We've got to get out of here. This place is going to collapse!"

He could see that Thomas was having no luck trying to move the desk. Henson, trapped beneath it, was an older man and was starting to lose hope. Tarantino got closer to him. "I'm a doctor," he said. "We're going to get you out, but you've got to calm down." Saying this, even Tarantino knew that if they didn't get Henson out quickly, he was going to die, and they would likely die along with him.

On the second floor, right above where Thomas and Tarantino struggled to free Henson, Mike Petrovich could feel his lungs filling with smoke. He looked at McNair. "I can't breathe," he gasped.

In a few moments, he felt as if he were going to black out. He told McNair he couldn't hold on any longer, so McNair picked him up and lowered him down to Correa before climbing out the window himself. As McNair jumped onto the dumpster, Correa looked around and could see gaping holes in the building that appeared to have been caused by a series of explosions. He noticed that in one hole, the large cement blocks were pushed in, and in another they were pushed out. Later, he would realize that he had seen the area where the fuselage of American Airlines Flight 77 had crossed through before it finally stopped.

When McNair reached the service road, he observed the same thing. He was amazed at the destruction. Huge holes had been punched into the side of the wall at ground level with piles of rubble next to them. He went inside one of the holes and could hear people crying out. Large air-conditioning units blocked the area, so he and another group of people began forming a chain to dig these survivors out. They threw computer monitors, chairs, and other debris out of the way, passing them back down the chain to the outside as they moved farther into the building, trying to get to the victims. At one point, they had to turn back as the smoke had taken all of the air. There was simply no way to breathe.

McNair ran back out onto the service road and secured a fire extinguisher, which he used on the electrical wiring. As McNair worked, some Pentagon guards ran up to him and told him to get out of the area.

"Another plane is inbound!" one of them said.

"What do you mean, another plane?" McNair said as he sprayed the wires with the fire extinguisher and then looked back at them, still totally unaware of what had really happened. Up to this time, he had figured the attack was some kind of accident or the result of a bomb. When someone explained to him what had happened in New York, McNair's reaction was cool and practical.

"Well, we've got fighter planes at Andrews," he said. "Why don't we scramble them and knock these things out?"

The guards just shook their heads. "We've got to get out of here, Colonel, now! Let's move!" McNair put down his fire extinguisher and went with them.

Victor Correa and Tony Rose were preparing to make another attempt to get into the Army Personnel Center, but by this time, it had become truly hopeless. There was no going back. The fire and smoke had completely inundated the area. Whoever was left behind was now gone forever. They retreated back toward the corridor in despair just as some Pentagon police ordered them out of the building.

"You folks need to leave now," one of them said. "There's another plane on the way in!"

Both Correa and Rose turned and looked at the police officers and said nothing, leveling a thousand-yard stare at them that let them know the two men weren't going anywhere. Correa looked at one of them, deliberately ignoring their commands to evacuate.

"Get us some masks," he ordered. The officer was dumbfounded that his orders were being dismissed like this. There was a tense pause. Then Correa looked at him again. "Get on the radio and see if you can get us some masks! We know the area. We can look for folks!" The officers ignored Correa in turn and repeated their order to leave. Seeing this was going nowhere, Tony Rose simply walked around the officers and headed toward A/E Drive. Correa, refusing to be ordered out, turned back toward the police. "Get us some masks, man," he said as he dismissed them and followed Rose. The police gave up and left.

PENTAGON COURTYARD—1007 HOURS

Under a tree in the courtyard, a medic worked carefully to cut all of John Yates's clothes off him, but Yates could feel nothing. Most of his nerve endings had been burned away. He was in no immediate pain but unaware that this meant he was in serious trouble. He just didn't know how long and hard the road ahead of him would be.

As the medic treated Yates, workers brought out Tracy Webb, his colleague, and sat her down next to him. Webb was distraught. Yates looked at her. "Hang in there, Tracy. You're gonna be OK."

As Yates said this, a Pentagon police officer walked into the courtyard and ordered everyone to evacuate. "We've got a report of another plane on the way in now. We've got to move!"

Yates became terrified. He had been through hell once, and now he was going to have to go through it again. It wasn't long before everyone was told to relax as the threat was downgraded. As patients were evacuated, a woman pointed to Yates and said, "He goes first."

Yates was put on a golf cart and then abruptly taken off by paramedics and laid back down in the grass. In a few moments, he felt himself being lifted onto a stretcher. He heard one of the paramedics shout angrily, "Somebody took my drug box!"

"You sure?" another voice asked.

"Yeah, it was right here. Now it's gone." As they talked, Yates realized they had nothing to intubate him with and nothing to give him for pain, but at this point, the only pain he could feel was that of a bad sunburn on the top of his head. The rest of his body was comfortably numb.

Sitting nearby, Marilyn Wills stared up at the smoke coming from the windows. Somewhere inside that inferno were her friends. Why had she not gone back for them? She lay in wait to be evacuated, but her physical injuries were nothing compared to the pain of losing people who were like family to her. At this point, she was more concerned with finding her friends than with her own condition, which was getting worse by the minute.

A/E DRIVE, PENTAGON—1008 HOURS

Tony Rose, now standing in the middle of A/E Drive, could hear cries and screams coming from inside the black hole blown through the wall just opposite where he was standing. He rushed inside and in one corner found a utility room with a door blasted off it. Entering the room, he found a broken steel cage, the secure entrance to the Navy Command Center, with a round circular hole blown through and smoke pouring out of it. Rose could hear the desperate wails and cries of the injured and dying coming from behind the wall on the other side of this hole. As he surveyed the area above the entrance, he could see that the ceiling was beginning to fall. It couldn't hold much longer. Nevertheless, there were people still alive inside, and they had to be saved. If the ceiling collapsed, they were doomed.

Rose climbed inside and began digging. In a few minutes, he was joined by Phil McNair. Rose looked at McNair and was startled by what he saw. His head was covered with blood, and his face was falling down around his eyes, but he was digging just as hard as Rose, trying to save people, unconcerned with his own serious injuries. In a few moments, Vic Correa arrived and immediately began helping the other two. The three men worked furiously in calf-deep water with slicks of burning jet fuel floating on the surface.

As Rose and the others proceeded to dig their way into the Navy Command Center, Craig Powell noticed the commotion and could see pieces of the ceiling fall to the ground near this small opening. It would only be a matter of seconds before it caved in. As he turned around, he saw Lieutenant Olin Sell, who had disappeared right after the initial blast. He grabbed Sell and headed for what was now being called the "tunnel." Behind them came Commander Jeff Stratton, another navy SEAL, who drove up in a golf cart he had found and began shuttling the survivors from the Army Personnel Center into the courtyard.

WEST WALL, PENTAGON—1008 HOURS

Firefighter Tomi Rucker of DC Fire remembered looking up into the sky at the exact moment that two F-16 fighter jets passed over-head, shaking the very ground she was standing on and sending a heart-stopping thud through her chest. She had seen the news footage of the World Trade Center towers and was now told the Pentagon had been hit. Alarms began sounding as the firemen mobilized. Rucker had been with DC Fire ever since leaving her job as a corrections officer some years before. Seeing Engine 34 begin to pull out, she had jumped aboard and now found herself at the Pentagon.

Getting across the river normally took five minutes, but it was a full half hour before they arrived. Rucker saw people running every-where. FBI agents were milling around, and one of them called out to her by name, which she found curious because she wasn't wearing a name tag. The agent asked her to find as many body bags as she could. Rucker obtained level A suits and body bags, then yanked the three-inch hose off the truck and ran toward the fire.

Rucker and other firefighters doused the flames with water, but it did no good. They remained inside for little more than twenty minutes, at which point they had to retreat due to the intensity of the heat. After coming out the first time, Rucker began worrying about her son. She called his school but got only a recording. Word was now trickling down of a major national catastrophe. Hundreds of firefighters had lost their lives in New York, and this enraged and emboldened everyone around them.

"We're going to get the people who did this," she said quietly to herself.

As the Fort Myer crew neared the site of the crash, Rusty Dodge could see shadows moving in the windows amid the blur of the flames. Jumping from the truck, he ran to the blown-out window and saw five people trapped inside. With some other rescue personnel, he helped get these people to safety. The last one to emerge told him that there was no one left in the area, but Dodge was not a man to just take some-one else's word for it. He had to be sure. He turned and headed inside, trying to keep from inhaling the smoke and calling out at intervals to see if anyone was still inside. No one answered, and in a few moments, he retreated to the outside, where he grabbed hold of a section of fire hose, helping to steady it for the point man. When the point man was suddenly called away, Dodge took up his position.

Meanwhile, Chris Evans and the other firefighters from Fort Myer had jumped off the truck as soon as it came to a stop, and rushed into the building. Running headlong into the blast site, Evans encountered heat so intense, it made his heart nearly jump out of his chest. Inside, he could see pools of burning jet fuel with multicolored flames. Bodies lay all around, but Evans could barely see anything else. One of the chiefs yelled in and told them not to move any of the bodies.

As Rusty Dodge aimed the powerful hose at the fire, he kept think-ing about his friend Joel Kanasky in New York and also about legend-ary fire chief Raymond Downey of the FDNY, Kanasky's boss. Dodge had accompanied Downey on calls while a member of RESCUE 1 in the early 1970s. He knew that Downey was the most highly decorated firefighter in the city of New York and a nationally known expert on high-rise building collapse. If there was something bad going down in Manhattan, Downey would be right in the middle of it.

Looking at the burning construction trailer, and the seared and blackened hulk of Foam 61, Dodge remembered something Downey had told him after returning from the bombed-out federal building at Oklahoma City in 1995: it was secondary outside fires that prevented rescue crews from reaching the scene quickly, thus allowing the pri-mary fire to get worse. Dodge looked at Wallace's truck, Foam 61, and then at a construction trailer and some outbuildings between the west wall and the highway. All around him were many small, isolated fires caused by propane tanks used by the pipe fitters during the renovation. These tanks had probably exploded from the heat generated by the initial fireball. Dodge now realized what Downey had been talking about. The secondary blazes generated by these propane tanks and other things were blocking access to the site for the fire and rescue crews now arriving on the scene.

Dodge quickly turned his hose on Foam 61 and then the construction trailer. Then he gave the hose to another fireman and headed toward the first floor of the west wall just as reserve units pulled up and began fighting the construction-trailer fire. The trailer fire was proving stubborn due to flammable chemicals that had been stored inside and around it. There had been repeated small explosions coming from this direction since the crash. He later learned that thankfully the chemicals had been properly caged, preventing them from becoming deadly missiles when they exploded.

A/E DRIVE, PENTAGON—1009 HOURS

Commander Craig Powell and Lieutenant Olin Sell had evacuated all of the people in Mike Petrovich's group and were now standing at the entrance to the Navy Command Center. They rushed past the door to the utility room and the broken cage, where they could clearly see the hole with people crawling in and out. Powell looked at the roof of the tunnel and saw that it was going to give way at any moment. He dropped to the floor and rolled in the water, then put a wet shirt into his mouth. He then walked to the opening and put his body in between the ceiling and the floor, holding it up with his arms.

While Powell held up the ceiling at the entrance, Tony Rose, crawling around inside the tunnel, found a hand sticking out from behind a pile of debris. He inched closer and found a sailor lying on his side. The man was badly wounded but kept motioning back into the blackness.

"There're people in there. They're still alive!" he shouted with all the strength he could muster. "You've got to get them out!"

"We will, partner!" Rose reassured him.

Over the next few minutes, Rose pulled survivors out between the legs of the injured sailor. Then he and some of the others, including Major General Paul K. Carlton, Jr., and Vic Correa, evacuated the sailor.

Rose crawled back toward the entrance through calf-deep water. As he made his way toward the light, he glanced up through the haze and saw something he would never forget. There, standing at the mouth of the tunnel, holding the ceiling up like Atlas with the world on his shoulders, was the big man he had seen catching his coworkers as they jumped from the second floor. It was Craig Powell. A memory suddenly came back to Rose from childhood—listening to Tennessee Ernie Ford records with his father and Ford singing the Jimmy Dean song "Big Bad John" about a legendary miner who had saved his fellow workers by holding up a mine shaft to allow them to escape and then perishing before he could get out. Rose didn't know this man's name, so he started calling him "Big John." He could hear the old melody in his head, and it gave him strength. He thought about his father, and he thought about heroes, and he moved forward again into the black hole, more determined now than ever to find survivors. With "Big John" holding up the ceiling, everything was going to be alright.

Lying in the tunnel a short distance from Rose, Dave Tarantino could see Jerry Henson pinned against the floor by a heavy desk with the walls of the cubicle and a bookcase piled on top of it.

Tarantino couldn't understand why the man was still alive. He had been in this heat and smoke for almost twenty minutes, whereas Tarantino had been inside for only twenty seconds and could hardly breathe. Through the smoke, Tarantino could see that Henson had sustained massive head injuries and burns.

Thomas was working hard to lift the desk off him, but the smoke was beginning to take its toll.

Outside, Tarantino heard a collective voice shout in his direction. "Everybody get out—it's going to go!"

He looked at Henson. "Let's go, man," he said.

Henson looked up at him, a hopeless expression on his face; "I can't get out," he said. "I can't move."

Tarantino could see there was no way that Thomas was going to free Henson. The weight of the desk and tangled debris was simply too heavy. But all at once, his eyes caught sight of a small space between Henson and the bottom of the desk, and an idea occurred to him. Remembering the old hip sledges from his crew days, he got down on his back and squatted in reverse, pushing up on the desk, cubicle walls, and bookcase with his legs. The strength of the former Stanford University crewman's legs was enough to raise the desk and debris a few inches, just enough to get the weight off Henson.

Tarantino reached down and pulled the older gentleman over the top of his body with his arms, moving him toward Thomas at the other end.

"Anybody else in there?" Tarantino asked Henson as he pulled him through.

"I think so," Henson told him.

Tarantino shouted into the blackness. "Anybody in there?" He waited a few moments, but all was silent.

Now, as Thomas went to pull Henson out, the old man's leg snagged on an electrical cord, and he stopped moving.

"Get your ass out!" Tarantino shouted at Henson as he struggled to hold up the enormous weight, steadily losing the battle with each passing second. The desk began to shift, and Tarantino felt his knees buckle.

"This thing's going to go!" he grunted, his knees quivering. "I can't hold it any longer!"

Henson struggled to free his leg as Tarantino fought to hold the desk up. In the nick of time, Henson untangled his leg, and Thomas grabbed him and pulled him through just as Tarantino let go and rolled sideways, the desk, cubicle walls, bookcase, and other heavy debris crashing to the floor in a heap.

Thomas pulled Henson to the outside as Tarantino got up and escaped back onto A/E Drive. As the men coughed and sucked air, Thomas walked up and ripped off Tarantino's name tag, which was by now melted and contorted from the heat. He walked over and handed the tag to Henson, who was lying on a stretcher. "Don't you ever forget this name," he said.

Standing at the entrance to the tunnel and holding the ceiling up, Craig Powell was now having trouble breathing. The impact from the woman in the courtyard had torn his quadricep muscle, and he couldn't squat down to get under the smoke, so he just stood there, breathing in the smoke and the "particle stew" that hung in the air all around him. Hot petroleum droplets seared his face and burned his lungs. Liquid metal dropped from above onto his uniform, burning through to the skin, but Powell held steady. He was a US Navy SEAL, imbued with the power of a positive mind that kept him going when everything looked hopeless. This was not something he was born with; it was something he had developed through years of hard training that taught a man to relax and function without emotion even when death had its arm around his shoulder.

As Powell held up the wall, Rose, Carlton, Correa, and McNair continued to evacuate survivors. The survival time inside the tunnel had now been reduced to approximately two minutes due to the intensity of the heat, the lack of oxygen, and the immediate danger of fuel floating on top of the water. One man would dig for a few minutes, then run back through the hole onto A/E Drive. Then another man would rush in and dig farther. In this way, the rescuers were able to get deeper and deeper into the area without getting too far from the oxygen supply. At one point, two petty officers, a man and a woman, were pulled out of the hole and stated that there were still others inside. "Jack Punches is still in there," one of them said. "We've got to get him out!"

After saving Thomas and Henson, Tarantino turned and went inside to look for Punches. Meanwhile, Craig Powell was fighting an ever-increasing pain in his lungs to hold the ceiling up. Since he couldn't squat, he couldn't get down under the smoke to get fresh air unless he released the ceiling, but if he did this, Rose and Tarantino and the others would be trapped alive, so he remained in position, his mind holding his body in place. He remembered Basic Underwater Demolition/SEAL Class 123 or BUD/S, where out of a total of one hundred and two men, only eighteen had made it, and he was one of them. He remembered the cold and the pain, and how it never seemed to end. He remembered going far beyond physical strength, beyond the voices in his mind that told him to give up, and into the realm of the spirit in order to survive the training. Now he was in this same place again, only this time, people's lives depended upon it. But there was something else holding him in position, a sense that this attack had to be reckoned with. These terrorist bastards had punched America in the nose. Now, Powell wanted to survive to punch them back. He wasn't going to die before he got his chance.

After some time, Tarantino, Rose, and Major General Carlton had found no other survivors. Thomas hadn't found his friend Bob Dolan. Repeated calls into the tunnel were met with silence, and they hadn't found Punches. Feeling the building shift constantly, they worried that the entire structure might come down on top of them at any moment. Recognizing the impending danger, they all retreated past Powell, who called into the black hole one last time to see if anyone was left. When there was no answer, he let go of the ceiling and rushed forward, leaving the tunnel to collapse in on itself. The Navy Command Center was now a crypt.

Tarantino and Thomas took Henson into the courtyard, where an IV was started on him. Tarantino caught his breath and went to get some water. As he looked back at the collapsed tunnel, he realized that Henson was the last person pulled out alive. He knew there were probably more still inside, still breathing but unable to call for help.

Thomas stared at the pile of debris that now blocked the tunnel entrance and thought of Bob Dolan. Maybe he had left the area before the attack. Dolan was his best friend. Not knowing whether he was alive or dead was an awful feeling.

IV

THE LIVING AND THE DEAD

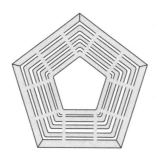

SOUTH PARKING LOT, PENTAGON—1005 HOURS

Around 10:05 a.m., Mike Defina had detected signs that the wall near the point of impact was beginning to weaken. Now, he stared intently at the upper west end of the wall. He could see that the expansion joint between the sections had been seriously knocked out of line. He figured the crack to be at least a foot wide. He then looked at the east end of the wall up toward the top part of the wedge and could see that it was showing signs of imminent collapse. The roofline was buckling, and there was debris falling around the edges of the hole that the plane had punched into it. He could see the Fort Myer firefighters nervously looking up and around. The fire was beginning to spread to the third and fourth floors and was now moving north toward the next wedge. All around the impact site, the concrete had turned snow white from the heat, indicating temperatures approaching two thousand degrees Fahrenheit. Looking at the windows, Alan Wallace and the others could clearly see fire advancing rapidly through the building. It was burning hotter now. If there were any more survivors, it was now or never.

TRIAGE AREA, SOUTH LAWN, PENTAGON—1009 HOURS

Ed Lucci watched as Kevin Shaeffer was transferred to the Walter Reed ambulance. He could clearly see the extent of Shaeffer's burns and knew the man had to be evacuated immediately. Along with Shaeffer, one of the "walking wounded," a man with a bandaged head who seemed to be talking just fine, climbed into the ambulance. Lucci walked up to the man.

"Get out!" he said. "We've got others in here who are worse off, and we need the space." Hearing the stern tone of Lucci's voice, the man promptly got up.

Lucci knew that in a situation like this, he had to be forceful. He recalled the Ramstein air show disaster in Germany in 1988 when a lot of less seriously injured victims were evacuated from the site because they were the first to reach the ambulances. With everything as disorganized as it was out here and no triage established, the highest-priority patients would likely be left behind. If he had to get a little nasty with people to control the evacuation, then so be it.

Apart from this, he was also worried that doctors arriving on-site would unnecessarily delay patient evacuation. Nearly three months before, he had been in Santiago, Chile, teaching disaster management to Chilean doctors. At the end of the course, they simulated a plane crash with multiple survivors at the site. Observing what happened when the doctors attempted to evacuate the wounded, he noticed that they allowed themselves to become embroiled in extended discussions and arguments about which patients were more or less critical and how to assign the triage categories. The end result was a slow evacuation, and slow meant a lower survival rate for the seriously injured patients. That wasn't going to happen here.

Lucci was also concerned about which hospitals to evacuate to. He knew that Walter Reed had the capacity to handle several major trauma patients, but it was not the closest hospital. The main consideration was time; if the evacuation was slow, some of the patients could die en route. He also knew that closer hospitals would probably be overwhelmed. He realized that the only way to get all of the patients evacuated was to put them inside the cars of passersby who would have to fight their way through traffic to make it to the hospital. He didn't like this option at all, but at the moment, he had no other choice.

The thing that was bothering him the most was wondering what they were going to receive from inside. There could be a lot of badly injured people, some of them firefighters, or there could be nothing but dead bodies. The waiting was killing him, but right now he needed to make sure he was prepared.

As Lucci watched, Marilyn Wills was brought out and placed inside the ambulance. Looking at her, he realized that she had some sort of upper-airway obstruction. Captain Rod Barlowe, who had been caring for her, told Lucci that it was not a good idea to send her back to Walter Reed in the ambulance.

"That's a twenty-to-thirty-minute ride, minimum," he said. "There's just a nurse in the back with two patients and a medic driving. What if her airway gets blocked on the way? She'll never make it." Glancing back at Wills, Lucci agreed, and the two men took her out of the ambulance and sat her down on a curb with the oxygen mask. They put some burn patients in the ambulance ahead of her.

By now, Wills did not look good at all. She was pale and limp, and even with the oxygen, she was gasping for breath. She had simply inhaled too much smoke. Lucci knew that they didn't have the right equipment with them to fix her problem. He suspected that her upper airway was burned and had swollen to the point where it was cutting off her air supply. She was placed on positive-pressure bag ventilation, and one of the rescuers was tasked with breathing for her. She needed to go to the closest hospital, which Lucci knew was Arlington General, but he also knew that there were probably more patients on the other side of the building and that they would likely go to Arlington as it was geographically closer. The decision was made to evacuate all of their patients to Walter Reed. Lucci figured he could take at least four patients out of the flood that would be going to Arlington General.

Lucci sent the Walter Reed ambulances on their way and then started placing critical patients in the backs of passing cars along with a health-care provider for each one. In this manner, they were able to evacuate most of the critically injured. Several doctors, dentists, nurses, and physician's assistants stopped and agreed to help. With no one left to accompany Marilyn Wills to the hospital, Lucci commandeered a

Subaru station wagon and took her to Arlington General himself. He placed an oxygen tank and some airway equipment in the back of the Subaru and told one nurse to drive and the other to sit in the passenger seat as he stayed in the back seat with Wills. En route, Wills began drifting in and out of consciousness, and Lucci knew something had to be done quick. He thought of a technique that was relatively new, a sort of shock therapy where you beat on the patient's back and shouted at them to breathe. He had observed respiratory therapists do it to patients on the ward back at Walter Reed with positive results.

"Listen to me," he shouted, pounding on her back. "You can't die now! You gotta breathe!" Marilyn looked at him for a moment, then passed out again.

As the tiny station wagon tried to make its way through a massive traffic jam, the nurses began blowing the horn and yelling at other drivers to clear the way as Lucci attempted to keep Wills breathing. The nurse in the passenger seat would periodically jump out of the car and walk out into traffic, yelling at the drivers and pounding on windows to get them to move. Lucci and the nurses were in uniform, but this didn't seem to matter to the other cars. Many people were desperately trying to get away from the Pentagon any way they could but were stuck in gridlock. Repeated rumors of incoming planes had thrown many people into sheer panic.

In a few moments, Lucci noticed that the tank was running out of oxygen. Wills was getting sleepy and turning pale. Her eyes rolled back in her head, and she wouldn't respond. He knew she had to be intubated or they were going to lose her, but he couldn't do it in the back seat of a Subaru.

"Stop the car!" he yelled. The nurse hit the brakes, and Lucci opened the door and pulled Wills out onto the highway. They were only two miles from Arlington General, but Wills was barely breathing. He knew that she was still too conscious to allow him to put a breathing tube down her airway. She was fighting him, and he had no drugs for sedation. He looked around at the angry cars blowing their horns for him to get out of the way, the nurses screaming back at the panicked drivers.

As he kneeled over Marilyn Wills, he noticed a private ambulance that was sitting in traffic. In a few moments, a couple of paramedics approached and asked if he needed help.

"A lot!" Lucci said.

In seconds, they brought up an oxygen tank, the difference between life and death. Wills quickly perked up again and began to look better. Her color came back. The ambulance driver agreed to take everyone to Arlington Hospital (Virginia Hospital Center). They loaded Wills into the ambulance and all got inside, leaving the Subaru abandoned in the middle of the road.

When they reached the entrance to Arlington Hospital, a full staff of nurses and doctors came out to attend to Wills. The ambulance driver had radioed ahead that they were coming. Wills was rushed to the ER, where she was intubated and placed on a breathing machine for twenty-four hours. She continued to go in and out of consciousness for some time. Someone gave her a pen, and she managed to write her husband's name, "KIRK," and then a phone number before losing consciousness completely for two days.

WEDGE ONE, PENTAGON—1009 HOURS

On A/E Drive, Vic Correa moved away from the collapsed entrance. Firemen began to flood into the area and evacuate it. Correa knew that once they were on the scene, it was their show and they called the shots. Someone walked up to him and said, "Sir, you need to look at your head." Correa stopped and looked at his uniform and felt his head. It was the first time he had paused to think about himself since the attack. Blood and other matter were smeared all over his uniform. He felt his head, where several cuts and abrasions had appeared. Someone led him to the medical clinic in the Pentagon gymnasium near the north wall, where he was treated.

In E Ring, Dan Fraunfelter shouted into the darkness and listened for voices, but none came. He didn't wait long. He heard the subcontractor call to him. "Dan, you'd better get out, now!" he said. Fraunfelter could hear the structural steel beginning to groan. He could almost feel the building move. He had seen the stress crack in the floor. Interior temperatures had been recorded at eighteen hundred degrees or more. He knew what was about to happen. The building was ready to go. Quickly, he turned and ran as fast as he could away from this section of the wedge.

Below Fraunfelter, near the crash site, Chris Evans had entered E Ring, where he found a foot still in a sock. The rest of the body was gone. Nearby were other bodies burned beyond recognition, their skin melted away by the heat. He had been told not to move or touch anything, but the heat made this impossible. It was so intense that he could stay inside for only a few minutes. Ahead of him, he saw darkness, smoke, and multicolored flames. Pools of jet fuel burned like gas jets. Debris rained to the floor from above. Suddenly, he heard the heat sensor on his air pack start to whine, indicating that his gear was now too hot to protect him. This was the first time in his ten years as a firefighter that Evans had heard the thing go off. The heat was simply too much. It was time to get out. As Evans backed away, he realized, to his horror, that in some places he couldn't distinguish bodies from debris.

In a corridor of C Ring, Tony Rose and Craig Powell, their uniforms blackened and shredded, their skin covered with white spots from the liquid metal, assisted Arlington Fire in mobilizing ten-man teams assigned to a fire captain as litter-bearers. As Rose stood there, he looked at the water rushing like a river past him toward a large drain covered by a grate. Looking closer, he saw something that made his blood run cold. It was the hand of a small child lying on the floor. Kneeling down, he gently picked up the hand and put it in his pocket. As he did, a finger floated past him in the torrent, then pieces of a leg and arm and various other human remains, all being carried into the drain by the surging water. Rose looked at Powell, and both men rushed to the grating and put their hands over the hole to catch these remains before they were washed away forever. One set of intestines was still connected to a body, even though they had been shredded. Rose and Powell worked frantically to try to collect what had once been human beings with families and homes, with memories and hopes and dreams, all gone in an instant. A cold, resolute anger was beginning to build in their hearts.

OFFICE OF MAJOR DAN PANTALEO, USMC, ROSSLYN, VIRGINIA—1009 HOURS

Dan Pantaleo was now convinced that the country was under coordinated attack from a foreign enemy. At 10:05 a.m., he along with the rest of his coworkers had heard of the attack on the Pentagon and the downing of United Airlines Flight 93 in Pennsylvania.

Outside, the streets of Rosslyn were beginning to gridlock with traffic. The wail of police and fire sirens filled the air, and, in the distance, rising above Washington, was the ever-present black cloud that now covered the surrounding landscape. Pantaleo looked in all directions. He had no car, and even if he had, he wouldn't have been able to get anywhere, so he just broke and ran toward the Pentagon as fast as he could.

SOUTH PARKING LOT, PENTAGON—1009 HOURS

Mike Defina and his fire crew from Reagan National Airport had arrived at the Pentagon at 9:42 a.m. and begun deploying. After surveying the area, he noticed the Fort Myer crew members attempting to fight the escalating inferno with their new Titan 3000, which was clearly out of action. Defina saw one of them trying to operate the water cannon on top of the truck but unable to aim it directly at the fire, so he ordered Foam 331 to pull up near the disabled fire truck and assist. The only other fire trucks in view at the time were a truck engine from Arlington County and Unit 105 on the north end of the wedge.

In a few moments, Foam 331 began to hit the fire with its roof and bumper turrets, dousing it with over six hundred gallons of 6 percent foam with an initial flow of three thousand gallons per minute. A four-person firefighting crew grabbed hand lines and rushed to put out vehicle fires and the fires from the diesel and propane tanks. Defina called for more units, with eight arriving on the scene within the first hour. National Foam Unit 345 was called up when 331 ran low on chemical. Battalion chief Glen Butler requested the dispatch of SERV-362, a mass casualty unit from Dulles International Airport, which responded immediately. Defina also called for a one-thousand-gallon foam trailer from the Metropolitan Washington Airports Authority that served both National and Dulles Airports.

In all his years as a firefighter, Defina had never seen such devastation. Though he had never before experienced a fire of this magnitude, through simulations and exercises he had been trained for it. He and others had received extensive instruction in dealing with fire aboard planes and in airport terminals. The initial heat was bad, but it was something he had been told to expect. The mass casualty units, SERV-329 and SERV-362, both arrived shortly and were able to treat up to one hundred and fifty patients each. Military officials looked to Defina and his crew for direction. It was the first time soldiers and firefighters had worked together outside of simulation and training exercises, and Defina could see that it was basically well coordinated. One stroke of luck was that Reagan National Airport's Paramedic Unit was familiar with the layout of the Pentagon, having responded to calls there on numerous occasions.

TRIAGE AREA, SOUTH LAWN, PENTAGON—1010 HOURS

On the lawn near the west wall, Bruno and Cruz-Cortez pulled themselves up after diving to the ground from an explosion, which had been caused by one of the pools of jet fuel igniting. These pools would continue to spontaneously erupt throughout the day and into the night.

After shielding the woman with the handbag from the sudden explosion, Bruno tapped Cruz-Cortez on the shoulder.

"I'm going back to help," he said.

"Be careful," Cruz-Cortez told him as the two hugged and Bruno disappeared.

All around now, Cruz-Cortez could see people approaching the area. When they offered their help, she turned them away, instructing them to attend to the more seriously wounded. All at once, out of the hole in Wedge One came two firemen and two civilians carrying a heavyset female on a stretcher. She was lying facedown and not moving. As they laid her on the ground, Cruz-Cortez overheard one of the firemen talking. "We found her buried under some furniture that was on fire," he said, then turned to Cruz-Cortez. "Hold this," he said, thrusting an IV bottle into her hand. Cruz-Cortez took the bottle and held it up while the worker inserted the IV and then moved on to the next person in line.

Cruz-Cortez sat next to the injured woman as she moaned in pain. Not knowing what else to do, she got up close to her. "Everything's going to be alright," she said softly. "The doctors will fix you up, and you'll be with your family soon." The woman continued to moan in agony, and Cruz-Cortez was not sure if she was hearing the words. Nevertheless, she continued to speak softly to her. "You're not alone," she said. "I'm right here. I know you're in pain, but you've got to be strong."

Looking up at the cloudless blue sky, Cruz-Cortez quietly said a prayer for the woman. When she finished, she looked around and saw two men from her unit nearby. She asked them if they'd seen Bruno.

"He's still pulling people out," one of them said. "With the firemen."

As Cruz-Cortez spoke with the men, a helicopter set down, and two paramedics headed toward the injured woman. As they approached her, she cried out that she couldn't breathe. The two of them tried to lift her up, but she was just too heavy, so Cruz-Cortez asked the two men from her unit to help. Working together, the four of them loaded the injured woman onto the helicopter. "We've got room for one more," one of the paramedics shouted over the earsplitting noise of the helicopter's rotor. Just then, Cruz-Cortez heard a shout, and a female army officer sprinted up to them.

"I've got a guy whose lungs might be collapsing," she yelled.

"We'll take him," the paramedic said. "Bring him up." As they waited, a fireman ran up to the paramedics. "Get this thing out of here. We've got another plane on the way in!" he shouted. The paramedic stalled for a moment while the injured man was brought to the helicopter and placed inside; then the door shut, and the machine took off. Cruz-Cortez watched as the helicopter disappeared. She looked around now in all directions after hearing what the fireman had said about another plane. She pulled herself up and began moving away from the area, still looking for April Gallop. As she started running, she saw someone snap her picture, but it didn't register. She kept on moving, looking everywhere for April.

WEDGE ONE, PENTAGON—1010 HOURS

Near the blast site, Lincoln Leibner continued to pull people out of the building, including a woman for whom September 11 had been her first day at work. Above his head, he heard the building groan. Something was going to happen. The wall couldn't take much more. Then he heard a shout.

At this same moment, Alan Wallace was preparing to go inside with one of the teams, when a loud voice cut through the din. "Hey . . . the damn building just moved!"

Then came another voice from a different direction. "Get out of there!" Everyone froze, and there was complete silence.

"I just saw the building move!" the first voice cried out again. "Don't let anyone go inside!" It was the voice of Captain Dennis Gilroy, who reached for his microphone and shouted into it:

> "No one goes inside! Get everyone away from the
> building now!"

Gilroy's eye had caught a slight movement along the upper cornice of the west wall, just to the right of where the plane had hit. He could see it beginning to slide, like the start of an avalanche. The collapse was only seconds away. He repeated his command, and the firefighters began retreating from the building, taking everyone in the vicinity with them.

As Chris Evans stepped out of the building, he heard the wall above him writhe and moan, the steel support beams whining as they began to bend and break. Outside, he could see Gilroy yelling at him and the others to get out, but the roar of the fires and all the other noise made the captain look like he was just opening and closing his mouth, like a nightmare without sound. Several firemen nearby were waving their arms at him, motioning for him to come toward them. All at once, he heard a loud creaking like the sound of an unoiled door hinge magnified a thousand times. Evans ran faster than he had ever run in his life, every muscle in his body flexed. Images of his kids ran through his mind as he hauled nearly eighty pounds of gear away from the building at breakneck speed.

Seconds later, everyone heard a low, guttural sound as the section of Wedge One where Peter Murphy and his marines had escaped, where Brian Birdwell had been rescued from certain death, and where Dan Fraunfelter had found the crack and guided fifty people to safety with his flashlight, collapsed into the hole, an iceberg of concrete breaking off into a sea of rubble.

Dan Fraunfelter watched the wall give way and fall into the chasm. It had held for approximately thirty minutes in heat that exceeded fifteen hundred degrees. He was amazed. Without the structural upgrades he and his people had installed, the wall would have fallen within several minutes of the attack, killing most of the firefighters and sealing many others inside.

After hearing the shouts, Leibner turned and ran away from the building, but he had trouble breathing, and his legs were weak. He stumbled forward just as he heard the wall collapse behind him.

As he made his way clear, someone grabbed him and handed him an oxygen mask. A female nurse sat him down, and he could see blood on his shirt. Was it his or someone else's? He didn't know, and it didn't make much of a difference. Today, blood was a common denominator.

At about the same time that Gilroy noticed the building beginning to fail, Mike Defina was on the radio, notifying the Arlington Command Post of the imminent collapse. As a result of this, they were able to get all of the rescuers out only seconds before the right side of the wedge caved in.

BIRDWELL HOME, LORTON, VIRGINIA—1011 HOURS

At her home, Mel Birdwell watched the collapse of Wedge One. She knew that this was right where her husband worked. Her son, Matt, punched the wall in frustration, and Mel jumped up and put her arms around him. Mother and son bowed their heads and prayed. In her heart, Mel Birdwell believed that her husband was dead.

"He's standing at the throne of God," she said quietly to herself.

WEDGE ONE, PENTAGON—1012 HOURS

The first floor of the Army Resource Services Office was now pock-marked with holes and crevasses blown through the floor by the pressure and fire. Jet fuel covered sections of the devastated suite in a patchwork. The remains of dozens of cubicles, pieces of furniture, and computer equipment lay heaped in piles, tangled and impenetrable. The collapse of the building now made finding survivors even more difficult.

After being ordered by high-ranking officers and firefighters to stay away from the building, Christopher Braman had simply run around one side of the Pentagon and reentered in another area, continuing to search for survivors. He was beyond the chain of command at this point. He was running along the knife edge of death, breathing in so much toxic material that his lungs were struggling to keep up. He continued to pray to God to help him maintain his strength. He had been diagnosed only a short time before September 11 with early arthritis in his vertebrae, the result of his many jumps from aircraft, but this would only occur to him several days later. He continued to go in and out, ignoring the pain.

Inside, Braman found a woman who was pinned down, unconscious, and burned all over her body. This was Antoinette Sherman, and she was in bad shape. She was nearly naked, her clothes having been blown completely off her. He picked her limp body up and carried it out onto the lawn and then headed back into the building. Braman would later learn that Sherman lived for only another seven days before passing away.

Somewhere in the blackness, Sheila Moody prayed to God. "Jesus, I know you didn't bring me here to die like this," she said. The smoke was beginning to overcome her, and she couldn't stop coughing. She curled up in a ball, her arms shielding her head, and waited for the end.

Back inside, Braman could see the devastation of the collapse, as if the building had been cleaved in two right down the middle. He headed through the first floor into the smoke until he came to a hole leading from the first floor to the second. Braman called into the darkness, and a voice suddenly answered him.

"I'm here," it said.

Braman moved closer. "I can't see you," he said.

"We're in here," the voice called out weakly. "Please keep coming."

On the other side, kneeling on the floor, Sheila Moody could speak no more. She was coughing hard, and, unable to talk, she began clapping. Braman heard the clapping and moved toward it.

Moody looked up to see the outline of a man walking toward her. In the dim light, Braman could see the figure of a woman on her knees with her hands outstretched, palms upward. Braman reached through the smoke and grabbed her hand. In the darkness, it felt as if he were clasping a wet towel, but he knew it could be melted flesh. He got closer and saw Moody covered with ash, her hands shielding her head. She was stiff and looked like a mummy, but she was still alive. All around were people in a similar desperate condition. Above him, clearly visible in an office window amid the flames, was a dead man, his outstretched hand still clutching a coffee cup. Braman picked Moody up and carried her outside. To her, Christopher Braman was more than just another rescuer; he was her guardian angel.

SOUTH LAWN, PENTAGON—1013 HOURS

Running across the Pentagon lawn, Major Dan Pantaleo saw the gaping black hole where the west wall had, only minutes before, collapsed in on itself. A phalanx of firefighters poured foam and water onto the blaze, surrounded by stretchers and medical equipment, people lying on the grass injured, helicopters constantly buzzing overhead, and the black smoke rising above it all.

As Pantaleo approached the wall, he met up with Eric Jones, who was busy pulling people out of the building. Together, he and Jones began doing whatever they could to assist, gathering supplies and helping to get people to triage stations. By this time, Arlington Fire was turning everyone away as throngs of people descended on the scene from every direction.

WEDGE ONE, PENTAGON—1015 HOURS

After evacuating everyone from Lieutenant General Nyland's office, marines Schuetz and Vera now ran back into the building and helped people escape down Corridor Five toward A/E Drive. There they linked hands with other rescue personnel so that they could enter the smoke without getting lost. By forming a chain in this way, they were able to save nearly fifteen people by guiding them out of their offices. They were then summoned by some sailors who needed their help back toward E Ring near the point of impact. They were able to move back into this area by climbing through holes in the wall in C Ring. When Schuetz and Vera reached E Ring, they saw marines, sailors, soldiers, and civilians all working together to rescue trapped office workers. The concrete dust was so thick that people were choking on it, and the service road connecting the rings was covered with more than a foot of water. The very walls seemed to move. In various places, they could see small pockets of fire flaring up intermittently as air rushed in through collapsing windows. To Schuetz and Vera, it was a vision of hell.

Standing in the middle of all this, Vera suddenly caught wind of a weird smell, something he had never encountered before. He wondered if this was the smell of burning flesh he had heard combat veterans talk about. Within a few moments, the heat became unbearable, and Vera and the others were forced to go back. As they did, behind the rasp of the raging fires, Vera swore he could hear voices calling out to him in the darkness, pleading for someone to save them.

Standing near the west wall, Ted Anderson and the other soldiers had finally backed away, allowing the firefighters to do their jobs. Anderson felt his stomach churn. In combat, nothing would have stopped him from rescuing his fellow soldiers, but here it was a different matter. The firefighters had successfully bridged a code that Anderson and every other American soldier had burned into the core of his being. In the quiet of his mind, Anderson knew that they had probably saved his life, but this knowledge didn't do anything to ease the anguish that he felt.

As they stood there watching the firefighters, rumors continued to circulate that there were other aircraft now in the sky that were unaccounted for. At intervals, a voice would come over a loudspeaker, advising of another inbound plane, and everyone, including the fire-fighters, would have to move away from the building into a safe area. Anderson looked at the faces of his fellow soldiers who, like him, were prevented from going inside to rescue their comrades, people who were dying with each tick of the clock. In some areas, the fires were so hot that fighting them would have been suicide. They were helpless to do anything about it, and they didn't like it.

TRIAGE AREA, WEST WALL, PENTAGON—1015 HOURS

Ben Starnes watched as an FBI agent walked toward the crowd, telling everyone in general to take their things and move to the rear.

"This is a crime scene!" the agent shouted as everyone began to move away.

In a few moments, however, a DC firefighter arrived and told everyone to move back to the original site. Starnes watched this ridiculous test of wills with the raging fire in the background, the firefighters trying desperately to extinguish the flames. There were people dying in the building, and these two idiots were fighting over who had the authority to position the medical personnel. It wasn't long before he had about all he could take and approached the FBI agent. "Hey, if you move us back there, we're going to have to cross those concrete barriers on the highway when the evacuation starts. That's only going to make things more difficult," he said, trying to control his temper. As he waited for the agent's response, a loudspeaker blared in the distance.

> "Attention! Clear the area now! There is a second plane inbound for the Pentagon. Please clear the area!"

This announcement sent hundreds of people fleeing into the woods. The FBI agent bolted past Starnes, and Starnes jumped from a concrete barrier and ran toward some trees. Moving quickly, he kept looking above the tree line for the belly of a jetliner, planning to dodge it somehow if he caught sight of it. Thoughts raced through his mind, the same thoughts that had plagued him in Kosovo. Would he live to see his family again?

FAIRFAX COUNTY FIRE AND RESCUE STATION,
FAIRFAX, VIRGINIA—1020 HOURS

Carlton Burkhammer, a member of Fairfax County's elite Urban Search and Rescue Team, grabbed his gear and prepared to head out.

His group of men and search dogs was renowned for its ability to go into heavily damaged buildings and locate survivors. This unit had been sent to many of the major disasters of the past ten years, including the 1995 terrorist bombing at the Oklahoma City federal building, the bombing of the US embassy at Nairobi, Kenya, in 1998, and the earthquake at Izmit, Turkey, in 1999. Each member was on call twenty-four hours a day and kept a packed bag in his car at all times. All seventy-two members of the team were part of the Federal Emergency Management Agency (FEMA) and were specialists in locating live people who had been buried under tons of debris. They knew how to probe through the inherently dangerous environment of collapsed buildings.

The team had been watching the televised footage of the World Trade Towers burning in New York from Station Fourteen of the Fairfax County Fire Department in Virginia. Their unit had been preparing to go to New York to assist in recovery efforts, when news came of the Pentagon attack. They were immediately ordered to reverse course and head for Arlington.

WEDGE ONE, PENTAGON—1025 HOURS

As soon as an "all clear" was given to reenter the Pentagon, Defina and Battalion Chief Walter Hood, along with several other battalion chiefs and their crews, entered the wedge with attack lines. They found victims burned to death where they stood, killed so quickly that the bodies didn't have time to fall. Some people were melted into desk and cabinet tops. Some were propped against walls. As Defina and the others moved through the smoke, they discovered that they only had a twenty-five-minute reserve supply of air.

As they moved toward C Ring, where the plane had finally come to rest, the reserve supply dwindled to almost nothing. Some of the men took off their masks and breathed in the smoke, still moving forward.

ARLINGTON NATIONAL CEMETERY—1025 HOURS

Just south of the Pentagon, Bruce Warner and others were crossing Washington Boulevard and climbing over a fence into Arlington National Cemetery. They had been warned of another incoming aircraft and were trying to take cover. All at once, Warner heard a loud bang. He couldn't tell if it had come from the Pentagon or was a sonic boom from one of the F-16 jets now patrolling the skies.

Everything was confusion and disorientation. The stronger men helped some of the ladies over the stone fence. Once over this fence, Warner could see that they were all on high ground, making them more vulnerable, so he immediately took charge and guided everyone over the hill and out of harm's way. An F-16 now cut the air overhead, and in the distance, Warner could hear the chopping sound of a Park Police helicopter surveying the damage.

In a few moments, Warner saw a gray C-130 naval electronic warfare aircraft fly over and head west. As the alarm sounded for a second incoming plane, Warner and the others took cover behind the numerous white tombstones that surrounded them. Finally, the "all clear" was given. As Warner looked up, he noticed that the headstone he had been hiding behind was the grave of a World War II veteran.

They are protecting us still, he thought to himself.

PENTAGON COURTYARD—1030 HOURS

John Driscoll's nose burned from the overwhelming stench of jet fuel as he emerged into a crowd of hundreds gathering in the center of the courtyard. To him, it was eerie to see such a large crowd of people in complete silence; it represented a sort of mass shock.

All at once, a woman, a civilian employee, began to cry. A coworker put his arm around her as the crowd started to move through an underground service tunnel that led out of the courtyard. Driscoll took the lead. The tunnel was long and began to curve around as they made their way to the outside. They came to a steel door that blocked their exit, so they turned around and headed back into the courtyard. Driscoll then led them to the level-one tunnel on Corridor Nine.

He had become familiar with this route because it was the practice-evacuation exit for his office.

As the group entered Corridor Nine, someone yelled that there was a bomb at the entrance. This caused the crowd to turn around en masse and quickly make its way back into the courtyard. Finally, the group was told it was safe to exit through Corridor Five into the south parking lot.

As Driscoll left, he was approached by a reporter, nearly out of breath, who wanted to ask him questions. Driscoll directed him to higher-ranking officers nearby and made his exit. The last thing he wanted to do was talk to a reporter. He walked outside and saw cars bumper to bumper on the freeway, people lying all over the place, some wounded, some not. There were no ambulances, and he figured they were tied up in traffic, trying to get to the scene. One thing that would remain with him was the sight of trash and junk lying around the area. It was everywhere, some of it the result of people just throwing it on the ground to make room inside of their cars for injured bodies that needed to be evacuated fast. In the middle of the road between the north parking lot and the Potomac River, he saw an FBI agent directing traffic. A slender woman with a ponytail, she was wearing a flak vest and blue jeans. She was yelling to people to move down to the tree line, shouting that there was another plane inbound within five minutes. Like Craig Powell and Ted Anderson, Driscoll knew that it was typical of terrorists to initiate an attack, then wait for the victims to get comfortable and believe the worst was over before hitting them with a second, more devastating strike that would catch them unaware.

Driscoll headed up into the tree line and moved along the river, realizing that if a plane hit out in the open now, a lot more people would be killed. At the memorial bridge, between Arlington National Cemetery and the Lincoln Memorial, two special forces soldiers turned him away.

"The bridge is closed," one of them said flatly.

Driscoll turned and continued to move up the river along the shore. When he reached the Roosevelt Bridge, between the Iwo Jima Memorial and the Kennedy Center, he climbed up the side of it and out onto the road, then crossed over the bridge and headed for his home in Foggy Bottom. By this time, it seemed as if the whole city were evacuating.

Driscoll stopped in the center of the bridge to behold a sight that would never leave his memory as long as he lived. He saw thousands of people fleeing the city on foot, like newsreels he had seen of refugees in World War II. Over his left shoulder was the Kennedy Center for the Performing Arts; to the left of that, the thin white stiletto of the Washington Monument; closer to the river, the white marble of the Lincoln Memorial with the Jefferson Memorial in the distance. To his right and above his head loomed the massive statue of four US Marines hoisting the American flag above Iwo Jima. Below the statue and along the river were thousands of white headstones in Arlington National Cemetery. Beyond these, he could see the roof of the Pentagon with an immense black cloud of smoke rising above it, thousands of feet into the air. It was a panorama that he wished every American could see. *A painter could paint one hell of a portrait from this position,* he thought as he turned and headed for home.

WALTER REED ARMY MEDICAL CENTER—1030 HOURS

When Kevin Shaeffer reached the Walter Reed emergency room, he overheard one of the nurses say that his chances were 50 percent. He had not realized how badly burned and in shock he was. He pulled her close. "Hey . . . I'm alive," he said. "I made it out. I'm going to live!"

The nurse looked at him and replied softly, "Yes, Kevin, you are. You are going to live."

Shaeffer lay still as the doctors worked for hours on his hands. At one point, they tried unsuccessfully to pull his wedding and navy rings from his fingers. Shaeffer came up off the operating table, grabbed the rings, and pulled them off himself, then handed them to the attending doctor.

"Now you can go ahead," he said. "Do what you have to do to save my life."

After this, Shaeffer passed out.

TRIAGE AREA, SOUTH LAWN, PENTAGON—1030 HOURS

On the scorched remains of the lawn outside the Pentagon, Roxane Cruz-Cortez continued to search for April Gallop and her baby. By now, one whole side of her body was beginning to hurt. With each step, the pain became more intense. She realized that this was where the wall had pinned her to the floor. Throughout the escape, she had seemingly felt nothing. Now, she was starting to feel the pain. Her chest and ribs felt as if they were being squeezed together in a vise. She tried to catch her breath.

"Are you OK?" a voice said. Cruz-Cortez felt a hand gently touch her arm. It was an air force officer, a lieutenant colonel.

"Have you seen a woman and a baby?" Cruz-Cortez asked.

"Yeah, I saw them putting her into an ambulance," the man said. Cruz-Cortez was relieved to hear this. "You need to sit down," the officer told her.

Cruz-Cortez pulled away. "I have to go back," she said.

"You're not going anywhere," the officer told her. "You need to see a medic." The officer asked her what happened, and Cruz-Cortez told him about the wall collapsing on her, but she continued to be stubborn and tried to go back toward the building. At this point, the officer took her to the side and sat her down. He began talking to her to try to keep her mind off the pain, but Cruz-Cortez was having trouble focusing on anything at all, much less what the air force officer was saying to her.

A few moments later, the officer and an army staff sergeant commandeered a white security vehicle and put Cruz-Cortez inside. They directed the driver to head for Arlington Hospital. When they reached the bridge, a police officer stopped them.

"The bridge is closed. There's been a bomb threat."

"We've got a wounded soldier here," the driver told him.

"I'm sorry, you can't go over," the officer told him. The army staff sergeant struggled to find a quick solution, then looked at the driver. "Take her to Fort Myer," he said, and the driver turned the car around.

By this time, cars and other vehicles were everywhere, blocking all exits and roads. The driver found himself trapped with no way out, so he pulled the vehicle up on the shoulder and began driving at high speed through the narrow space. Cruz-Cortez listened as a lady in the passenger seat began yelling at the driver in Spanish to slow down. The driver responded in Spanish that he had no choice; he had to get to the hospital. Understanding the dialogue, Cruz-Cortez came out of her pain and rose up, speaking in Spanish.

"Sir, please be careful; I'll be alright," she said. "Just take your time."

In an impromptu triage area set up in the parking lot by the south entrance, Sheila Moody heard someone cry her name. She turned to see Louise Kurtz, seated in the back of a police car. Kurtz jumped out of the car, ran over to Moody, and sat down next to her. In reality, she was able to move only because, like Kevin Shaeffer and Brian Birdwell, her nerve endings had been all but burned away, and she simply couldn't feel the incredible physical damage that had been done to her. In truth, she and her supervisor, Juan Cruz-Santiago, would be the worst of the burn victims in the attack.

Moody struggled to breathe as she sat next to Kurtz. Paramedics moved among the injured, assessing who should be evacuated first. As they passed Kurtz, she called out that she needed help. It was then that Moody got a good look at her friend. She had literally been baked alive. Her original facial features were gone, her skin twisted and contorted, her eyelashes and eyebrows burned away. A short time later, both women were evacuated to local hospitals.

WEDGE ONE, PENTAGON—1030 HOURS

Ed Plaugher's Arlington firefighters were running out of oxygen. The bulk of his entire department was inside the building, many of them trying to put out the stubborn rooftop blaze that refused to be contained. For the past half hour, he had been trying to find fresh oxygen cylinders for his men. He was angry that the equipment hadn't been updated to include advanced respirators that didn't require air tanks, but Congress had not yet come through with the requested funds.

Near the west wall, Alan Wallace worked to salvage equipment from the burned hulk of Truck 61. As he attempted to retrieve breathing apparatus, he realized that he could not extend his left arm. He couldn't reach forward, and he couldn't reach inside the compartment. He quickly grabbed a wrench with his left hand and beat on the apparatus until it came off; then he went over and sat down. It had now been almost an hour since the plane had hit the building. Dennis Gilroy walked over to Wallace, who was sitting next to Skipper.

"Can you go on, Al?" he said.

Wallace was sucking air. "I can't catch my breath," he said, wheezing. "There's something wrong with my arms too. I can't move 'em, and my shoulder's screwed up."

Wallace sat on the ground, exhausted, as he watched Defina's big fire trucks from National pump a thousand gallons of water and foam per minute onto the blaze. These trucks were now plugged into the massive forty-eight-inch hydrant that nearly circled the Pentagon. The fire was beginning to come under control. Gilroy called an EMS crew to tend to Wallace and Skipper, and they were taken to one of the triage areas being set up.

EAST WALL, PENTAGON—1030 HOURS

Returning from the hospital where he had been treated for minor cuts and bruises and smoke inhalation, Lincoln Leibner hitched a ride with some doctors, eventually arriving at his office in the Executive Support Center on the east side of the Pentagon. One of his coworkers walked up to him.

"The secretary wants to know what hit the building," one of them said, referring to Secretary of Defense Rumsfeld. "He doesn't know if it was a cruise missile or a small plane."

"Where's the secretary?" Leibner asked them. This was something he was going to tell Rumsfeld about himself, in person.

NATIONAL MILITARY COMMAND CENTER, PENTAGON—1033 HOURS

After helping to evacuate the wounded for over half an hour, Secretary of Defense Donald Rumsfeld reached the NMCC, where a teleconference was in progress between the president, the vice president, and the chairman of the Joint Chiefs of Staff. Reports that there were several unaccounted-for planes inbound for Washington were coming in at a rapid pace. Rumsfeld placed the nation on Force Protection Condition Delta, a heightened national security level involving the closing of all national borders, military control of the skies, and many other measures to be implemented by both military and civilian law enforcement.

Approximately ten minutes earlier, President Bush, on board Air Force One en route to Offutt Air Force Base in Nebraska, had issued a general order to all US fighter jets to shoot down any aircraft deemed to be controlled by terrorists. Sorties were now being flown nationwide.

Within fifteen minutes of the attack on the Pentagon, intelligence analysts with the National Security Agency had picked up a phone call via secure satellite from one of Osama bin Laden's terrorist camps in Afghanistan to a phone number somewhere in the former Soviet Republic of Georgia. The analysts listened carefully as the caller relayed that he had heard "good news" concerning events in the West and indicated that there was "more to come." NSA officials surmised that the caller was receiving American media reports detailing the strikes from satellite television and/or radio as events occurred and relaying them to fellow terrorists in that part of the world.

At the same time as this was happening, Rumsfeld saw Major Lincoln Leibner walk into the room, looking as if he had been in a firefight, his uniform blackened and cut up. Leibner walked up to Rumsfeld and saluted.

"It was a passenger jet, sir, and it didn't crash into the building," he said with a voice masking rage. "It was flown into it." This was the first time Rumsfeld had heard anything about a civilian jetliner being the cause of the attack.

Around noon, Rumsfeld was told of the transmissions picked up by the NSA. He knew that they did not provide hard evidence against Bin Laden, even though the caller was identified as a known al-Qaeda operative. In less than an hour, though, the CIA had collected the passenger manifests for all four aircraft used in the attacks. The information started rolling in, hard and fast.

At least three of the hijackers were linked to al-Qaeda. Of the three, Nawaf al-Hazmi (alias Rabia al-Makki) and another well-known al-Qaeda operative, Khalid al-Mihdhar, both Saudis, had been aboard American Airlines Flight 77. Both were known to have fought on the side of the Bosnian Muslims during the Balkan Civil War of 1995, and it was believed they had fought alongside Chechen rebels in Grozny in 1998, subsequently attempting to reenter Chechnya only the year before but being turned away at the border. A short time after this, both of them showed up in Bin Laden's training camps in Afghanistan. Their next appearance was in Malaysia in 2000, where they attended the Kuala Lumpur summit. Intelligence reports would later indicate that this meeting was where the final plans for something called the "planes" operation were finalized. In addition to all of this, both of them had connections to Abd al Rahim al Nashiri, the mastermind of the attack on the USS *Cole* in the port of Aden in 2000.

There was more. For several years prior to September 11, al-Hazmi and al-Mihdhar had traveled back and forth from Afghanistan to Indonesia to the United States using US visas obtained through the Saudi Arabian consulate. The CIA knew them well and had been tracking their movements as far back as the beginning of the Clinton administration. After the US used cruise missiles to destroy an al-Qaeda training camp near Khowst in 1998, Bin Laden opened a new camp in an abandoned Russian copper mine near Mes Aynak.

Al-Hazmi, his brother Salem, and al-Mihdhar were some of the first terrorists trained at this new camp, which had been opened with the approval and direct support of the Taliban, the fundamentalist Islamic government of Afghanistan. Upon being told of all this, Rumsfeld knew that Bin Laden was most likely the man behind the attacks and that he was being protected by the Taliban. The decision of where to strike first would not be a difficult one. He immediately ordered preliminary plans to be drawn up for review by the president and the Joint Chiefs centered on Afghanistan. He then asked someone to get him any available intelligence on involvement by Iraqi president Saddam Hussein. When the director asked him what the intensity of the strike plans should be, Rumsfeld looked at the man with a cold stare.

"Go massive," he said.

WEDGE ONE, PENTAGON—1040 HOURS

Deep inside Wedge One, Staff Sergeant Williams, part of a seven-member squad from a combat engineer battalion based at nearby Fort Belvoir, was searching through the debris for survivors. The heat had burned everything in sight, and there was little hope now of finding anyone alive. Due to the intensity of the heat, they could not remain in any one area for more than twenty minutes at a time. The metal on the floor was so hot, it would cause first- and second-degree burns just from touching it.

Working under halogen lights in the blackness, Williams and his team used wooden beams to shore up the unstable ceiling and handsaws to cut through the surrounding concrete. They moved at a slow pace until they came upon three victims. Williams recognized one of them as the husband of one of his coworkers. As he turned to go back out, his eye caught something on the second floor above. Right next to where the plane had cut through a section of the wedge was a stool with a Bible lying on top of it. Nothing around this stool was burned, and the floor was seemingly suspended in thin air.

Williams did not consider himself a religious man, and he knew what other people would say about this. Some would claim it was divine revelation, others that it was concocted, but Williams had to admit what he saw was inexplicable.

BIRDWELL HOME, LORTON, VIRGINIA—1045 HOURS

A distraught Mel Birdwell heard the phone ring. Picking it up, she heard a voice tell her that her husband was still alive. It was the husband of Natalie Ogletree, the woman who sat and prayed with Brian in a burned-out corridor of the Pentagon. The man told Mel that Brian had been taken by ambulance to Georgetown University Medical Center. Mel thanked him, grabbed her son, and left immediately.

TRIAGE AREA, WEST WALL, PENTAGON—1045 HOURS

When Ben Starnes returned to the triage area, he could see that all of the aid workers were now massed behind the concrete barriers of the highway. At this point, it seemed that anyone with a bullhorn was in charge. A DC fireman walked along, shouting through the contraption at the assembled crowd.

"I need all medical personnel to gather round," he said.

Starnes looked at the man and then shouted back, "Everyone here is medical personnel! You need to clarify whether you want doctors, nurses, medics, EMTs, rescue workers, or corpsmen."

The man looked at Starnes for a moment as if shrugging off an insult, then began pointing to different areas where he wanted people to go. Starnes walked to the designated area for doctors. As he walked along, he counted almost thirty doctors, mostly military, from all branches of the armed services, as well as a few civilians.

One of the local ER physicians, a man named Casey Jason, grabbed a bullhorn and tried to gain control of the situation. He said that he wanted a pool of doctors, a pool of nurses, and so on. As patients were evacuated, he wanted to assign one doctor and one nurse to each patient. Starnes heard this and walked up to him. "No, no, no, you can't do that," he said, pulling Jason to the side. He told him who he was and explained his level of experience. He then advised him to form between four and five teams and have them set up aid stations with the exclusion of burn patients. Starnes was able to convince Jason that a team approach was the only rational way to do things. It was something he had learned from hard experience.

Jason handed the bullhorn to Starnes, who took control. He asked the crowd of doctors to raise their hands if they were ATLS (Advanced Trauma Life Support) or ACLS (Advanced Cardiovascular Life Support). Seven individuals raised their hands, and he asked them to come forward. One of these was an ENT surgeon from the navy. Injuries from burns were a common occurrence aboard aircraft carriers and other naval vessels, and navy ENTs were trained to pay particular attention to these kinds of wounds. Starnes could see that what he had on his hands was barely containable chaos. People were milling around, wondering what to do and scared out of their wits that another plane was going to drop out of the sky at any moment. The frequent false alarms didn't help. As he scanned the crowd, he saw Lieutenant Colonel Rick Bonnecarrere, a plastic surgeon and an old friend, and Lieutenant Colonel Larry Lepler, a pulmonary critical-care doctor. He knew that Bonnecarrere and Lepler were good men, so he walked up to them individually and made them team leaders. He then walked through the crowd, assigning doctors and nurses to various teams.

After the teams were formed, Starnes told each leader and his individual group to gather supplies and set up in separate areas that Starnes designated by pointing at them with his finger. He also assigned an additional physician to each team, based on level of experience, along with an ICU nurse and a medic. The problem facing him was too many people and no organization, so he asked the members of each team to go to their areas and wait until they were called upon to help. He began using color designations to separate the injured into zones indicating severity of injuries, red being the most serious.

Starnes designated the site where the triage units were set up as the "Red Zone" to differentiate it from the masses of personnel and supplies that were flooding the disaster site. Once the five teams were in place, Starnes figured they would be able to adequately tackle patient flow despite the obstacles between them and the west wall of the Pentagon. They would act like a spider's web to catch patients as they were brought out and separate them by severity of injury.

Starnes searched for and found a Walter Reed National Military Medical Center pharmacist and set him up in a central area where he controlled all drugs to be administered. Colonel Oster was by now continuously on his cell phone in contact with Goff in the command suite at Walter Reed. He asked what narcotics were needed, and Starnes told him there was the potential for a maximum of three hundred and fifty casualties and that he would need approximately one thousand milligrams of morphine and ten thousand milligrams of Demerol. Oster repeated this into his phone.

Starnes saw a representative from the District of Columbia Fire Department and told him that the concrete barriers that were obstructing the area would have to be taken down. Within thirty minutes, a truck with a jackhammer had arrived to remove the barriers. Starnes marveled at the support and response he was getting from people. He had never seen anything like it. Anytime he asked for something, it was there.

He maintained constant radio contact with DC Fire and Command and Control. Starnes requested an adequate power supply, food, water, blankets, and porta-potties as well as more tents to cover aid workers and patients from the weather. Starnes asked two orthopedic surgeons to set up what was called a GP medium for a morgue, away from the patient care areas and closed off to cameras and the media.

"Soon we're going to have bodies," he told them as he stared at the Pentagon. Sadly, he and the other surgeons would sit idle throughout much of the rest of the day. The morgue would see most of the business.

During the setup of the Red Zone, Starnes had occasionally glanced at the west wall with its mass of demolished concrete crumbled into a wide crevice torn into its side. He saw the giant lime-green fire trucks pouring water onto the site, but the one vehicle that had caught his attention when he first stepped off the bus was the red fire truck with the number "61" on the side, dwarfed by the lime-green trucks and sitting right next to the impact site, its rear end on fire. Now, walking among the patients, he noticed one firefighter sitting off to himself on a bench with a helmet next to him, the number "61" on the front. It was Alan Wallace, eating a piece of fruit, his back and arms bandaged.

Starnes approached Wallace. "I saw your fire truck," he said.

Wallace slowly raised his head and looked up at him. "It saved our lives," he said. Wallace took a breath of oxygen from a nearby tank and stared off at the burned shell of the firehouse. "I can't understand why we weren't all cut to pieces," he said, his voice trailing off and his hand reaching down for another breath of oxygen. "I just never expected it." He looked up at Starnes. "We didn't have time to think about anything. That damn plane came out of nowhere."

Starnes could see Wallace's smoke-blackened face and tired eyes, but his soul was strong and unyielding, and he occasionally flashed a smile. The American spirit was still within him, and it was far from dead.

Heartened by this, Starnes turned and went back to work. As he walked away, he heard Wallace call to him.

"Doc," he said, "I was inside the Pentagon, spraying my fire extinguisher. I heard a woman call to me, but I couldn't see her. They pulled me out of there so fast, I couldn't . . . You think she made it out?"

Starnes looked at him but didn't have an answer. Not wanting to speculate but figuring the woman could very well be dead, he shook his head. "I don't know," he said as he turned and walked back to the triage tent.

As Starnes approached the tent, he heard shouts and looked back toward Wallace. Two soldiers, a man and a woman with minor burns to their faces and hands, approached Wallace. They were Sean Boger and Jackie Kidd, the two air controllers who had been in the tower of the firehouse and had escaped alive. Wallace saw them and let out a sound akin to a laugh and a cry at the same time. Starnes saw them hug each other. He wondered how many other scenes like this were being played out everywhere. His heart was in his throat.

Just then, the naval ENT surgeon came running up to him.

"The towers are gone!" he said.

Starnes turned and looked straight at him. "What did you say?"

"I said the towers, the World Trade Center towers, they're gone!"

"You mean the tops of the towers are gone," Starnes said, trying to reassure himself.

"No, man," he said. "Both the towers, the north and the south, are gone. They've completely collapsed into the ground! They're estimating between twenty and forty thousand dead!"

Starnes looked back at the fire trucks shooting water onto the Pentagon. He couldn't believe what the ENT was saying. It had to be a rumor. He thought back to a night, more than ten years before, when he stood on top of the north tower of the World Trade Center, the wind feeling like it was going to pick him up and carry him away. He remembered looking over the side and the terrifying feeling it gave him. Now, standing on level ground, he couldn't fathom what those people in New York were going through. It was all of man's fears combined into one single horror—fear of heights, fear of fire, fear of loud noises, fear of smothering in closed spaces—all coming at you at once. All Starnes could do was hang his head.

HIGHWAY 27 OVERPASS—1100 HOURS

As the triage was being set up on Washington Boulevard, Noel Sepulveda was standing on top of the tunnel over Highway 27 with a bullhorn. He was organizing the medical units by color, just as Starnes was doing down the road. All at once, he heard a voice call to him. "Sergeant, get over here!" He looked around to see air force surgeon general Carlton beckoning to him.

Damn, I'm in trouble now, Sepulveda thought to himself as he approached the general.

"Sergeant, what the hell are you doing?" Carlton asked. Sepulveda explained that he was using the color-coded system for triage.

"Where did you learn that?"

"I was a medic in Vietnam," Sepulveda replied, at which point Carlton made him the on-site medical commander.

As the day wore on, Sepulveda felt pressure in the back of his head getting worse. At times, his eyes couldn't focus on anything. When he rubbed the back of his head, he could feel a large bump. He was unaware that the pressure wave from the explosion of American Airlines Flight 77, which had thrown his head into the light pole, had created a subdural hematoma, a ruptured blood vessel that all morning long had been leaking a small amount of blood into his brain.

Still, he would remain on-site, helping victims and first responders for several days.

MARINE BARRACKS, HENDERSON HALL—1100 HOURS

After being given morphine intravenously, John Yates was taken to a triage area at the marine barracks at Henderson Hall. More IVs were started on him, and he was placed on a stretcher. As he looked up, a white-haired navy chaplain stood next to him. Yates gave him his wife's name and phone number and asked him to call her. Soon, he would be placed in an ambulance and taken to the burn unit at Arlington Hospital.

When Ellen Yates received word that her husband had been wounded, she immediately called the Pentagon, but the line was dead.

She then tried his cell phone and pager but came up empty. Every line of communication was down. Ellen Yates was a firm believer in the hand of fate, that everything happens for a reason, so she somehow knew that her husband was OK and that they would both make it through this ordeal. She calmed herself and tried to go about her routine, attempting to contact her husband at intervals.

TRIAGE AREA, SOUTH LAWN, PENTAGON—1130 HOURS

After delivering Marilyn Wills to Arlington Hospital, Lieutenant Colonel Ed Lucci and the nurses had hitched a ride with the Arlington ambulance crew back to the Pentagon. The driver radioed to his headquarters that his ambulance had been "requisitioned" and diverted by the Department of Defense, which in this case meant Lucci.

When they arrived near the west wall, Lucci noticed gurneys and medical supplies in the open field near the overpass, but most of the medical personnel were underneath the overpass. When he reached them, they told him that there had been another plane scare, and they moved under the overpass for protection. Lucci looked and saw a special forces medic standing nearby who agreed to go into the courtyard of the Pentagon, where Lucci was sure most of the critical patients would be.

Catching a ride on another ambulance that was headed through one of the tunnels into the courtyard, Lucci and the medic arrived to find chaos, with no one really knowing what was going on. They walked into the courtyard and saw several hundred people but no wounded and no casualties. Lucci looked around but couldn't identify one single patient. This was odd. He had to find out what was going on. There were medical personnel and equipment scattered all over the yard and a tall air force officer who had a crowd of people gathered around him. Lucci couldn't tell his rank, but he appeared to be in charge. He walked up to the officer and offered his help. The man smiled at him.

"Great, I'm putting you in charge of the medical operations in here. You take your orders from the fire chief over there," he said, pointing to a man standing opposite him. He then gave Lucci a radio. "I've got to get over to the Emergency Operations Center," he said, and left. Lucci later identified the man as the air force surgeon general, Major General Carlton.

Lucci began to set up the triage area just as Starnes had done on the outside, with "immediate," "delayed," "minimal," and "expectant" areas. The "expectant" area was right next to the "immediate" area, so they moved this away to a stage that had been set up. Lucci didn't want living patients seeing badly burned patients and corpses, which he knew the firefighters would eventually bring out of the building.

As time wore on, Lucci began to sense that there would be no more patients coming out. Everyone still inside the building now was either dead or trapped in the rubble, waiting and hoping someone would find them. Firefighters emerging from inside the rings told him of the sickening heat and the body parts scattered in isolated pockets—so many burned and charred pieces that in some cases it was difficult to tell debris from human remains.

Lucci stood in the courtyard, preparing the area for casualties as a makeshift morgue was set up. The army was flying in its special morgue unit from Puerto Rico, the Army Reserve 311th Quartermaster Company, also known as the Mortuary Affairs unit. There was no doubt now that most of what would be brought out of the Pentagon at this stage would be dead bodies.

While this was going on, the Arlington Fire Department massed on the outside of the west wall, preparing to enter through the blast site. Several attack teams entered and quickly realized that the fire raging inside was burning so hot that no human being could survive long enough for them to make a difference. As soon as they were in, they were back outside again. Soon, however, some units made it around the worst of the fires and proceeded toward the courtyard.

Once the fires were relatively under control, the firefighters who entered the building encountered sights of the most horrific sort—battlefield-type casualties known only to war veterans who recalled them continuously in their dreams, sights that these firemen would not forget for the rest of their lives. Numerous bodies littered the floor, burned into stiff, black contortions, their arms outstretched. One woman was sitting in her chair, dead, her hands melted into her face. Most floors were under an inch of water, and the combination of smoke, steam, fire, and burning debris and flesh was almost more than any of the men could take, yet they pressed on. No one saw any evidence of survivors, and witnesses would later recall feeling that nothing could live through that kind of heat.

Some hallways were so full of smoke that the firemen couldn't see each other, let alone their own hands and feet. Other hallways were clear but their fire alarms still sounding. Every once in a while, the firemen would see an office, its contents untouched, keys still on the desk, photos of loved ones perched on credenzas without a scratch. One had a newspaper still on the desk with a cup of coffee next to it but no evidence of a human being.

One firefighter came across a golf cart that was still running. He guessed that someone must have tried to use it to escape the blaze, but where this person was now was anyone's guess. He just hoped whoever it was had survived.

Inside the courtyard, Ed Lucci waited for bodies to be brought out, but nothing was forthcoming. He was hearing reports that firefighters were sweeping the rings for survivors but that the going was slow. All around him, he could see debris and body parts from the plane, tagged with FBI identification labels. The fact that this site had become a crime scene and an emergency area at the same time was causing problems everywhere. The FBI didn't want anything touched, and they were getting in the way of the fire companies and rescue workers who were just trying to do their jobs.

WEDGE ONE, PENTAGON—1300 HOURS

Carlton Burkhammer peered through the bus window at the demolished west wall. He had seen this type of structural collapse many times. He and his teammates with Fairfax County Search and Rescue were used to this sort of thing. It was their specialty. Surveying the damage, they were heartened by the prospect of "live finds."

Earlier this morning, Burkhammer had trouble paging the other members of the team, who had been advised to gather at Station Eighteen. A bus was ready and waiting with a police escort at around twelve o'clock, but it took an hour before everyone was assembled and on their way.

When they finally got inside, things turned out to be far worse than expected. The building was highly unstable, and the concern was that more of the wedge would collapse. They were unaware of the structural upgrades that had been made to this section.

Burkhammer sent in two reconnaissance teams, one to the left of the crash site and one to the right, both accompanied by search dogs. The job of these teams was to locate possible survivors beneath the rubble and then radio for backup when someone was located. The members were outfitted in "flash gear," full plastic face shields, oxygen, and powerful searchlights mounted on their helmets to see in the dark.

It was only a matter of minutes before the teams came upon bodies. They would roll them over to make sure they were dead, but after coming across nothing but corpses and scattered remains, after some time, they became disheartened. The initial blast appeared to have killed everyone within a specified swath. Outside this "death alley," most of the survivors had already been evacuated or made their way to safety on their own power.

As he moved through Wedge One with his team, it didn't take Burkhammer long to realize that the left side of the building was more unstable than the right, where the team could gain access to all five floors. As he walked, Burkhammer passed an exposed steel beam that read "May 2000," the mark of the ironworker indicating recent upgrades. As he surveyed the scene, he could also see how the plane had entered the building and how it had initially moved through the first and second floors. The skeleton of the fuselage was still there, tangled up in a twisted cage of metal and debris.

The heat and smoke in this section were nearly unbearable, even with protective gear. In a few moments, one of Burkhammer's men collapsed from dehydration and had to be carried out. The worst thing was that they were not finding any survivors. He could see the dejected look on the men's faces. A search dog let out a low whimper. These dogs were trained to find people by using their heightened sense of hearing and smell, but in here, it was useless. The dogs were as depressed as the men.

TRIAGE AREA, WEST WALL, PENTAGON—1300 HOURS

As Ben Starnes looked across the highway and beyond, he could see people approaching from every direction, walking to the Pentagon from their homes and surrounding shops and gas stations. It reminded him of stories he had heard as a child about the Amish who would walk miles to help a fellow farmer when his barn caught fire. People were now walking up to Starnes, asking what they could do. Without hesitation, he would give them each a task to accomplish.

By early afternoon, there were so many people arriving on the scene to help that Starnes had to direct them to stay clear of the area. He kept most of them in reserve as litter-bearers to carry patients when the time came, but hardly any victims were ever brought out. As the afternoon wore on, he realized that there were two kinds of people in this place—the living and the dead, and not much in between. This was something that doctors like him had a hard time with because it rendered them almost useless. He remembered something Jim Goff had said to him about war: Rule number one is that in war, people die. Rule number two is that doctors can't change rule number one.

As Starnes stood thinking, he looked up and saw a woman walk into the area, coughing, her face blackened. She walked up and sat down in one of the chairs. She was cleaned up, given oxygen, and wrapped in a blanket. She was silent for a moment. Then Starnes heard her speak.

"I was inside," she said. "I couldn't see anything, but I heard this clicking noise and then a man's voice. He told me to walk toward him, but I couldn't see him, but I could hear this clicking noise, and I walked toward it. I thought I was dead, and then I was outside."

Starnes suspected that this was the woman Alan Wallace had asked him about. She had been saved by the noise of a fire extinguisher. So many others, unable to see, on this day would be saved by a voice or a noise of some kind.

Starnes watched as supplies and food were unloaded along with a box full of Bibles outside the main tent. Over to one side was a make-shift pharmacy with two pharmacists and a cardboard sign that read "Pharmacy." This was a major accomplishment. All drugs were now controlled in a central location. Evacuation routes had been established, and some three hundred yards away were a group of approximately six helicopters waiting to evacuate patients. By early afternoon, every-thing had been coordinated and they were ready for their first patient, but none came. In the distance, Starnes saw water being poured onto the blaze and firefighters coming in and out of the building. There just had to be wounded people somewhere. Maybe they were being evacu-ated into the courtyard or to other areas of the building, but with the cell phones down in DC and northern Virginia and poor communica-tion otherwise, he had no way of knowing.

More news continued to come in about New York, and each report was even more grim than the one before. Information also came in about the second-plane scare they had endured, and the news was that this airliner had in fact been shot down over Pennsylvania by US fighter jets. A loud explosion and mushroom cloud of smoke had been observed somewhere in the countryside eighty miles southeast of Pittsburgh. Only later would they discover that the passengers aboard this plane, United Airlines Flight 93, had made a valiant stand against the terrorists and sacrificed their lives to keep the plane from crashing into another target. One of the passengers who charged the terrorists was Jeremy Glick. His parents lived next to Starnes's sister-in-law in New Jersey.

Starnes continued to get word sporadically that patients would be forthcoming, but after several hours, nothing had happened. As he stood there thinking, he realized that with both towers collapsing, the entire south part of Manhattan would likely be reduced to rubble or at least closed down for several weeks. Sloan Kettering hospital, where his father was to undergo his surgery the next week, would also likely be closed or without power for some time. His father would have to wait.

PENTAGON COURTYARD—1310 HOURS

After watching John Yates being loaded into an ambulance and taken away, Phil McNair had wandered off through one of the corridors and out into one of the triage areas. People were talking to McNair, but when he responded, they just looked at him, puzzled. McNair soon realized that he was talking, but the words weren't coming out right.

His lungs and throat had been damaged from smoke inhalation. Some nurses sat him down and began cutting some of his uniform off and inserting an IV.

"I'm OK," McNair said. "I just need some oxygen." His words were no more than a low wheeze.

"Look, Colonel," one of them said. "You've been inside breathing God knows what. You could die. Now, just let us do our job."

McNair was soon carried to Arlington Hospital, where a crisis tag was placed on him because his carbon monoxide level was nearly seven times above normal. Meanwhile, at their home in Stafford, Virginia, Nancy McNair had watched the images on TV and had clearly seen the helipad and the entrance of the airplane. She knew that her husband worked right where the plane had entered, and she was almost beside herself with panic, thinking he was surely dead.

ARLINGTON HOSPITAL—1315 HOURS

When they arrived at the burn unit of Arlington Hospital, paramedics carried John Yates inside. They cut off his watch, his wedding ring, and his claddagh, the traditional Irish friendship/love ring his wife had given him. Then they proceeded to cut his bracelets off. A nurse walked up to him and took hold of his arm. "I'm going to put a catheter in, Mr. Yates," she said. "I'm sorry, but it's going to hurt." As she said this, Yates passed out. He would not regain consciousness for two days.

Meanwhile, Ellen Yates listened to a navy chaplain as he told her, over the phone, about her husband. "I just want to tell you that I've prayed with your husband, John," he said.

"Is he alive?" she asked.

"I just want you to know that I've prayed with him."

"That's good. Is he alive?" Ellen Yates demanded.

The chaplain told her that he really didn't know; that he had last seen her husband at the Navy Annex. Ellen hung up the phone and continued working. She was from a small town in the Adirondack Mountains of New York and was a very direct and straightforward person. She didn't like being led "down the primrose path." Before long, another call came in for her.

"Ellen Yates?"

"Yes."

"Your husband is here at Arlington Hospital."

"What's wrong with him?"

"We're still assessing him," the nurse said.

"What's wrong with him?" Ellen Yates asked again in a stronger voice.

"He's been severely burned," the nurse finally told her.

WALTER REED ARMY MEDICAL CENTER—1320 HOURS

In a dimly lit room with multiple phone lines hanging from the ceiling and two large television sets turned to CNN, Jim Goff stood among a group of people he didn't know well—high-ranking military people. He preferred the company of working surgeons like himself, but most of them were at the Pentagon. All elective cases had been canceled, and all cases scheduled for this day were presently being completed. Here, he was stuck in the control room with people who made the decisions but didn't do the work.

Checking around, Goff found that he currently had four rooms configured and available to take care of trauma cases that he was sure would be coming through the door at any time. The blood bank was well stocked, and an active blood drive was going on with volunteers too numerous to count. The surgical teams were organized and ready.

Initially, there had been a flurry of activity with several casualties in the ER, one man being sent to Washington Hospital Center with severe burns and another undergoing an emergent tracheostomy in the ER from burns he had received to his throat, but then there was nothing. From this point on, no one was brought in and nothing was happening. Goff wondered about Starnes and whether patients were being treated adequately in the field and whether this was the reason no one had been evacuated to the rear. He wondered if patients had been sent to hospitals other than Walter Reed. These questions weighed heavily on everyone. Television sets showed that the Pentagon was still burning, and reports indicated that the fires were too hot in many areas for the firefighters to go in. Goff knew that if no personnel could get in, no one would be coming out alive.

PENTAGON COURTYARD—1330 HOURS

Ed Lucci looked at a pile of body bags stacked against a wall and equipment scattered from one end to the other. The heat from the fires inside the building could be felt all over, and the smell of jet fuel permeated everything. Firefighters continued to go in and out through A Ring. Presently, Lucci heard glass shatter as some people threw a fire extinguisher through the window of a drug cabinet to get at the contents inside. The supplies were needed in the triage areas.

Tony Rose, Craig Powell, and Olin Sell, still wandering the area helping people, also saw this happen. "Don't break it open," Powell said. "We'll just pick it up and carry it out." With this, Powell and Sell grabbed the big cabinet and dragged it back through the building. Rose followed right behind them, pushing a gurney stacked with bandage materials.

As the three men made their way toward the triage areas, a guard blocked their path and told them to stop. Powell and Sell simply bulldozed the man, knocking him to the ground and nearly trampling him underfoot as they moved. "Get the hell out of my way," Rose shouted at the guard as the three men moved toward the courtyard.

After delivering the supplies, the three men headed back into the building. Presently, a man appeared out of nowhere and gave them a power sprayer to fight flare-ups with. Powell rigged it to work off pressure from the hydrants, but the sprayer couldn't keep up with the water flow. The three of them ran back inside to help with evacuating the bodies, most of which were now covered with white sheets.

In the courtyard, firefighters from Arlington continued to move in and out of the wedge. As a firefighter would appear, medical personnel would run up and ask him for any news regarding survivors, and the response was always the same: too much heat and a lot of scattered body parts. This went on for some time.

ARLINGTON HOSPITAL—1400 HOURS

Ellen Yates approached the nurse at the station. "Which room is John Yates in?" she asked firmly. It seemed like hours since she had last heard about her husband, and she was in no mood for small talk. The nurse pointed to a room along the hall.

Inside this room, John Yates lay unconscious, his head and neck swollen to the size of a basketball, his body wrapped from head to toe in bandages. He dreamed that he was being taken by ambulance to a baseball field and then put on a helicopter and flown away.

Through the light in the doorway, Ellen Yates appeared and stared at her husband, then just as quickly marched back out to the nurses' station. "No, that's not him. I'm looking for John Yates," she said. The nurse took her gently by the arm and led her back to the room. She pointed at the patient lying in the bed.

"That's your husband," she said, "That's John Yates."

WEST WALL, PENTAGON, 1515 HOURS

Lieutenant Colonel Ted Anderson had spent much of the afternoon watching firefighters go in and out of the building and moving back and forth across the highway whenever someone shouted to get to cover because another plane was coming in. The hardest thing for Anderson to cope with at this moment was the thought that the people the burning man had been screaming about had envisioned someone coming to save them before they died and no one had come back for them! He found this very hard to deal with, and he knew it would haunt him for a long time to come.

As Anderson stood near an operations tent, a call came from inside the building. The National Military Command Center, or NMCC, the most secure part of the Pentagon, commonly known as "the tank," was taking in smoke. The NMCC was the nerve center of the Pentagon, a self-contained room from which commanders could communicate with American forces around the world, and now it was threatened. Anderson knew that the NMCC was vital to coordinating the nation's military defenses and could not be compromised without serious consequences. Carbon dioxide levels were increasing, and the internal temperature of the "tank" was rising from the heat of the fires surrounding it. This heat threatened the lives of those inside as well as the expensive computer network. There was also another problem. Due to the high level of security in this area, personnel had been ordered to hold fast. They couldn't evacuate under any circumstances, and their ventilation system was not functioning. Anderson knew the people in there had the capability to create their own oxygen. The main concern was the smoke and their inability to get away from it. They could all die quickly of smoke inhalation if something wasn't done.

After some discussion, a battalion fire chief developed a plan for a squad of his men to go in and surround the NMCC to prevent the fire from reaching it, to form a sort of cordon between the fire and the "tank," and also to report on conditions within that area of the building. The firefighters immediately gathered their hoses and equipment, checked their oxygen levels, and put their masks on. Anderson was impressed with the military-like precision that these men displayed in suiting up for a life-threatening mission. They were really soldiers themselves, not much different from him and his comrades.

As Anderson stood there watching them, one of the firefighters looked around and said, "Hey, we don't know where we're going! We need someone to take us in there."

Anderson stepped up. "I'll take you in," he said. "But we're going into a burning building. Does anyone have any gear for me? I mean, even a coat and a helmet would be much appreciated."

Another one of the firefighters looked at him. "Hey, pal, we don't bring extra gear to a fire, and you ain't gettin' ours!" Anderson gave the fireman a hard glance for just a second and then watched a wry smile come across the man's face. Anderson smiled and then started laughing along with the others. He was part of a team now!

Anderson was issued some basic gear. As he put it on, he looked at the burning building. *What have I done?* he thought to himself. He and his fellow soldiers had been prevented by the firefighters from going back into the flames to rescue his comrades. Now he was being allowed back in to save the folks in the NMCC. Nothing made sense.

Once inside, Anderson led the fire squad through a labyrinth of hallways, back corridors, and tunnels. He instinctively knew where the facility was located, and even in the midst of such destruction and confusion, he still managed to take them in the right direction. In the meantime, the personnel inside the NMCC worked feverishly to rewire their ventilation system.

Anderson and the firefighters soon reached the NMCC and found that it was more secure than they had first thought. The firefighters pinpointed the fire and radioed its exact location back to headquarters. Then they took air-quality samples and tested the oxygen levels. As a result, they determined that the NMCC personnel could remain active and secure within the "tank." As they stood there, a message came over one of the radios that another aircraft was inbound. Anderson peered past the NMCC into the darkness. Now he was caught between the fire and a possible second attack without any real protective gear on. He knew he was going to be a lucky man if he made it through this day alive.

TRIAGE AREA, WEST PARKING LOT, PENTAGON—1530 HOURS

The young lieutenant colonel looked to be career military, probably West Point, Starnes figured. He had seen and talked to this man earlier in the afternoon but couldn't remember his name. The clean, pressed shirt he had been wearing the first time he saw him was now covered with black soot. The man looked haggard and tired and stank of jet fuel just like every other survivor Starnes had seen. In fact, the smell of burned jet fuel now covered everything and everybody in the general vicinity.

Starnes listened as the man told him how he had gone into the inner courtyard through a tunnel on the south side and then come back out. "You've got no idea what it's like in there," he said, describing yellow and black body bags stacked all over the place and how he and another man had spent time trying to move some of the bodies to a more secure location. "We're going to get the bastards who did this," he said, staring away with a blank expression on his face.

Starnes could see that the man was clearly disturbed but quickly regained his composure. These professional officers had been trained for war through hypothetical situations and theories. Now, it was real.

"It's like nighttime in there," the man said. "The building is torn all to pieces, nothing left but twisted metal and crumbled concrete." As he said this, he delivered a message from inside the courtyard that Lucci needed medical supplies. The man volunteered to carry them in on his back. He told them that the new plan being discussed was to evacuate some survivors into the courtyard as opposed to the triage areas on the outside of the building. Starnes knew that in some cases the patients had to be taken to whatever site was closest, depending upon how badly they were injured, and figured it to be a good idea, especially with someone like Ed Lucci in there directing things. He knew Ed from Walter Reed and knew him to be a consummate professional.

Without further delay, Starnes and the others loaded the lieutenant colonel and another soldier up with endotracheal tubes, burn blankets, bandages, and backboards.

"You want to come with us?" he asked Starnes.

Starnes shook his head. "I'm in charge. I've got to stay out here."

The man looked at him. "What you see in there, you won't forget for the rest of your life. I know I won't," he said.

Starnes had seen enough war casualties in Kosovo and didn't need any more images in his mind. He wanted to help people who still had a chance.

"I don't need to see any dead bodies," he said.

"Alright," the man said as he headed back toward the burning building. Watching the two men fade into one of the holes, Starnes thought about the differences between those who had seen war and death up close and those who had not.

WASHINGTON METRO—1700 HOURS

After saving Jerry Henson's life, Dave Tarantino continued to help in the courtyard for several hours, assisting firefighters and doctors. Sometime in the late afternoon, he boarded the metro to go home. Sitting on the train, his uniform torn and blackened, he noticed some passengers staring at him, some of them crying. Tarantino reflected on what he had just been through. He had been a navy man most of his life, trained to deal with fire on a ship at sea, where a man couldn't run away. He had been a rescue worker in Istanbul, Turkey, right after the catastrophic earthquake of 1999, where tens of thousands of people were killed. He had seen bodies and live human beings pulled from under the rubble. He had been shot at in Haiti and trapped in disaster zones and had recently returned from nine months' duty in Iraq, but he had never been through anything like what he had just endured.

Nearby, Ted Anderson looked into the weary face of the fire chief who told him that his firefighters weren't finding any more people alive in the building. This indicated that there might not be any more survivors. Night was coming on, and fighting a fire at night was a different thing altogether. He wanted the military personnel to leave. Anderson was angry, but he was also exhausted, a scarred, hollow shell of the man he had been that morning. As he reflected on it, he was angry that the firefighters had kept him and other army personnel from rescuing those twenty people who had burned to death only inches from safety, but he also realized that these men had probably saved his life. It was a tragic irony he would spend the rest of his life trying to forget.

Anderson and an army buddy who had been with him walked away in silence and headed for the Pentagon metro. Reaching the station, they boarded the train, which was full of passengers.

Anderson looked at the faces of the riders as they stared back at him with his blackened skin and torn clothing. In the background, Anderson could hear people crying. The train was like a church during silent prayer, only here the eyes were wide open, the heads unbowed; everyone just staring at each other and saying nothing as the train pulled away.

TRIAGE AREA, PENTAGON—1800 HOURS

In one of the outside triage areas, Vic Correa watched as the Third Infantry Division honor guard arrived. He took one last look at the still-burning Pentagon, then simply turned and walked toward home. It took him a long time, but when he finally reached his house, his wife, Oretta, was shocked at the sight of him. He was completely disheveled, his uniform drenched in fuel and blood. She ran to him, and he stuck his hand out at her.

"Stop!" he said firmly. "I want to be alone."

TRIAGE AREA, WEST PARKING LOT, PENTAGON—1900 HOURS

Ben Starnes wrung his hands and gathered his things. He and the other army doctors had been informed that they were being rotated out. Fresh critical-care specialists were being brought down to relieve them. Starnes walked down Washington Boulevard and looked out at the monuments.

In the distance, he could hear fighter jets as they flew their sorties over Washington as they had been doing regularly throughout the day. He thought about the war in Kosovo, about the two dead chopper pilots he had been unable to save. September 11 had been a repeat performance. He had been trained to use his skills to save people, yet all he had done here was wait, just as he had in Kosovo. As he turned to go, he saw three helicopters appear low over Washington, two Black Hawks escorting a blue-and-white helicopter. The helicopters landed near the Washington Monument. It was Marine One. The president had come home.

V

SHADOWS

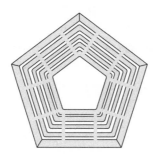

Carlton Burkhammer and firefighter Brian Moravitz were weary but focused and nowhere near ready to give up. They had both been on the job for hours, still hoping to find someone alive in the rubble. As they made their way through the wreckage, they spotted a seat, still intact, sitting on the floor. The seat turned out to be from the cockpit of American Airlines Flight 77 and was still connected to a piece of the metal floor. As they looked closer, they saw two metal boxes, each around two feet in length. Burkhammer was sure these were the plane's black boxes even though he had been told to look for orange ones. As he approached them, he could see that they were originally orange but had been burned black by the fires. Both boxes had handles on either side, and one had been ripped open. They notified the FBI by radio, and agents dispatched people from the National Transportation Safety Board to retrieve them. Burkhammer had hoped to at least find a live person in the wreckage, but finding the boxes meant they might be able to catch the people responsible for this. Both men were heartened by the find, even though when the recorders were recovered around 4:00 a.m. on Friday, September 14, they were immediately analyzed, and nothing was found of any significance.

After most of the victims had been evacuated to hospitals, Detective Don Fortunato remained on-site with technicians, sifting through debris by hand. With a flashlight, Fortunato picked up small pieces of clothing, ductwork, concrete, and now and again pieces of bone and teeth. Fortunato carried a bag with him, and when he came to personal belongings, a wristwatch, a pair of keys, or pieces of a body, he would carefully place them in a bag and keep crawling. If he spotted some remains or belongings farther away, he would start a new bag to keep them separated. Fortunato's experience as a detective helped him deal with the sheer ugliness of it all. It was hard for him to pick up the body parts of a human being like the last few pieces of an old jigsaw puzzle that had long since disappeared.

The rescue team of Tony Rose, Craig Powell, and Olin Sell was now joined by Jeff Stratton. These men continued to go in and out of the building, recovering bodies until night came on and the fire chief told them to stand down. Rose went to help in the morgue while Powell and Sell were given a ride to the metro station by Stratton. Powell continued to wonder about Captain Jack Punches, the officer they had been unable to rescue. Powell thought that maybe if he had held the ceiling a mere ten seconds longer, they would have found him.

When Kevin Shaeffer's wife, Blanca, arrived at his bedside, she could see that her husband was fighting for his life. He was covered with third-degree burns on his hands, arms, and back and had second- and third-degree burns to his head and face. He had incurred severe lung damage from breathing in a fine mist of jet fuel from the initial explosion. Over the next several days, he would fight one infection after another. He would go into cardiac arrest twice, the doctors bringing him back to life both times with electric shock. Following the second cardiac arrest, doctors doubted that he would make it through the night. They turned to his wife and advised her to have him medically discharged from the navy so that he would die on active duty, thereby securing payment of full benefits.

In the days and weeks that followed, Victor Correa wandered in a kind of shock, trying to put himself back together. He thought about his father and wished that, like him, he had joined the special forces so that he could be on the front line with a gun, killing these thugs who called themselves soldiers. Correa understood the code of war, the code of the soldier, but attacking women and children was the act of a coward. He knew that America was in for a long fight and hoped people would not soon forget what had happened this day. He knew he would never again have the luxury of forgetting.

Juan Cruz-Santiago watched as sixteen of his coworkers from the Pentagon walked into the room one by one. This was the second night they'd come to see him at the hospital. Then he noticed something strange. Each of them wore a number. Why did they have numbers on their clothes? he wondered. He looked into their faces, and they all stared back at him with the same lifeless expression.

"It can't be! You're all dead!" he screamed as he awoke in the darkness, his body bathed in sweat. He shook his wife, Veronica, pulling at her nightgown as if he were looking for something. She turned and looked into his panic-stricken face.

"Juan, what's wrong?"

"Do you have a number?" he said. "What is your number?"

At the main gate of Dover Air Force Base, Delaware, Mike Flocco stared hard into the eyes of an air force guard.

"Look, my son was at the Pentagon, and nobody's told me anything for three goddamn days!" he said. "I want to know what's going on!"

The guard was taken aback at Flocco's despair, the anguish of a father who wanted answers so that the pain of not knowing, the worst pain in the world, would stop.

"Can you fly me down there?" Flocco said. "I've been in the trades for thirty-eight years. I know things about buildings," he pleaded. "I can help. Just get me down there!"

The guard looked at him. "I . . . we can't do that, sir," he said.

"Well," Flocco said, "can you give me an escort? 'Cause if I can't fly, I'm driving—and I'll be doing it at high speed."

The guard knew he was serious. He thought for a moment, then walked around to the rear of Flocco's car and took down the license plate number.

"I'll put it out over the wire, Mr. Flocco," he said. "You're all clear."

"Alright," Flocco told him, taking down his phone number. "I'll call you at intervals," he said as he sped away.

Mike Flocco only got as far as Kent Narrows near the Chesapeake Bay Bridge that day due to gridlock and the fact that any and all approaches to Washington, DC, were closed for security reasons. He learned later that he never could have approached within ten miles of Washington, let alone the Pentagon.

Five days after the attack, the Floccos received confirmation of something they really knew on the morning of September 11. Their only son was gone.

In a hospital bed two days after the attack, Marilyn Wills woke up to find her husband, Kirk, at her bedside. She couldn't speak. Her lungs had been badly burned. Kirk gave her a pen and paper, and she wrote some words. "Where's Marian? Where's Regina?" Wills looked wide-eyed at her husband. She glanced around and could see that she was strapped to the bed, her body bandaged from the burns. He just shook his head, then began to relate what had happened.

The doctors and her husband knew that Marian Serva was dead but had instructed him not to tell her. On Friday, he finally told her that her friend was gone. Wills took the news as poorly as expected. Why had she been spared and not Marian? Who would Marian's young daughter have to depend on now? In her mind, Wills could see the two standing together, smiles on their faces, happy.

"Where are my girls?" she said. "I want to see my girls!"

Shortly thereafter, Portia and Priscilla Wills were brought into a new room at Walter Reed Army Medical Center to see their mother. In the hallway outside, Ed Lucci paused to look at the woman he had saved in the middle of Washington Boulevard. Wills looked back at him with a blank stare. She didn't remember him. Lucci smiled at her and walked on.

The last thing John Yates remembered hearing before losing consciousness on September 11 was a nurse telling him that she was going to insert a catheter and that it was going to hurt. Now, he opened his eyes to see his wife, Ellen, sitting next to him. He was lying in a hospital bed, his body wrapped in clean bandages. His mind was clear now for the first time since that fateful morning. It was Thursday, September 13, and Yates had been prepped for one of many surgeries he would undergo in the coming months. The nurses had readied him to be transported to the operating room, but they were waiting for something. As Yates lay incapacitated, Ellen asked him if he wanted to speak with President Bush.

Yates stared at the light in the doorway and watched as First Lady Laura Bush walked into the room and over to Ellen. The two women hugged each other as if they were lifelong friends.

Then through the door walked George Bush. The president slowly approached the bedside, saying nothing as his hand gently touched the bedsheet. Yates could see tears in his eyes as he reached over and touched his arm, the tears expressing the sadness of a good man who had genuine empathy for other people. Yates would not remember if the president said anything that day or what his exact words were, but it didn't matter. His eyes said it all.

Throughout the next year, Yates would endure enough pain for several lifetimes. On one occasion, he underwent eight hours of surgery. He was intubated and put on a respirator because he couldn't breathe. His body was immersed in a tank of antiseptic solution and the dead skin scraped from his body in a procedure that rivaled the tortures of the Spanish Inquisition. He spelled words with his hands because he could not write or speak. At night, he thrashed around in his bed with horrible, violent nightmares. Two and a half months after September 11, he returned home, but he could not care for himself. His wife became his full-time caregiver.

Yates became depressed, and his wife began seeking psychological counseling for him. One day, Yates summoned enough strength to pick up the phone. He dialed the number for a company called Mental Health Resources in Fredericksburg, Virginia. On the line came a woman named Mary who would eventually diagnose Yates with post-traumatic stress disorder.

"No," Yates said, "that's for Vietnam vets who think they're going to die at any moment!" In the coming years, Mary would convince Yates that he indeed suffered from this condition. Slowly, she brought him back from the darkness.

Sheila Moody spent a month at Arlington Hospital, recovering from her injuries. Sleep was something she tried to avoid, as it brought on nightmares about terrorists coming to kill her. Sunny days now filled her with a sense of dread. Later, she was transferred to Walter Reed, from which one weekend she was allowed to go with her family back to Rome, New York, where the townspeople lined the road into town in the pouring rain, waving signs that said "Welcome Back" and "We love you." Seeing these people, along with the firemen and policemen from the town, people she didn't even know, showing concern for her and her family would help Moody make it through the many dark days that lay ahead.

A week after the attacks, Fort Belvoir firefighter Rusty Dodge finally received word on what had happened to his friends in New York. Joel Kanasky had been with Chief Raymond Downey arranging for water rescue training in downtown Manhattan when the north tower was hit. Upon seeing the first plane crash, Downey yelled for Kanasky to get his equipment and then made a fast run for midtown. Fifteen minutes later, after a second plane hit the south tower, Kanasky and Downey arrived at the scene and got to work just as they had hundreds of times before with Downey standing amid the chaos and taking charge. The fearless ex-marine was last seen in the lobby of the Marriott Hotel in the south tower of the World Trade Center. Kanasky, who had gone back to get his gear at RESCUE 1, was last seen entering 7 World Trade Center and had reportedly gone deep inside the structure to ride out the collapse. Both men were officially listed as missing. Miraculously, Kanasky made it out of the building, but Chief Downey was killed.

Reports were coming in of whole companies lost in the tragedy. One estimate ran as high as four hundred individual firefighters dead and many more missing. Dodge hung his head. If the reports were true, he knew it was the greatest single disaster to befall American firefighters in history. Many old friends from the 1970s worked in that downtown area, and many of them were now gone forever. Their faces flashed across his mind one after the other. It was hard for him to accept that so many of them had been killed in less than an hour. He sat in silence, remembering.

Sometime on the morning of Wednesday, September 12, rescue workers at the Pentagon pulled out the body of army major Stephen V. Long, who had succumbed to carbon monoxide poisoning. He had come to the Pentagon on this day for a simple meeting, not knowing that his life would end there. He had made it all through Grenada and the Persian Gulf War without being killed. Had fate allowed him thirty-nine years of life just so that he could play this one critical part? Did he know that his moment had come, that he had gazed upon the beauty of the earth for the last time? In the end, it didn't matter. "No greater love hath a man than that he lay down his life for his friend," the Bible says. Finding himself alive, Stephen Long chose death to save the lives of others. He had stayed true to the Ranger creed.

In the months following September 11, Major Lincoln Leibner was alert to everything and everyone around him. His mind was in combat mode, and as he had served in Bosnia and Panama, he was ready for anything. If the Pentagon could be attacked, then any place could be a target at any time. He now had the mindset almost of a medieval warrior who was wise to the potential danger surrounding him. He could no longer walk into a restaurant or a place considered "safe" and relax. He knew that even though life had improved for humankind and was more comfortable and pleasant, the same old evil that had inhabited the world since the dawn of man still lurked in the shadows.

John Driscoll finally arrived home on the evening of September 11 after having simply walked all the way from the Pentagon. When he came through the door, his wife noticed that he was covered with sweat, and his shoes were blackened and torn. As she approached him, she looked down to see one of his hands still tightly clenched around a crushed Starbucks coffee cup.

It was a bright, beautiful day as Sergeant Major Tony Rose stood in his front yard, watching a little girl wave to him on the street. The sunlight seemed to illuminate her pretty hair and dress as she smiled at him.

Then everything went dark, and Rose was suddenly back inside the Pentagon near the drain, picking the small hand up off the floor and putting it in his pocket. He sat straight up in bed, bathed in sweat. Of all the nightmares he would experience, this was the one he couldn't shake—the one that kept coming back.

In a room in the burn unit of Washington Hospital Center, Brian Birdwell lay in agony. His wife, Mel, sat by his bed, her clothes stained with his blood, her hair disheveled. She hadn't bathed in three days. The only part of her husband she could touch was his feet, so she rubbed them. His pain was so intense that he couldn't sleep, so she stayed awake with him, talking and reading the Bible. A knock came at the door, and Mel told whoever it was to come in. As she looked up, First Lady Laura Bush walked into the room and hugged her. Her smile was soft and her voice quiet and reassuring. She then turned to Brian. "I've got someone here who wants to see you," she said. As Birdwell looked up, he saw President Bush walk into the room.

"How are you doing?" he asked with a gentle smile. He told Birdwell that he was proud of him and that he was his hero. Then he came to attention and saluted him. Seeing this, Birdwell didn't know what to do. He was aware that there was no one in the US military higher than the president; therefore, protocol dictated that you always saluted him first. Birdwell could barely move, but he brought his bandaged arm up ever so slowly, the pain from burned ligaments making it difficult to get his hand to his forehead. He kept it there for a moment until the pain forced him to let go. During this time, the president stood at attention and never moved. Finally, Birdwell dropped his arm, and the president, a tear in his eye, lowered his.

In Section 64 of Arlington National Cemetery, a baby reached out and touched a cool white tombstone, running her fingers along the grooves of a name: "Patrick Dunn, CDR, US Navy."

Somewhere deep in her soul, the little girl knew that her daddy was gone. No matter how old she got, something inside would always remember his voice speaking to her on that fateful day, saying, "I love you," kissing her as she lay in her mother's womb, and then walking into the bright sunshine, never to return.

Allie Dunn cooed as she looked at the many gravestones all around and the blue sky above. Behind her was the west wall of the Pentagon. Next to her was her mother, Stephanie, who held her up and pointed her hand at the name.

"That's your daddy," she said as a tear ran down her cheek.

It had been five months since her husband had been killed, and every minute of it had been painful, but she would keep coming back here to this place as long as she was alive to let Pat know that she and Allie were alright and that they had not forgotten him.

Getting to her feet now, she put Allie in her stroller, picked out by her husband only days before he died and decorated with the Naval Academy colors of blue and gold. Wiping her eyes, she turned and quietly pushed the stroller away.

Three weeks after the attack on the Pentagon, Commander Craig Powell was informed that they had found the body of Captain Jack Punches in the rubble. He had apparently left the Navy Command Center only a few minutes before the plane crashed and had died because he was openly exposed to the fireball and the shockwave. Ironically, had he remained inside, he might have survived.

Over the next year, Commander Powell was transferred out of the Pentagon and given command of Special Boat Team Twenty based at Norfolk, Virginia. His men know him as Commander Powell, his friends as Craig, but to Sergeant Major Tony Rose and the survivors of the Navy Command Center, who crawled out of a dark hole into the light on that terrible morning, he will forever be known as "Big John."

Dave Thomas finally helped recover the body of his friend Bob Dolan, who was buried at sea with Thomas in attendance. Dolan was the best friend Thomas had ever had. He would remember his friend the way he was on that fateful morning, smiling as always—happy to be alive and serving his country. He would never be forgotten.

At a funeral service for the members of the Army Personnel Command killed during the attack, Phil McNair stood in Arlington National Cemetery, peering at the black hole on the Pentagon's west wall. All of the trees, grass, and foliage were still burned away, the scorched area providing a fitting backdrop to the preacher as he spoke. In his hand, McNair held a photo of himself and Neil Hyland drinking beer in Hawaii some years before. They were both smiling, and everyone around was happy. After the memorial service concluded, McNair walked over to Hyland's father and gave him a copy of the photo. The old man looked at it and was silent for a moment, then just stared straight ahead, never looking at McNair.

"Yep," he said softly, "that looks like Neil. That looks like my boy."

Christopher Braman and Eric Jones continued to work for several days after the attack. The work was gruesome in the extreme. Some of the bodies would leak brain matter as they were lifted and carried to the refrigeration trucks, where several chaplains of varying denominations performed last rites over them. The building was strewn with pieces of human bodies in every state that could be imagined, but they were all blessed before being loaded into the trucks. As this was being done, Braman and Jones continued to go in and out of the building. The smell of jet fuel permeated the air, so much so that they had to apply Bengay to their nostrils. Some remains they found were just a pile of vertebrae and ashes, but they were handled by the men with dignity as if they were a complete human body. In some cases, the only way to identify whether the remains were from a man or woman was by a piece of clothing or jewelry. Braman found a pelvic bone with a piece of women's underwear attached to it. Another set of remains was that of a woman who had flesh on her hands and arms up to her elbows, and then the rest of the body was a skeleton. He identified these remains as that of a woman from her painted fingernails and her engagement ring. In one section of the building, Braman found four men in a line together, one right behind the other, frozen where they died as they tried to escape.

On Thursday, September 13, 2001, Braman, working on the lawn, saw a flash of red coming from the ruins of the Pentagon, like the sudden appearance of a cardinal's wing. Looking closer, he realized it was a flag, a Marine Corps flag, fully intact and still standing on the fourth floor of the gutted Pentagon, fluttering in the breeze with everything else having fallen away from it. Braman grabbed Dan Pantaleo. "Look at that," he said, pointing up at the building. "You are going to get that flag," he said, "even if we have to stand on each other's backs to get you up there, but you are going to be the one to get it."

Pantaleo couldn't believe what he was seeing. The flag, which had been carried into battle at Tripoli, Château-Thierry, Guadalcanal, Iwo Jima, and Khe Sanh, the flag of the US Marine Corps, his Marine Corps, had survived the blast of a fuel-laden jetliner and the collapse of thousands of tons of concrete right next to it, and it was still standing and in almost pristine condition. It was the flag from Peter Murphy's office, only thirty feet from the impact site.

In no time, a cherry picker was located, and Pantaleo was hoisted up onto the exposed flooring where the flag stood. On what remained of the wall next to the flag was a clock stopped at the exact moment of the attack. On the desk nearby was a Bible, and on the floor was a giant Webster's dictionary, open in the middle. Pantaleo grabbed the flagpole and found the wooden pole seared onto its stand, so he just took the flag and the stand and climbed back into the cherry picker and was lowered to the ground. When he reached the ground, he and Braman hugged each other to the cheers of onlookers. It was a moment desperately needed by those present and by the nation itself. The next morning, it would be on the front page of the *Washington Post*.

Pantaleo walked through the crowd and handed Peter Murphy's flag to General Michael J. Williams, assistant commandant of the Marine Corps. The two saluted each other, and then the flag was presented to Murphy, who wept.

On Friday morning, Christopher Braman looked at the men around him. "Guys, I'm goin' home," he said as he turned and walked with Eric Jones toward a Red Cross tent, where both men were given clean clothes and bags to hold their uniforms. Both Braman and Jones still had the same clothes on that they were wearing on September 11, drenched in jet fuel and covered in human remains and blood. These were put into the bags, and the two men walked into an open area where a large crowd of reporters stood waiting to interview them, but the two men ignored them and kept on walking.

At some point, the two men parted, and Braman walked toward his Jeep. As he walked, he passed a grievance area set up by the Salvation Army for people with relatives who were missing or deceased. Next to one of these tents, he could see a little girl with curly hair standing next to her mother. Braman was transfixed by this little girl, unable to take his eyes off her. He found himself still staring at her as he got into his Jeep and drove home. His house was only fifteen minutes away, but he would not remember leaving the Pentagon.

When Braman arrived home, he dropped the bag containing his uniform on the front porch as his wife opened the door and threw her arms around him like Vise-Grips. The two held each other for several moments, and then he went upstairs, got into the shower, and just stood under the water, unable to get the images out of his head. His wife sat next to the shower stall the entire time and then followed him into the bedroom as he put some clothes on and lay in the bed, staring at the ceiling, his wife holding on to him for dear life.

Braman stared at the wall for several moments and then jumped up. "I gotta go!" he said. "I gotta go, hun!" His wife watched as he ran down the stairs and jumped into his car. As he put the keys in the ignition, he continued to think about that little girl he had seen near the Red Cross tent. His three girls were safe at home, but that little girl was still over there, waiting for someone to bring her daddy out. Her daddy was still inside that building, and he might still be alive! He had to go back in there and find him!

Braman drove back toward the Pentagon. As he approached the exit, thoughts of the little girl and then his three daughters raced through his mind. He stared at the empty highway and then glanced at the Pentagon, smoke still rising from the west wall in the distance. He had to go back in; he had to find that little girl's father and bring him out! As he thought this, he felt his foot slip off the accelerator. The car fell out of gear and slowed as Braman felt the emotion suddenly well up within him, paralyzing his body and filling his chest. The car coasted into an abutment and rolled to a stop, and then everything came down at once.

Braman laid his head on the steering wheel and started crying, thinking about that little girl. If only he could give her that extra day of hope she needed to believe that her daddy would be coming home to her. If only he could stop time so she wouldn't have to grow up without a father . . . "I can't tell her he won't be coming home . . . I can't tell her that!" he said to himself, and then he cried to her, "I will bring your daddy home for you. I'll bring him back to you . . ."

EPILOGUE

PHOENIX RISING

The old soldier stood at the podium and spoke of D-Day, June 6, 1944. He had been commander of the 121st Engineer Battalion of the US Army's Twenty-Ninth Division, which during the Normandy Invasion had waited for hours under continuous fire on Omaha Beach while some of the men set charges to blow up a massive Nazi fortification. He recalled that horrible day, lying there, seeing men all around him die and watching his own men accomplish their mission in the midst of a living hell.

"Dealing with combat," he told the audience, "is a question of attitude. You know there's constant danger, but you can't let the fear drive you. I knew what I had to do, what I was supposed to do, and I went about doing it."

At the end of the speech, the old soldier stepped down from the podium. He was harboring a pain in his heart worse than anything he had experienced during World War II, but he had told no one. He was a soldier. He was one of many heroes who bore his crosses in silence.

When he got home and was finally alone, retired Major General Robert R. Ploger broke down. His son Robert Ploger III and his new wife, Zandra, had been on board American Airlines Flight 77. Both had died in the attack on the Pentagon. A year later, the major general would pass away at his apartment in Ann Arbor, Michigan, a man whose heart had been broken for the last time. Glancing up at the wall that day, one of his sons would notice the huge diploma from the US Military Academy at West Point. It had been personally presented to his father in 1939 by Franklin Delano Roosevelt.

On January 25, 2002, Ben Starnes's father died of cancer. In the weeks following, Starnes would sit for long periods of time on his back porch, just staring into space. His father had been his mentor and his closest friend. To him, his dad was like those two big towers, standing strong for several decades and then gone in a flash. In the following years, Starnes would serve two tours in Iraq but would always feel as if he and the country had crossed some kind of line on September 11—a line we would never cross back over again.

Mere months after the attack on the Pentagon, Mike Flocco had walked slowly into the cavernous work site where men labored at a fever pitch to rebuild what had been destroyed on September 11, 2001. The goal of the Phoenix Project, as it was named, was to completely raise Wedges One and Two from the ashes in record time—by the stroke of midnight on September 10, 2002. This was thought impossible by most experts, as it had taken the previous Pentagon renovation team nearly four years to do what the Phoenix Project was proposing to do in less than a year's time.

A large clock was erected near the jobsite with a terminus of September 11, 2002. Workers of every type and description, of every race, ethnicity, and religion, of every trade and skill, and from every corner of the nation descended on the ruins of the west wall.

"Just give us all the ducting we need and stay out of our way," Flocco's foreman, Mark DePriest, had said to one official. And for the next year, they did just that.

For these men, no one personified the reason for this effort more than Mike Flocco, known in the union as "Floc." He was one of them, a man who had worked with his hands all of his life to support a family and build a home. He was an American and a patriot, and he wasn't ashamed of these things. Most of all, on that terrible day, he had lost his only son.

After he had been informed of Matt's death, Flocco made a call to his New Castle jobsite and asked to speak with the foreman. He had trouble talking to anyone during those dark days. "I won't be comin' in for a while," he said. "My son didn't make it." With this, he hung up the phone. That afternoon, five hundred men, mostly workers from his union and work site, arrived at the Flocco house in Brookside, Delaware, carrying forty cases of beer and fifteen gallons of whiskey. Into Mike Flocco's hands, they shoved a bag containing six hundred dollars in cash. One of them looked at him.

"Floc, we're not leaving you, man. We're here for you."

In the months to follow, Mike Flocco sat for long periods of time, drinking and listening to Willie Nelson records. He had always loved Willie Nelson. He remembered going to concerts and getting the feeling that Nelson was a simple, humble man like himself. After a while, though, Willie Nelson and the whiskey gave him no solace. The loss of a child was the worst pain he had ever endured. He felt as if he just wasn't strong enough to get through it, but then he learned of the Pentagon Phoenix Project. Maybe helping to create a proper monument to his son and his fallen comrades would ease the pain a little.

On January 16, 2002, Mike Flocco finally arrived at the Pentagon, just over four months after he had attempted to drive into Washington to find out what had happened to his boy. As his eyes scanned the open area where the old west wall had been, he could still see signs of the destruction of that day—pieces of concrete, burned and charred, small pieces of debris still lying in places. He was met by a woman named Charlotte Hartman, who quietly led him into the building.

He was getting closer now. He could feel it. Hartman held his arm as they walked together between the newly erected columns. Nearby, workers stopped what they were doing and turned to watch. Presently, the woman came to a halt in an area of bare concrete. She pulled Flocco gently to a spot in the center of the floor.

"Stand right here," she said. "This is where Matt died."

With this, she abruptly turned and left him alone. Mike Flocco looked down at the floor. He could feel his son's spirit all around him.

"I'm here, kid," he said softly. "I'm here to put this building back together for you."

In the silence, he felt the emotion well up inside. He just wanted to hug his son and tell him he loved him once more. All around him now, Mike Flocco no longer heard the sound of hammers or power tools. All was quiet. He was standing in a holy place, a place where many spirits had been taken from the earth in one terrifying instant. Somewhere he could hear Matt speaking to him, telling him to go forward, telling him to do good things; to love as many people as he could, to live life for others each and every day. It was not something he could hear with his ears or his mind. It was coming from his heart.

It was here in this place that Mike Flocco finally understood what salvation meant. Matt had been robbed of his physical life, but through his selflessness, he had been given eternal life. Mike Flocco breathed in the spirit of his son and took it with him away from this place.

All through the early months of 2002, workers on the Pentagon project put in sixteen-hour days. At the same time, on the other side of the world in Afghanistan, army Green Berets, Delta Force, navy SEALs, and army rangers hunted Osama bin Laden tirelessly over windswept mountains more than fifteen thousand feet above sea level, across barren treeless plains, through heavy snow, and into darkened caves. The clang of hammers at the Pentagon rang in unison with the bullets and shells fired from the guns of America's soldiers.

Some good men would die, like Phil DeFilipo, the superintendent of the United Sheet Metal Workers' Union, who collapsed dead of a heart attack one morning at the Pentagon jobsite, and Petty Officer First Class Neil C. Roberts, a navy SEAL, who died fighting al-Qaeda among the lonely peaks of the Hindu Kush, and Master Sergeant Jefferson Davis and his fellow Green Berets, known as Texas 12, all of whom died from friendly fire because they got too close to the enemy, and Sergeant Philip Svitak, the army ranger who was cut down by enemy fire as he rushed from his helicopter. But within a year, the crumbled west wall of the Pentagon would again rise from the ashes with every upgrade from the previous renovation, plus some new modifications.

***

On September 11, 2002, a memorial service was held in remembrance of the victims of the attack. Once again, the sky was a brilliant blue, and the sun shone down upon the newly renovated west wall of Wedge One, completed in record time by the workers of the Phoenix Project.

In the months leading up to the ceremony, Mike Flocco lived in an RV at College Park, Maryland, working long hours like everyone else. He slept at night with a navy flag draped over his small bed and during the day worked with an ex-navy sheet metal mechanic at the exact site where his son had died. Now, standing on stage with the president of the United States, Flocco understood that America, like the very earth itself, was about rebirth, about tearing down and rebuilding, and its very engine was freedom.

Relatives of the victims arrived to find a single red rose placed on each of their seats. President Bush and other officials gave short speeches. When they were finished, Mike Flocco extended his arm to shake hands with each one, the fresh tattoo of his son's name just visible past his shirtsleeve. Secretary Rumsfeld pulled Mike close and whispered in his ear: "I'm an old navy man, and we respect what you've done here."

Seated in the stands for the official unveiling were Tony Rose, Marilyn Wills, John Yates, Phil McNair, Mike Petrovich, Victor Correa, Sheila Moody, David Tarantino, Dan Pantaleo, Frank Probst, Christopher Braman, Ted Anderson, and a host of others, many of them with visible scars, some with scars hidden from view. They would never forget September 11. It would wake with them in the morning and go to sleep with them at night, and one day when their souls finally passed from this earth, they might once again see their friends.

Alan Wallace also attended the ceremony. He didn't consider himself a hero. In fact, most everyone in attendance was a hero in one way or another. It was comforting to know that all these people had responded in the way they did. He had wondered many times whether heroism was dead. Now he knew that though it may become dormant, heroism never dies, awaiting that moment when it is most needed.

As the ceremony ended, Wallace glanced at the graves in Arlington National Cemetery up on the hill, shining white in the sun just as they had on that bright morning. That graveyard was much more than a collection of pretty white stones. It was a clear and constant reminder.

As he turned to leave, he thought of something he had heard long ago, like an echo across the ages: that the price for forgetting the cost of freedom is payment in blood.

AUTHOR'S NOTES

The prologue, set on September 11, 1941, is a dramatic vignette of real events. Some of the dialogue, such as Clarke's observation that the Pentagon provided the "largest target in the world for enemy bombs" and Roosevelt's reply to him, was actually stated days later during a meeting, rather than during this trip to the site, but was included for effect. All other aspects of this story are true.

It is not the author's intention to slight General Brehon Somervell. He was in reality the driving force behind the building of the Pentagon and probably did more than anyone else to see the project through, but he was a forceful personality and not very diplomatic, and this was part of the reason he was unable to persuade FDR to see things his way. He wanted a different site for the structure, and he was entirely justified. The swamp that Roosevelt selected required an enormous amount of manpower and equipment to accomplish the task, and additional pilings had to be set to provide a stable foundation.

The description of the final moments of Aerographer's Mate Second Class Matt Flocco, USN, is based on a statement given to his father, Mike Flocco, by his superior officer, Lieutenant Nancy McKeown. According to Mr. Flocco, McKeown stated that moments after the plane hit, she heard a weak voice cry her name twice. Since it was established that Earhart died instantly from blunt force trauma and no one else was in this immediate area, this voice was surely Flocco's. As Flocco was seated behind Earhart facing away from him, the pressure wave would have knocked him to the ground. It is certain that instead of trying to get out, he attempted to save his friend first. This belief is based on the position of his body as it was found by rescuers. Classified photographs of the death scene show Flocco lying in a serene position parallel to Earhart, who lay facedown on the floor. This is also consistent with statements made to the author by Major Dan Pantaleo, USMC, who was one of the first people to see Flocco's body and who was in charge of transporting it for burial. Research was performed on how Flocco's body would have ended up with his left foot crossed over his right and his hand over his chest. If he stood up and fell down, his body would not have ended up in this position but would have been outstretched or slumped. It is certain that he straddled his friend's body, trying to get him to wake up; in the course of doing this, his head was too high above the floor, and he began to take a large amount of smoke into his lungs. He became very weak in seconds and fell to his left, ending up in the position in which he was found. The author believes this to justify the description of Flocco's final moments as depicted in this book.

The description of the hijacking of American Airlines Flight 77 was based on information contained in the *9/11 Commission Report* and the testimony of former solicitor general of the US, Theodore Olson, whose wife, Barbara, made two calls to him from the plane. Mr. Olson declined to be interviewed for this book, so all information was gleaned from the *9/11 Commission Report*, news articles, and the internet.

Mrs. Olson stated in the first call that only one pilot was nearby and in the second call indicated that there were two pilots present, subsequently asking her husband what she should tell the captain to do. These calls took place from roughly 0920 hours to 0933 hours, ending just four minutes before American Airlines Flight 77 hit the Pentagon. This, coupled with a statement given by the FBI that indicated that the "footprint" or radar signature of the aircraft showed that an experienced pilot was at the controls, suggests that pilot Charles Burlingame was in control of the aircraft until it neared Washington, at which point Hani Hanjour took over, and the captain was moved to the rear. There is no way of knowing whether the passengers organized themselves and attempted to take the plane, but the fact that they were unaware of the New York attacks at the time of Mrs. Olson's call and the fact that there were many children on board suggest that they remained calm and believed, until the final moments, that the terrorists were going to land and negotiate. In addition, the smooth movements of the plane even during the dive into the Pentagon indicate that there was no struggle inside the cockpit. The families of some of the victims insist that their loved ones would have fought the hijackers rather than let them carry out their plans.

Judging from some of the personalities on board, the author believes this is probable, but again, they knew nothing of the New York attacks or United Airlines Flight 93, and the presence of innocent children aboard likely caused them to refrain from doing anything, in the hope that everyone could be saved.

The description of the hijacking is also based on testimony given by the mother of Renee May, a flight attendant aboard American Airlines Flight 77 who contacted her mother by cell phone after the plane had been seized by terrorists.

It is the author's stated belief that the following personnel, in light of their supreme sacrifice and heroic actions above and beyond the call of duty, should rightfully be awarded the Navy Cross or Silver Star, depending upon branch of service, and in the case of Mr. Wallace and Mr. Ho'opi'i, appropriate civilian awards for exceptional bravery. It is the author's belief that Aerographer's Mate Second Class Matthew Flocco, who could have escaped to safety, sacrificed his own life in order to save the life of his friend.

Commander Craig Powell, USN
Sergeant Major Tony Rose, USA (Ret.)
Lieutenant Colonel Victor Correa, USA (Ret.)
Aerographer's Mate Second Class Matthew Flocco, USN
Commander David Tarantino, USN
Staff Sergeant Christopher Braman, USA
Lieutenant Colonel Ted Anderson, USA
Eric Jones
Alan Wallace
Lieutenant Colonel Ed Lucci
Isaac Ho'opi'i
Major Stephen V. Long

These individuals, above all others, put themselves at tremendous risk time and again to help locate and save victims of the attack, and many of them sustained injuries that still plague them. The government should do what is right by these people.

This manuscript was written using a combination of over forty different news articles, approximately seventeen interviews conducted personally by the author, and several texts, including the American Society of Civil Engineers' *Pentagon Building Performance Report* and the *9/11 Commission Report.*

When this book was started, in the summer of 2002, news articles were the only source of information. Subsequent interviews in the years 2003 and 2004 vastly supplemented the information gleaned from these articles. Half of the articles used as information sources were federal or government sponsored, which placed them in the public domain. The other half were from several major US newspapers as well as all of the major news networks. The author used these sources for information only. Direct text was not copied, with the exception of quotes that were later changed based on the personal interviews.

IN REMEMBRANCE

Paul Wesley Ambrose
Specialist Craig S. Amundson, USA
Yeoman Third Class Melissa Rose Barnes, USN
Master Sergeant Max Beilke, USA (Ret.)
Yeneneh Betru
Information Systems Technician Second Class Kris Romeo Bishundat, USN
Carrie Blagburn
Lieutenant Colonel Canfield D. Boone, USA
Mary Jane Booth
Donna Bowen
Allen Boyle
Bernard Brown II
Electronics Technician Third Class Christopher Lee Burford, USN
Captain Charles Burlingame III, USN (Ret.)
Electronics Technician Third Class Daniel Martin Caballero, USN
Sergeant First Class Jose Orlando Calderon-Olmedo, USA
Suzanne Calley
Angelene C. Carter
Sharon A. Carver
William Caswell
Sergeant First Class John J. Chada, USA (Ret.)
Rosa Maria "Rosemary" Chapa
David Charlebois
Sarah M. Clark
Julian Cooper

Asia Cottom

Lieutenant Commander Eric Allen Cranford, USN

Ada Davis

James Debeuneure

Captain Gerald Francis DeConto, USN

Diana Borrero de Padro

Rodney Dickens

Lieutenant Colonel Jerry D. Dickerson, USA

Eddie Dillard

Information Systems Technician First Class Johnnie Doctor, Jr., USN

Commander Robert Edward Dolan, USN

Commander William Howard Donovan, Jr., USN

Lieutenant Commander Charles A. Droz III, USN (Ret.)

Commander Patrick Dunn, USN

Aerographer's Mate First Class Edward Thomas Earhart, USN

Barbara G. Edwards

Lieutenant Commander Robert Randolph Elseth, USN

Charles S. Falkenberg

Dana Falkenberg

Zoe Falkenberg

Storekeeper Third Class Jamie Lynn Fallon, USN

James Joe Ferguson

Amelia Virginia Fields

Gerald P. Fisher

Darlene "Dee" Flagg

Admiral Wilson "Bud" Flagg, USN (Ret.)

Aerographer's Mate Second Class Matthew Flocco, USN

Sandra Foster

First Lieutenant Richard P. Gabriel, USMC (Ret.)

Captain Lawrence D. Getzfred, USN

Cortez Ghee

Brenda C. Gibson

Colonel Ronald F. Golinski, USA (Ret.)

Ian J. Gray

Diane Hale-McKinzy

Stanley Hall

Carolyn Halmon

Michele Heidenberger
Sheila Hein
Electronics Technician Second Class Ronald John Hemenway, USN
Major Wallace C. Hogan, Jr., USA
Staff Sergeant Jimmie I. Holley, USA (Ret.)
Angela Houtz
Brady Kay Howell
Peggie Hurt
Lieutenant Colonel Stephen Neil Hyland, Jr., USA
Lieutenant Colonel Robert J. Hymel, USAF (Ret.)
Sergeant Major Lacey B. Ivory, USA
Bryan C. Jack
Steven D. "Jake" Jacoby
Lieutenant Colonel Dennis Johnson, USA
Judith Jones
Ann Judge
Brenda Kegler
Chandler Keller
Yvonne Kennedy
Norma Khan
Karen A. Kincaid
Lieutenant Michael "Scott" Lamana, USN
David Laychak
Dong Chul "D.C." Lee
Jennifer Lewis
Kenneth Lewis
Samantha Lightbourn-Allen
Major Stephen Vernon Long, USA
James T. Lynch, Jr.
Terence Michael Lynch
Operations Specialist Second Class Nehamon Lyons IV, USN
Shelley Marshall
Teresa Martin
Ada Mason-Acker
Lieutenant Colonel Dean Mattson, USA
Lieutenant General Timothy Maude, USA
Robert J. Maxwell

Renee A. May

Molly McKenzie

Dora Menchaca

Patricia E. "Patty" Mickley

Major Ronald D. Milam, USA

Gerard P. "Jerry" Moran, Jr.

Odessa V. Morris

Electronics Technician Second Class Brian Anthony Moss, USN

Teddington Hamm Moy

Lieutenant Commander Patrick Jude Murphy, USN

Christopher C. Newton

Khang Nguyen

Draftsman Second Class Michael Allen Noeth, USN

Barbara K. Olson

Ruben Ornedo

Lieutenant Jonas Martin Panik, USN

Major Clifford L. Patterson, Jr., USA

Robert Penniger

Robert R. Ploger III

Zandra Flores Ploger

Lieutenant Darin H. Pontell, USN

Scott Powell

Captain Jack Punches, USN (Ret.)

Aviation Warfare Systems Operator First Class Joseph John Pycior, Jr.,
    USN

Lisa Raines

Deborah A. Ramsaur

Rhonda Sue Ridge Rasmussen

Information Systems Technician First Class Marsha D. Ratchford, USN

Martha Reszke

Todd Reuben

Cecelia E. Richard

Edward Veld Rowenhorst

Judy Rowlett

Sergeant Major Robert E. Russell, USA (Ret.)

Chief Warrant Officer Fourth Class William Ruth, USA

Charles E. Sabin

Marjorie C. Salamone
John Sammartino
Colonel Dave Scales, USA
Commander Robert A. Schlegel, USN
Janice M. Scott
Lieutenant Colonel Michael L. Selves, USA (Ret.)
Marian H. Serva
Commander Dan F. Shanower, USN
Antionette "Toni" Sherman
Diane Simmons
Donald Dean Simmons
George Simmons
Cheryle Sincock
Chief Information Systems Technician Gregg Harold Smallwood, USN
Lieutenant Colonel Gary F. Smith, USA
Mari-Rae Sopper
Robert Speisman
Patricia J. Statz
Edna L. Stephens
Norma Lang Steuerle
Sergeant Major Larry Strickland, USA
Hilda E. Taylor
Lieutenant Colonel Kip Paul Taylor, USA
Leonard Taylor
Sandra Carol Taylor
Sandra D. Teague
Lieutenant Colonel Karl W. Teepe, USA (Ret.)
Sergeant Tamara C. Thurman, USA
Lieutenant Commander Otis Vincent Tolbert, USN
Staff Sergeant Willie Q. Troy, USA (Ret.)
Lieutenant Commander Ronald J. Vauk, USN
Lieutenant Colonel Karen J. Wagner, USA
Meta L. Waller
Specialist Chin Sun Pak Wells
Sandra Letitia White
Staff Sergeant Maudlyn White, USA
Leslie A. Whittington

Ernest M. Willcher

Lieutenant Commander David Lucien Williams, USN

Major Dwayne Williams, USA

Chief Petty Officer Marvin Roger Woods, USN (Ret.)

Captain John D. Yamnicky, Sr., USN (Ret.)

Vicki Yancey

Shuyin Yang

Information Systems Technician Second Class Kevin Wayne Yokum, USN

Chief Information Systems Technician Donald McArthur Young, USN

Edmond Young, Jr.

Lisa Young

Yuguang Zheng

INTERVIEWS

Lieutenant Colonel Benjamin Starnes, USAMC/Interviews, various
    between July 2002 and March 2003
Lieutenant Colonel Edward Lucci, USAMC/Interviews, August,
    September, and October 2002 (also taped interview)
Alan Wallace, Fort Myer Fire/Rescue, Fort Myer, Virginia/Interview,
    August 21, 2002
Lieutenant Colonel James Goff, USAMC/Interviews, various between
    September 2002 and January 2004
Commander Craig Powell, SPECBOATU 20/Interview, December 8,
    9, and 11, 2003
Sergeant Major Tony Rose, USA (Ret.)/Interview, February 14, 16,
    and 18, 2004
Colonel Victor Correa, USA/Interview, March 17, 2004
Colonel Phil McNair, USA (Ret.)/Interview, April 13, 2004
Lieutenant Colonel Marilyn Wills, USA/Interview, May 19 and 26,
    2004
Lieutenant Colonel Sean Kelly, USA/Statement, July 17, 2004, via
    email from Iraq
Sergeant Roxane Cruz-Cortez, USA/Interview, July 18, 2004
Michael "Mike" Flocco/Interview at his home, September 20, 2004
Major Dan Pantaleo, USMC/Interview, September 24, 2004
John Yates/Interview, September 27, 2004
Frank Probst/Interview, September 28, 2004
Blair Bozek, Senior Defense Analyst, USAF/Interview, September 28,
    2004
Commander David Tarantino, USN/Interview, October 18, 2004

SOURCES

ABC News KGO TV, San Francisco, Oakland, San Jose
All Hands (Magazine of the US Navy)
American Lives, by *Newsday* and *Tribune* reporters
American Society of Civil Engineers, *The Pentagon Building
    Performance Report*, January 2003
American Survivor Relief Fund website
Arlington National Cemetery website
Army Link News
Army News Service
Army Times
Associated Press
Aviation Week
Baltimore Sun
BellaOnline, the voice of women on the web
CBS News
Chicago Tribune
Christian Patriots in Action website
CNN archives
Center for Cooperative Research
DCMilitary.com
DefenseLINK, American Forces Information Service
Detroit Free Press
Government Executive (https://www.govexec.com/)
Honolulu Advertiser
Larry King Live, Interview with Secretary of Defense Donald
    Rumsfeld, December 5, 2001

Leatherneck magazine (magazine of the US Marines)

Marine Times

MSNBC archives

Navy Times

NFPA Journal

No Ordinary Time: Franklin and Eleanor Roosevelt: The Home Front in World War II, by Doris Kearns Goodwin, c. 1994

Okmulgee Daily Times

Pentagon *9/11 Commission Report,* July 2004

Seattle Times

Shadow Warriors, by Tom Clancy with General Carl Stiner and Tony Koltz, c. 2002

SouthCoast Today

Space.com

The Flagship

The Vindicator

The Virginian-Pilot

United States Air Force

United States Department of Defense (www.defenselink.mil)

US Medicine Information Central

US Navy Office of Information, US Navy

USA Today

Virginia Fire Chiefs Association

Voices of 911 (https://hereisnewyorkv911.org/)

Washington Post archives

Wikipedia, the free encyclopedia of the web

WorldNetDaily

ACKNOWLEDGMENTS

Thanks to my wife, Mary Starnes, for all of her love and support throughout the writing of this book.

Thanks to my mother, the late Martha Starnes. God rest her soul. Without her tireless efforts, this book would not have come to be.

Thanks to my brother, Lieutenant Colonel Benjamin Starnes, USAMC, for initially suggesting this project and for taking time out of his busy schedule to assist me in gaining access to military personnel and also for acting as a proofreader and for prodigious moral support. His help was invaluable.

Thanks to Sergeant Major Tony Rose, USA (Ret.), and Colonel Phil McNair, USA, who provided extra help and assistance in getting this project completed. Thanks very much to Colonel McNair for furnishing diagrams of the Pentagon.

Thanks to Mike and Sheila Flocco for providing photographs and diagrams of the Pentagon and also for their gracious hospitality in welcoming me and my brother into their home.

Thanks to Commander David Julian, USN, associate director, Office of Family Policy, Office of the Deputy Under Secretary of Defense, for acting on my behalf to secure interviews from Pentagon personnel.

Thanks to Mr. Bob Rieve, executive director of the UDT/SEAL Association, Fort Pierce, Florida, for his help in securing the interview with Commander Craig Powell.

Thanks to Mr. Bob Zielendorff of Manhattan, New York, for his help in securing interviews with military personnel.

Thanks to Ms. Karen Soule, PAO, Fort Jackson, South Carolina, for granting permission to interview Colonel Victor Correa.

Thanks to Ms. Jayme Loppnow, 130th Engineer Battalion, USA, for granting permission to interview Sergeant Roxane Cruz-Cortez.

Thanks to Mr. Don Jackson for his advice and suggestions.

Thanks to Mr. Tracy Shurtleff, systems engineer, Boeing Company, for providing technical information on Boeing aircraft.

Thanks to Captain Larry Rousseau of the Fulton County Fire Department, Station 9, Fulton County, Georgia, for providing information on fire and its effects and on various firefighting methods.

Thanks to my good friend Mr. Dave Rogers for proofreading the manuscript and for all his help and advice.

Thanks to Colonel Thomas N. Britton, USA (Ret.), for acting as a proofreader and also for much valuable information concerning the military and the history and layout of the Pentagon.

NOTE: The following people either declined to be interviewed or no contact information could be found for them; therefore, their accounts were taken primarily from secondhand sources. Every effort was made to produce an accurate narrative using available source material.

Mr. Theodore Olson, former solicitor general of the United States
Lieutenant Colonel Theodore "Ted" Anderson
Staff Sergeant Christopher Braman, USA
Lieutenant Kevin Shaeffer, USN (Ret.)
Mr. Juan Cruz-Santiago
Mrs. Louise Kurtz
Mr. Isaac Ho'opi'i
Lieutenant Colonel Brian Birdwell

DISCLAIMER

Due to the overwhelming number of participants and responders involved in this tragedy and the difficulty in tracking them down for interviews or in finding any information whatsoever about them, it is a certainty that many people were regrettably left out of the narrative. This in no way diminishes their heroic efforts or participation, and this book is not intended to be taken as a complete account of what occurred that day.

The description on page 86 is based on testimony of Mike Flocco, who was intimate with his son's daily movements at the Pentagon, classified autopsy photos viewed by the author, statements made to Mike Flocco by Matt's supervisor, Nancy McKeown, who did not want to be interviewed about 9/11, and a reenactment of what probably happened based on the position of the bodies per the photos, so it is a supposition. Mike Flocco believes that his son was on his way back down from submitting his morning report when the plane hit, but it is more likely that he was seated at his cubicle. McKeown heard a voice cry her name twice, coming from the weather room right next to her office. As Flocco and Earhart were the only people in this room and Earhart was killed instantly, this was most surely Flocco's. The position in which his body came to rest in death on the floor indicates that he was hovering over Earhart, trying to get him to wake up. Flocco had just completed a navy firefighting course required of all naval personnel, but he ignored the advice to stay close to the floor to get air because he was concerned for his friend, so he tried to rouse him by strad-dling the body, thereby putting his head in the smoke and in doing so, died of smoke inhalation. If a reenactment is performed in which the actor straddles a body lying facedown on the floor and imagines losing strength from lack of oxygen, smoke filling the lungs, and he lets his body weaken and fall naturally to the left, the body will end up in the exact position that Flocco was in in the autopsy photo. The autopsy photo is supported by statements made to the author by Major Dan Pantaleo, USMC, who was one of the first to enter the weather room and see the position of the bodies and was also the one who removed Flocco's body from the room so that it could be transported for burial. Still, what happened in that room on the morning of September 11, 2001, is known only to God.

The capitalization and style of military titles in this book adheres to the standard recommendations outlined in the *Chicago Manual of Style* publishing guide instead of to specific American military style preferences. This has been done in an effort to ensure the book is eas-ily readable for civilian readers. For example, military titles are not capitalized, except when they are used as part of a name; the words "army" and "navy" are not capitalized unless used as part of a full proper name; and military titles are spelled out instead of abbreviated.

ABOUT THE AUTHOR

Lincoln M. Starnes was born in Salisbury, Maryland, in 1962. As a boy, his interests were history, exploration, and motorcycles. As a young man he taught himself to play banjo, guitar, and harmonica and developed a love of jazz, rock 'n' roll, and the blues. In his early twenties, he worked in Montana and Wyoming, where he climbed mountains and explored the backcountry in his off time. In 1985, he graduated from the University of Virginia with a degree in English. For the past twenty-one years, he has worked as a courier for FedEx. He lives in Georgia with his wife and daughter.